GULF OF ST. LAWRENCE

CMAC

MIRAMICHI R.

PRINCE EDWARD IS.

CAPE BRETON IS.

NEW BRUNSWICK

NOVA SCOTIA

HN RIVER

L

MICMAC

OCEAN

IC

INDIAN PEOPLES
OF THE
DAWNLAND

THE ABENAKIS
AND THEIR NATIVE AMERICAN NEIGHBORS
≫ FROM PRE-CONTACT TIMES TO THE EARLY 18th CENTURY ≪

CARTOGRAPHY BY : H. Stacy Miller Moain

SCALE

0   20   40   60   80   100 MI.

Dawnland
Encounters

Dawnland Encounters

Indians and Europeans in Northern New England

Compiled and edited with
an introduction by

Colin G. Calloway

University Press of New England
Hanover and London

The University Press of New England

is a consortium of universities in New England dedicated to publishing scholarly and trade works by authors from member campuses and elsewhere. The New England imprint signifies uniform standards for publication excellence maintained without exception by the consortium members. A joint imprint of University Press of New England and a sponsoring member acknowledges the publishing mission of that university and its support for the dissemination of scholarship throughout the world. Cited by the American Council of Learned Societies as a model to be followed, University Press of New England publishes books under its own imprint and the imprints of Brandeis University, Brown University, Clark University, University of Connecticut, Dartmouth College, University of New Hampshire, University of Rhode Island, Tufts University, University of Vermont, and Wesleyan University.

The author gratefully acknowledges permission to reprint extracts and/or documents from the following sources: the *Collections of the Maine Historical Society* and the *Province and Court Records of Maine*, Board of Trustees of the Maine Historical Society; Massachusetts Archives Vols. 30, 32, 52, Massachusetts Archives at Columbia Point; Ayer Manuscript #423, The Newberry Library; *Massachusetts Officers and Soldiers, 1723–1743* (1979), New England Historic and Genealogical Society; *The Narrative*, The Connecticut Historical Society; *Documents of the American Revolution* edited by K. G. Davies, Irish Academic Press; *Indian Tribes of the Upper Mississippi Valley* by Emma Blair, The Arthur H. Clark Company; 1729 storehouse register at the Chicago Historical Society; MG 11, Series Q, MG 1, series F3, Mg1 series C11A, National Archives of Canada; *L. C. Wroth: Voyages of Giovanni da Verrazzano*, through permission of The Pierpont Morgan Library, New York, PML.60196; quotation from *Adventure in the Wilderness: The Journals of Louis Antoine de Bougainville*, by Edward P. Hamilton. Copyright © 1964 by the University of Oklahoma Press; Timothy Bedel letter in the Stevens Transcripts, Office of the Vermont Secretary of State; Manuscript 777601, Eleazar Wheelock to Joseph Louis Gill, Dartmouth College Library; Elkins Journal, The Vermont Historical Society.

Printed in the United States of America

∞

5   4   3   2   1

Cataloging-in-Publication Data appears on page 297.

This was always for Marcia

Contents

Preface

This book grew out of another. In the course of researching and writing *The Western Abenakis of Vermont, 1600–1800: War, Migration, and the Survival of an Indian People* (Norman: University of Oklahoma Press, 1990), I compiled a mass of data on the western Abenakis in time of war and upheaval. Every so often, as I waded through the materials on the "French and Indian Wars," I came across intriguing snippets on another dimension of the relations between Indians and Europeans. Not only were there long periods of peace in northern New England during which Indians and Europeans dealt with each other on a daily basis, but further investigation uncovered frequent instances of coexistence and cooperation, hints of social experiments that cut across racial or ethnic lines. By presenting many of these examples in this volume, I hope to offer a view of relations between Indians and Europeans that is more balanced, more complex, and ultimately more fascinating than the picture that emerges from narratives of the "French and Indian Wars." The Columbian Quincentennial in 1992 promises to generate a flood of books and exhibits on the theme of encounter between the Indian and European worlds, but such works inevitably emphasize initial meetings. Indians in northern New England have been in contact with Europeans and their descendants for close to five hundred years: from before Verrazzano's voyage in 1524 to the present. This volume begins with the first encounters and traces the story of interaction up to the end of the eighteenth century, by which time the Europeans in the area had asserted their independence as Americans.

Traditional histories portrayed the New England frontier as an impenetrable wilderness that hardy, God-fearing English pioneers wrested from the Indian inhabitants and their unscrupulous French backers in Canada. The "French and Indian menace" casts a long and sinister shadow across the pages of New England's history: Pioneers working their fields keep a wary eye on the forests and a musket within easy reach; families huddle behind barred shutters as faceless Indian warriors filter out from behind trees with murderous intent. In the long struggle, so the story goes, English muskets and courage prevailed against Indian tomahawks and treachery; English axes and plows transformed the wilderness into a world of communal villages and farms; and English Protestantism triumphed over French Catholicism.

Today historians adopt a more sophisticated approach to the study of Indian-European relations in New England. Many of the old stereotypes have been cast aside; many of the old assumptions discredited. Few scholars now accept outdated notions about the frontier as a steadily advancing line where "civilization" met a "savage wilderness." Most view frontiers as areas where two or more cultures meet and overlap, not just as battlegrounds between inveterate foes.

Northern New England has not yet received its fair share of this revisionist attention. Recent scholarly enquiries tell us much about southern New England, about Puritan-Indian relations and about governmental policies and tribal responses. But we still know relatively little about the north, about Indian relations with other European groups, or about individual interactions. Geography and historians have combined to place northern New England on the periphery of Indian-white history; it remains a backwater, too easily characterized as a non-man's land between New England and New France.[1]

Yet, as the documents in this collection illustrate, northern New England offers rich testimony to the range and complexity of Indian-white relations in general and to colonial European-Indian relations in particular. Inevitably, many of the documents attest to the violence, treachery, and mutual misunderstanding that were all too common on the frontier—Indian war parties always made more urgent news than did Indian traders, hunters, and farmers, and English treatment of native New Englanders was often myopic, vicious, and cynical. But other documents show that the northern New England borderland—the Abenakis' dawnland—was more than a war zone; it was also a middle ground where Indians, French, English, and other individuals coexisted and cooperated as often as they fought, and where natives and newcomers shared some common history. Indians and Europeans encountered each other as representatives of social and political units, but they also interacted as human individuals whose perceptions, motivations, and reactions were always influenced, but not necessarily dictated, by their membership in a particular society.

A collection like this cannot tell the whole story. The purpose of the extracts is to convey for students and general readers the flavor and variety of Indian-European relations in this fascinating borderland region. Not every treaty and land transaction negotiated between the English and the Abenakis is included; nor are the frontier conflicts that dominated and disrupted life in the area for almost a century described in the detail so often served up in the old histories. Readers will find a sampling of treaty proceedings and military accounts that reflects the ways in which Indians and Europeans dealt and fought with each other; but they will also find selections that illustrate alternative areas of interaction in trade, religion, and everyday life.

The records furnish ample evidence to fuel old stereotypes about Indian cruelty, English treachery, or French intrigue. Yet our preoccupation with conflict and conquest has often blinded us to other sides of human interaction. *Dawnland Encounters* tries to redress the imbalance and suggests a fuller and richer story of Indian-European relations in northern New England. If there was treachery and hostility, there was also trust and harmony; if there was confrontation and conflict, there was also cooperation and conversion; and if there were occasional acts of genocide, there was also the genesis of new societies—born out of the meeting of Indian and European in northern New England's dawnland.

Since the volume is intended for general readers and as a starting point for student discussion rather than as a research work for scholars, I have tried to limit editing to minor changes that make the documents more readable without destroying their original flavor. Many of the documents selected already show the heavy hand of successive editors. I have tried to establish some consistency in capitalization and punctuation. Seventeenth- and eighteenth-century writers littered their documents with capital letters, often with no consistency and for no apparent reason. To retain these would be distracting to the eyes of many twentieth-century readers. Consequently, I have lowercased the capitals unless it seemed that the writer intended to add special emphasis or draw particular attention by his use of capitals. On the other hand, proper names that appear lower case in the originals have been capitalized, and capitals are used consistently at the beginning of sentences. Punctuation has been altered only in places where the original sentence was lengthy or unclear, although the pen strokes used by some writers at the end of sentences have been replaced by periods. Abbreviations and ampersands have been spelled out in full, but otherwise spellings have not been altered. Occasional obvious slips of the pen or typographic errors have been corrected without comment. Treaties and formal proclamations have been reproduced with a minimum of change. French documents have been presented in their English translations where available, or translated for this volume. Editor's omissions are noted by three ellipsis points and a row of ellipsis points if the omission includes a paragraph or more. The occasional words added to clarify the text are placed in brackets, as are introductory material and follow-up comments to the documents.

COLIN G. CALLOWAY
Bellows Falls, Vermont,
and Laramie, Wyoming

Introduction

Dawnland Frontiers

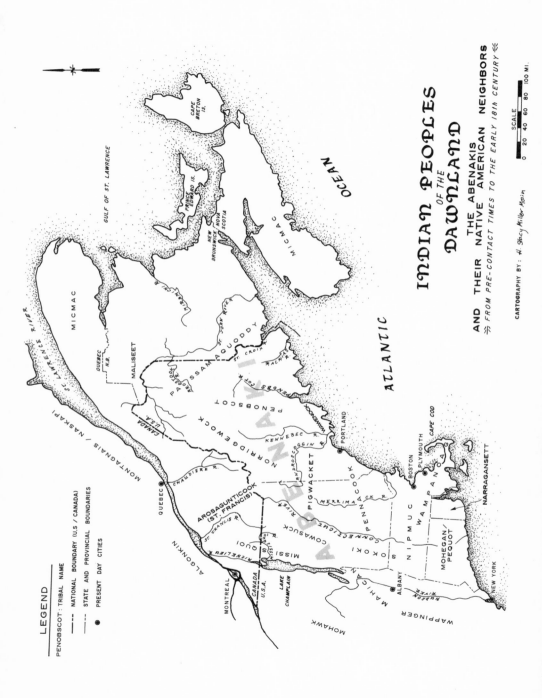

LEGEND

PENOBSCOT: TRIBAL NAME

— · — NATIONAL BOUNDARY (U.S./CANADA)

———— STATE AND PROVINCIAL BOUNDARIES

● PRESENT DAY CITIES

INDIAN PEOPLES
OF THE
DAWNLAND

THE ABENAKIS
AND THEIR NATIVE AMERICAN NEIGHBORS
⇾ FROM PRE-CONTACT TIMES TO THE EARLY 18th CENTURY ⇽

CARTOGRAPHY BY: H. Stacy Miller-Morin

SCALE

0 20 40 60 80 100 MI.

Northern New England—the present states of Maine, Vermont, and New Hampshire—is an area rich in beauty and resources. From Maine's craggy Atlantic coast to the shores of Lake Champlain, towering mountains, deep green forests, sparkling lakes, and tinkling brooks feed the needs and spirits of human inhabitants and visitors. Sea coast, lakes, and rivers provide a bounty of fish; forests of white pine, birch, beech, fir, spruce, hemlock, maple, oak, and ash harbor a wealth of wildlife; fertile valleys produce an agricultural cornucopia that belies the short and precarious growing season. Rivers and streams rise from the Green Mountains of Vermont and the White Mountains of New Hampshire, wending their way through the woods into the Champlain and Connecticut valleys or east to the Atlantic, providing highways of travel and arteries of communication. Harsh winters, with frequent heavy snows and sub-zero temperatures, give way reluctantly to late springs, pleasant summers, and spectacular autumnal displays as the year turns full circle. For people accustomed to long waits, hard work, and limited material comforts, northern New England is a perfect place to live.

The Abenakis thought so. For countless generations before Europeans set foot on the continent, northern New England was their homeland. "The people of the dawnland" were the first to see the sun rise at the start of each new day and among the first to see Europeans at the dawning of a new era. Traditions and legends, lives and deaths, linked the Abenakis to this land. Spiritual places—Mount Katahdin in Maine, Guardian's Rock in Lake Champlain—reminded them of their special relationship to the Creator; stories told through the winter instructed them about their role in the world. Their collective memory recalled simply that northern New England had been the Abenaki homeland since time immemorial; but modern archaeological re-

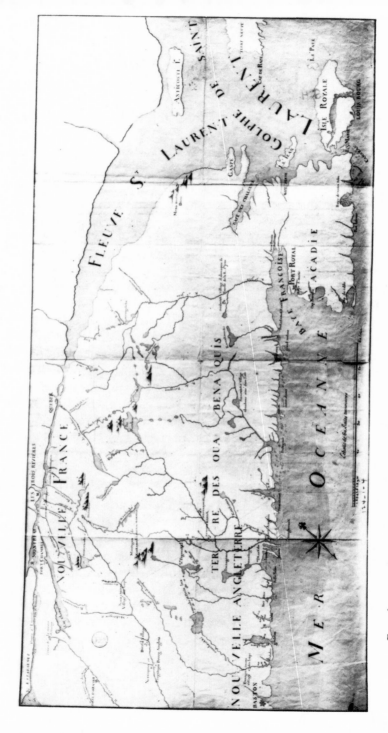

French map of 1713, attributed to Father Joseph Aubery. The map depicts northern New England as Abenaki country and shows the location of some Abenaki villages. *Courtesy of the Newberry Library.*

search yields increasing evidence that the Abenakis and their ancestors inhabited the dawnland for well over ten thousand years.[1] The New World was already old by the time Europeans reached the dawnland.

The Abenakis comprised numerous scattered bands of the eastern Algonkian family. Anthropologists group them into two main branches, the division based on linguistic rather than political distinctions. In Maine, tribal movements and confusion in nomenclature have produced disagreement over the precise identification of several groups and of people who appear in early records as "Etchemins,"[2] but the tribes associated with the various watersheds—the Penobscots, Sacos, Androscoggins, Kennebecs, and Wawenocks—were all eastern Abenakis. Northeast of the Penobscots lived the Passamaquoddies who, while not strictly recognized as Abenakis, featured prominently with them in Indian-European relations in Maine. The English often lumped Abenakis and Passamaquoddies together—along with Micmacs and Maliseets—as "Eastern Indians." In Vermont and New Hampshire, western Abenaki groups occupied the Green and White mountains and the shores and tributaries of the Champlain, Connecticut, and Merrimack valleys. The Missisquois, Winooskis, and other groups inhabited the east shore of Bitawbagok (Lake Champlain); the Cowasucks and Sokokis centered on the upper and middle Connecticut River; and Pennacook communities nestled in the valley of the Merrimack. Western Abenaki Winnipesaukees and intermediate Pigwackets and Ossipees lived in the White Mountains.

The broad application of the term "Abenaki" obscures some precise identifications but reflects the flexibility of relations among the Indian inhabitants of the dawnland. The Abenaki homeland stretched from southern Quebec to northern Massachusetts, but, bounded by Sobagw (the Atlantic) on the east, and by Bitawbagok's one hundred miles of water on the west, it was relatively secure. Abenaki warriors repelled occasional Micmac forays from the northeast, Mohawk incursions from the west, and, until relatively late, English invaders from the south. As Lieutenant John Montresor noted at the end of the French and Indian wars, no nation was "more jealous of their country than the Abenaquis."[3]

Each Abenaki band was a distinct and autonomous yet fluid community. Leaders lacked the authority to make decisions for the whole community, since their influence was personal rather than institutional. They exerted authority only so far as their followers were willing to comply with their advice, and their prestige was tested in daily life. Leadership was not only "weak" in European terms, it was also often irrelevant in situations where decisions were made by the people who carried them out. Few Europeans comprehended that decisions had to be reached by consensus and that leadership rested on voluntary obedience, and they regularly accused Abenaki chiefs of duplicity and dismissed Abenaki society as anarchical.

Abenaki social and political organization reflected a life that revolved around the rhythm of the seasons. The core unit of society and subsistence was a small band composed of linked families. These family bands regularly congregated at the river falls and rapids when smelt, shad, bass, and salmon made their spring runs upstream to spawn. Eastern Abenakis went down to the sea to fish, harvest shellfish, hunt sea mammals, and, in time, trade with European sailors who visited the coasts for similar purposes. Abenaki family bands congregated into village farming communities in the late spring and early summer. Hunting and fishing were the mainstays, and early European explorers found no corn being grown north of the Saco River. In the Champlain and Connecticut valleys, however, horticulture preceded Europeans by several centuries. Abenaki men cleared fields in rich bottomlands around the village, and Abenaki women cultivated corn, squash, beans, and tobacco, supplementing the diet with nuts, berries, and maple sugar in the spring. Bands also gathered for social occasions, for midwinter ceremonies, and to mobilize warriors and resources for war.

Abenakis constructed their villages close to woods and water, taking advantage of a rich and varied resource base. So productive were forest, field, and stream that large stores of corn, smoked fish, dried meat, nuts, and dried berries could be set aside in root cellars lined with birchbark or mats as sustenance for the lean winter months ahead. The bands dispersed in the fall to hunt deer, moose, beaver, bear, and other woodland animals, continuing the hunt through the winter when deep snow hindered the escape of hoofed prey from hunters on snowshoes. Migrating flocks of ducks and geese, along with partridges, wild turkeys, and passenger pigeons added to the spring and autumnal larders.

Nature furnished the bounty, but the native inhabitants of the dawnland recognized their spiritual and ecological obligations. They revered the natural balance and maintained symbiotic relations with the animal world. The tales of Gluskab, or Glooskap, the trickster hero, reaffirmed the harmonious relationship that eastern Abenakis shared with their universe in the old days. After Europeans arrived, traditional balances were disrupted as axes bit into Abenaki forests and guns slaughtered Abenaki game. Many Abenakis believed that Gluskab departed in anger, leaving his people unprotected to face the troubles ahead.

The expansion of European power, peoples, and cultures that began in the fifteenth century soon brought strangers to the edges of the dawnland. The Atlantic coast and estuaries and the Champlain corridor provided access routes by which European trader-explorers circumscribed Abenaki territory. Long before English Pilgrims crossed the ocean, fishermen skirted the coasts of Maine and Newfoundland, returning home to Europe with large hauls of salted or dried cod. Rumors of a fabled city named Norumbega and the search for a northwest passage lured other adventurers. The newcomers soon realized that behind the dawnland's forbidding exterior lay a bountiful land. Like most other early Europeans, Captain John Smith, the hero of James-town, was struck by the desolation of Maine's coast and called it "a Countrie rather to affright, then [sic] to delight one." Yet, like those who followed, he was quick to see the dawnland's potential: "From Penobscot to Sagadahock this Coast is all Mountainous and Isles of huge Rocks, but overgrown with all sorts of excellent good woods for building houses, boats, barks or shippes; with an incredible abundance of most sorts of fish, much fowle, and sundry sorts of good fruites for mans use."4

The myth of Norumbega faded, but other myths grew out of the dawnland, as Christopher Levett indicated in 1628 in an account designed to promote English colonizing efforts in the area:

> And to say something of the country. I will not do therein as some have done to my knowledge, speak more than is true; I will not tell you that you may smell the corn fields before you see the land; neither must men think that corn doth grow naturally, (or on trees,) nor will the deer come when they are called, or stand still and look on a man until he shoot him, not knowing a man from a beast, nor the fish leap into the kettle, nor on the dry land, neither are they so plentiful, that you may dip them up in baskets, nor take cod in nets to make a voyage, which is no truer than that the fowls will present themselves to you with spits through them.

But for land-hungry Englishmen, the reality Levett described was attraction enough. Not only were there "fowl, deer, and fish enough for the taking, if men be diligent"; there were also vines, plum trees, strawberries, gooseberries, raspberries, walnuts, chest-nuts, parsley, herbs, lands suitable for farming, meadow, and pasture, "and as black fat earth, as ever I saw in England in all my life."5 It was clear, by the early seventeenth century, that the Abenakis would have to share their world. The first European explorers, sailors, and soldiers of fortune were the advance scouts of a vast *Volkerwanderung* that was to reshape the human geography of northern New England.

The newcomers came from many places and with many purposes. Sailors and fishermen from the seaports of western England competed with Normans, Bretons, and Basques in northern waters. These fishermen touched Abenaki shores, where they established temporary bases for drying fish and mending nets and boats. Some began to stay year-round in permanent coastal settlements, severing their ties to homes in Devon, Cornwall, Dorset, and Somerset, initiating trade and intercourse with Abenaki inhabitants of the forests that edged the sea, and adapting Indian techniques of procuring and processing marine resources.[6]

As West Country fishermen and their descendants clung to and then cultivated the eastern shoreline of the dawnland, English Puritans from Massachusetts began to bring social, political, and religious change. East Anglians predominated, but the Puritans represented a broad array of dissent, driven to New England by a variety of political, religious, and economic oppressions. Between 1630 and 1660, some twenty thousand migrated to America, where they became a "markedly aggressive colonizing population." They established tight communal villages, developed particular attitudes toward the New World wilderness and its native inhabitants, and put those attitudes into sometimes gruesome practice in their relations with the Indians of southern New England. Fueled by continued immigration, they pushed into southern Maine and overland to the Connecticut Valley, impinging on the lands of the Abenakis.[7]

The eighteenth century brought additional variations to the developing "English" culture of northern New England. Beginning in 1718 and continuing in successive waves, Scotch-Irish Presbyterians arrived from Ulster. They migrated to New Hampshire, settled Londonderry in 1719, established satellite communities to the north and west, developed a commercially successful linen trade, and made a significant economic and political impact on the region. They also added their distinctive traits—and the potato—to the culture of the Merrimack Valley and parts of Maine and Vermont. At the same time as Indians and Europeans were adjusting to each other's presence, English and Scotch-Irish on the New Hampshire frontier were coming to accept each other's differences in dialect, diet, religion, customs, and history.[8] Scottish and Irish refugees from Old England's northern and western frontiers appeared on virtually every American frontier, and northern New England received its share of expectant immigrants. Rhode Island, Connecticut, and Massachusetts sent a stream of population north to the dawnland. The trickle became a flood after the French defeat in 1760 opened the north to settlement: "Up the Connecticut Valley trooped pious men and women from Connecticut, solid citizens with Bibles and pinched faces and an eye for town meetings and account books." Others ascended the Saco, Kennebec, Penobscot, and Merrimack, and farmers from the lowlands of Scotland settled in Ryegate, Vermont, on the eve of the American Revolution. Northern New England's immigrant population leaped from 60,000 to 150,000 in just fifteen years. It kept growing after the Revolution: the population of Maine soared from 56,000 in 1784 to almost 300,000 by 1820.[9]

As settlers moved north, following the rivers into the backcountry, they abandoned seventeenth-century Puritan ideals of tightly settled and closely organized communities, creating in their place country towns where life focused on the family farm rather than on the village.[10] Growing mercantile interests, acceptance of other religious groups—Presbyterians, Quakers, Anglicans, Baptists—the increasing secularism of life, and the religious revivalism of the mid-eighteenth century completed the transformation from English Puritan to New England Yankee. The English advance did not constitute a straight line edging into the wilderness, it comprised a series of encroachments into Abenaki country as settlers bulged westward from the coast of Maine and pushed north up the Champlain, Connecticut, and Merrimack valleys.[11]

Old England and her borderlands were not the sole source of immigrant population for northern New England. New Netherland fell to the English in 1664, but Dutch influence remained prominent on the upper Hudson and spilled over into the Champlain Valley. Traders like John Lydius enjoyed extensive influence among the Indians of the region, and settlers of Dutch descent settled on Abenaki lands around Lake Champlain during the Revolution. In Maine, Palatines, Wurttembergers, and German Swiss brought a German flavor to the area between the Kennebec and Penobscot rivers after 1740. Black slaves from the British West Indies represented another source of population. By the 1760s, blacks counted for 4 percent of Portsmouth's population, 1 percent of New Hampshire's total population. We know little about their lives, and much less about their interactions with Indians, but they formed the northern tip of an evolving society in which blacks drew on both African and Yankee cultures.[12]

Meanwhile, French traders, priests, and soldiers entered the dawnland from the north. Black-robed Jesuit priests traveled deep into the Abenaki heartland in search of a harvest of souls. They won converts, established missions, catered to what they saw as the Abenakis' spiritual and secular needs, and sometimes assumed leadership roles in Abenaki communities. French entrepreneurs operating out of tiny, fortified coastal outposts engaged in lumbering, cod-fishing and fur-trading. French traders visited Abenaki villages in search of a harvest of furs and cultivated relations with Abenaki hunters and chiefs, exchanged goods for pelts, and pulled Abenakis into the commercial orbit of western Europe. French officers functioned as war chiefs, leading Abenaki war parties against English settlements. French men married Indian women, learned Indian languages, and adopted Indian ways.[13] French influence became evident in the names, clothing, offspring, and actions of Abenakis, and the Franco-Abenaki connection frightened and frustrated New Englanders for a century and a half. Captain John Smith heard of Frenchmen who lived "as one nation or family" with the Indians east of Penobscot Bay. The Reverend Cotton Mather referred contemptuously to eastern Abenakis as "Frenchified Indians" and denounced the war party that François Hertel and the Abenaki chief Hopehood or Wohewa led against Salmon Falls in 1690 as "being half one [and] half the other, half Indianized French and half-Frenchified Indians."[14]

The intrusion of new peoples into what was once exclusively Abenaki country generated a nightmare of competition, conflict, and chaos. Successive waves of biological, technological, military, religious, and demographic changes buffeted the dawnland. A terrible epidemic of smallpox or plague devastated the New England tribes between 1616 and 1619; it reached the Abenakis and swept along the coast of Maine in 1617.[15] Smallpox hit again in 1633–1634 and in 1639, and in 1646 Abenakis were dying of a disease that caused them to vomit blood. Jesuit Pierre Biard noted that the Indians of Maine and Nova Scotia were no strangers to disease as early as 1616 "and often complain that, since the French mingle with and carry on trade with them, they are dying fast and the population is thinning out." The English took a more providential view of biological cataclysm: "The Indians are tractable," wrote Deputy Governor of Maine Thomas Gorges in 1642. "The Lord sent his avenging Angel and swept the most part away."[16] New diseases from Europe continued to decimate Abenaki populations—smallpox ravaged the dawnland in the 1730s and again in the 1750s—and disrupt Abenaki society. Diseases killed the young, who provided their families with food, shelter, and protection, and cut down the elders, who provided the community with wisdom, legend, and ceremony. The newcomers themselves were not immune in an age of precarious mortality. Europe itself was still a disease-ravaged land; an un-identified epidemic swept the English towns in the Connecticut Valley in 1690, and an epidemic of diphtheria or "throat distemper" swept northern New England's colonial population in the 1730s and 1740s.[17]

The Europeans brought other changes to the country they invaded as they endeavored to fit their New World into Old World patterns. English colonists not only wanted to take over the Abenakis' land, they also wanted to permanently alter that land. The Indians and Europeans who were now inhabiting a single world represented two sets of ecological relationships as well as two sets of human communities. Both peoples were essentially members of small folk communities, and both lived lives that followed the rhythm of the seasons; but whereas Indian villages were mobile and fluid communities, the English sought to establish fixed villages. They regarded Indian mobility as wasteful improvidence rather than as an effective alternative use of the land. English colonists intended to transform the environment they inherited into "a world of fields and fences," and the influx of farmers radically changed the landscape.[18]

The influx and movement of European settlers also produced changes among the settlers themselves. Part of the process by which English—or Scots, Irish, Dutch, German, French—men and women became Americans involved rubbing shoulders with the Indian inhabitants of their new homelands.[19] Colonists in northern New England may not have interacted as closely with the Abenakis as did their counterparts in New France, and not even the French automatically jettisoned their Old World values, lifestyles, and social pretensions when they took up residence in the dawnland.[20] Nonetheless, Europeans added Abenaki words to their vocabularies, ate Abenaki foods, employed Abenaki practices in hunting, farming and maple sugaring, learned the uses of Abenaki herbs, inherited a network of Abenaki trails through the dawnland, and adopted Abenaki modes of travel

by moccasin, canoe, and snowshoe.[21] European sailors who bent
their backs to the oars of cumbersome wooden boats looked with
envy at the ease with which Abenaki canoeists maneuvered their
light birchbark craft, and the canoe quickly became the standard
mode of travel for Indian and European alike on dawnland rivers, lakes, and coast. In 1704, the New Hampshire Assembly
passed a law requiring all householders to keep "one good pair
of snow shoes and mogashuns" for the better pursuit of enemy
raiders in wintertime.[22] Puritan pens and pulpits may have pro-
claimed the forest a howling wilderness and denounced the Indians as its satanic inhabitants, but in reality English colonists
often shared the forest with the Abenakis and benefitted from
their knowledge and woodland wisdom. The chapters in this
volume reflect this aspect of contact as well the history of confrontation.

The first contacts between Indians and Europeans in the
dawnland generally were amicable. European invasion is usually
regarded as bold, aggressive, and brutal in its treatment of Indian inhabitants, but, as the extracts in chapter one indicate,
first encounters were actually marked by hesitation and uncer-
tainty as Europeans and Indians came to terms with new neighbors and a new situation. European visitors came with stereotypical expectations about noble and ignoble "savages" and
judged the natives by European standards. They described
much of what they saw in negative terms and dismissed Indians
as lacking any real government, laws, religion, or morals. As
James Axtell observes, the cultural interface often wore a scowl
"because European ships carried not only fish hooks and trade
goods but large ladings of cultural arrogance." But Europeans
noted positive as well as negative aspects in Indians and their
ways of life. They did not always understand Indians' actions,
but they were not always blind and hostile either. Like other
people, they operated from their own cultural framework and
viewed things through their own distorting lenses, interpret-

ing—and frequently misinterpreting—what they saw in terms they understood. Like other people, they also sometimes acted carelessly, dishonestly, and cruelly. Indians seem to have looked at the strangers and their new technology with a mixture of interest and fear, with a degree of awe and repulsion, and with some cultural disdain of their own. They may have wondered whether the newcomers were human, but they usually extended the hand of hospitality. As Verrazzano's account indicates, Indians in Maine had learned to distrust Europeans as early as 1524, but for the most part hostilities between Indians and Europeans in northern New England occurred only after misunderstanding and mistrust marred initially peaceful relations.[23]

Northern New England was the scene of spiritual and religious as well as military and diplomatic encounters. Anglo-French rivalry was a clash of faiths as well as empires, a contest for souls as well as colonies. At a time when wars of religion were tearing Europe apart, Catholic and Protestant princes competed to extend the one "true religion" to the New World and to exclude rivals from an unprecedented fallow field. In the dawnland, Jesuit missionaries like Sebastien Rasles dedicated their lives and labors to winning Abenaki converts, discrediting Abenaki shamans, and saving the Indians' souls, concurrently securing their allegiance for the king of France. New England Puritans shuddered at the thought of black-robbed papists controlling Abenaki hearts and minds and dispatching them to commit murder and mayhem on the frontier, and they stepped up their own efforts to make inroads among the tribes. French missions in Maine, Vermont, and Quebec attracted Abenakis in numbers that attest to the zeal and appeal of the Jesuits. Many Abenakis embraced Christianity and impressed the missionaries with evidence of their new-found faith, although Europeans frequently mistook quiet native civility for tacit acceptance and agreement. Missionaries attempted to impose a revolution on Indian society, but Indians responded to Christianity in a variety of ways and, as Kenneth Morrison has reminded us, religious change did not necessarily equal conversion. Abenaki responses varied from total acceptance to outright rejection, while many adopted a syncretistic approach that melded the best of old and new beliefs. Abenaki society included zealous converts and diehard traditionalists. The documents in chapter two illustrate the contest of Catholic, Protestant, and Indian beliefs in the dawnland and show that the contest failed to produce total victory for either—or any—of the "true religions"; instead, the dawnland's religious mosaic now included Indians who adhered to traditional beliefs as well as English, French, and Abenaki Christians whose individual faiths, as in every age, defied accurate or appropriate measure.[24]

Indians and Europeans frequently tried to formalize their relations and to regulate their encounters by diplomacy and protocol. Some of the treaties Europeans made with Indians displayed, or rather concealed, a Machiavellian intention to delude and deprive. The English employed a repertoire of deceptive practices in their efforts to acquire Indian land, dominate Indian trade, or disregard Indian rights. Treaty texts reflected little of the mistranslation, misinformation, and duplicity that marked English conduct. Ethnocentric English officials were less interested in the justice of Abenaki arguments and grievances than they were in obtaining Abenaki lands and forcing compliance from a position of strength.[25] Nevertheless, as the documents in chapter three illustrate, treaty and council proceedings were not always forums for dispossession of gullible Abenakis. Dawnland diplomats also endeavored to arrange mechanisms for avoiding and settling disputes. Europeans in Indian country adapted their procedures to accommodate native protocol, and Abenakis regularly employed diplomatic proceedings to voice their concerns, complaints, and demands. Abenaki delegates were forceful spokesmen, confident of their power, and when occasion demanded were more than a match for the newcomers in making bellicose and threatening speeches. On other occasions, they displayed genuine commitment to negotiating peaceful solutions to problems. Colonial English officials in the wake of victory were capable of tremendous arrogance as they dictated terms to defeated and dispirited Indians—as some of the treaty extracts attest—but at other times French and English alike adjusted their expectations to the reality that Abenakis still called the tune in the dawnland.

War was a recurrent feature of dawnland life and is the focus of chapter four. Interethnic and international rivalries overlapped as the superpowers of the Old World glowered at each other across Abenaki territory, engaged in a tug of war for Abenaki allegiance and the land they called Acadia, and turned the dawnland into a buffer zone and battleground. Disruptions in native economies upset intertribal balances of power, generated increasing Iroquois intrusions across Lake Champlain, and placed the Abenakis in an increasingly perilous world. Puritan wars of conquest in the south sent Indian refugees fleeing north, and English pressure on Abenaki lands sparked new conflicts. French and English colonists marched to war to the sound of drums beaten in Paris and London, although they did not replicate the carnage enacted on European battlefields. Indian allies and dawnland terrain and tactics dictated the nature of the conflict fought in northern New England. French raiding parties, augmented by Indian warriors, struck south across the dawnland, burning English settlements and carrying off captives, scalps, and plunder. English militia, with Indian scouts to the fore, retaliated against Indian villages. Bound by ties of religion and mutual self-interest to the French in Canada, Abenaki warriors supported the cause of the fleur-de-lis every time Old World rivalries spilled over into contests for New World hegemony. In these conflicts, they often served far from home and fought alongside warriors from tribes as distant as the Great Lakes. But they also fought for their own reasons, on their own terms, and on ground of their own choosing. The net result was over eighty years of warfare that disrupted normal patterns of life.

War produced hardship and suffering for Europeans and Indians alike. Trade ground to a standstill; villages were abandoned; houses and lodges were burned and not rebuilt, crops were destroyed and fields not replanted; and men who served with militia companies or war parties could not hunt, farm, or provide for their families. Famine and poverty struck individuals and villages far from the front lines. English towns felt the impact of war in the taxes they paid and the sermons they heard as well as in the sons they lost. War and threats of war severely limited the expansion of New England settlements between King Philip's War (1675–1676) and the Treaty of Utrecht (1713) and even curtailed population growth by adversely affecting marital patterns and fertility behavior.[26] War drove English settlers into confinement in garrison towns and caused Indian villages to disperse in woodland retreats. Only with the fall of New France in 1760 did the threat of war cease to restrict the options and direct the lives of the dawnland's Indian and European occupants. Until then, caught up in the maelstrom of conflict, they fought and died or survived as best they could the toll war took on their lives, communities, and families.

Colonial contests masterminded in Paris and London, executed from Montreal and Quebec, Albany and Boston, were often fought by farmers and hunters who, whether they were Indians or Europeans, were part-time soldiers with other lives to live. The ranks of the regular British army in North America were filled with individuals whom Fred Anderson describes as "permanently marginal members of British society." These included convicts and social misfits, as well as men from the impoverished backcountry regions of Scotland and Ireland and people dislocated by the rapid economic changes of the times. By contrast, the young men who swelled the ranks of provincial

New England armies were only *"temporarily* available for service." They were farmers, artisans, and laborers who were needed at home.[27] And, as a verse etched on a powder horn by a soldier at Fort Number Four and Pierre Thury's account of Abenaki women and children kneeling in chapel praying for their warriors' safe return remind us, dawnland warriors were human beings with fears and families of their own.[28]

Settlers and Indians who met in conflict sometimes knew each other from peacetime contacts. John Lovewell's men exchanged personal insults with their Pigwacket adversaries during their famous fight in 1725; in King George's War, settlers in Gorham, Maine, fought Indians with whom they had played as children; the two Indians who acted as negotiators between the besieging Franco-Indian army and the commander of Fort Number Four in 1747 were "formerly acquainted with Captain Stevens"; and when Tomhegan raided the Androscoggin Valley in 1781, the settlers recognized the Abenaki leader because he had often been in their homes.[29] Indians fought Indians as well as Europeans, and kinship ties and individual attachments that developed during the course of everyday life often made the choice of allegiance difficult.

Between bouts, Indians and Europeans resumed war-torn lives and reopened avenues of commerce and cooperation. Warriors who had disappeared to don war paint returned to English settlements to peddle pelts. English trader-settler-soldiers like Phineas Stevens at Fort Number Four on the Connecticut River set aside their muskets and picked up their ledger books, in some cases continuing accounts with Indian customers who had been temporarily called away to fight.[30] The fur trade was part of a wider exchange between Indian and European worlds. Exchange often meant different things to Indians and Europeans. Europeans approached trade as hard-bargaining to make a profit; Indians saw it as an exchange of gifts that cemented friendship and established mutual obligations. Indians' refusal to behave according to profit incentives and market forces puzzled and frustrated European traders, just as the Europeans' refusal to honor reciprocal obligations by simply sharing what they had often appalled the Indians. But trade was a natural component of contact as participants engaged in exchanges of goods and furs, and with currency a scarce commodity in colonial settlements, it remained an integral part of the barter economies of all dawnland inhabitants.

The economies of New France and New England overlapped in the dawnland as French and English traders competed for Abenaki commercial allegiance. Indians also competed for the benefits to be derived from European commerce: Early in the seventeenth century, Abenakis and Micmacs fought for the coveted position of middlemen in passing along European trade goods to the tribes of New England. Abenaki trappers and traders frequented European communities, became tied into European colonial economies, and adjusted from gift exchanges to market forces. The fur trade disrupted and decimated Indian society. It facilitated the spread of European killer diseases, armed the tribes with deadly new firearms, introduced alcohol, disturbed Indian relations with the animal world, eroded native craft skills, and promoted dependency on Europeans and their products. Merchants peddled liquor to stimulate demand among people who enjoyed limited material needs, and cynically extended credit to Indian customers as a sure way of acquiring Indian lands when those customers defaulted.[31] But, as the selections in chapter five illustrate, the fur trade also engaged Indians and Europeans in an area of interdependence and common endeavor. The fur trade functioned as a bridge between cultures, and participants avoided open ruptures that would terminate a commerce that was beneficial to both parties.[32] Likewise, although land swindles were common, there were instances when Abenakis and Europeans worked out mutually satisfactory land transactions, and agreements for shared use of lands sometimes functioned effectively until they broke down under the increasing pressure of English settlement.[33]

Economic interaction produced lively borderland societies. The Baron de Lahontan said that Sokokis, Pennacooks, and other Indians came "in shoals" to trade at Chambly before 1685, and English frontier communities like Fort Number Four and Fort Dummer, which served as defense outposts in time of war, saw Indians and settlers mix freely in peacetime commerce.[34] For these societies, war was an interruption to brisk trade and functioning reciprocal relations between colonist and Indian.

Contact, conversion, conflict, and commerce created a mingling of peoples, and a melding of cultures in the dawnland. Traders, interpreters, soldiers, and settlers who lived on the frontier knew the Abenakis much better than did government officials living in colonial cities. Abenakis who frequented English settlements and visited Boston and Quebec—or even London and Paris—understood the newcomers better than did their relatives who kept their distance in the woods. Even Deerfield in the middle Connecticut Valley, famous as an English outpost against French and Indian attacks coming out of the dawnland, included a handful of Indians, blacks, and Frenchmen in its population.[35] Individuals emerged who personified the nature and complexity of these encounters. Such people demonstrated that the gulf between Indian and European was not impassable, and chapter six contains some of their stories.

Some Europeans entered Indian country voluntarily; others went against their will but attained status in Indian society through adoption. The New England frontier produced volumes of narratives by people captured by Indians. Captivity narratives became an important genre of early American literature and helped to establish the image of Indians as bloodthirsty savages. They frequently described the sufferings of their heroes and heroines in sensational terms, thereby emphasizing the final triumph of English courage and Puritan virtue over the forces of evil. Recent studies have challenged and qualified the notion that Indian captivity was always a fate worse than death, suggesting instead that the abduction and adoption of white captives was simply a process of acculturating and assimilating Europeans into Indian society.[36] Many Europeans taken captive in the dawnland became ethnic converts, and they and their offspring added a European strand to the cultural fabric of Indian communities. Others were sold to the French and made new lives for themselves in French Canada. Thus, even if Abenakis regarded the English as enemies, they also on occasion regarded them as potential Abenakis and clung to their adopted captives with tenacity and affection.

Former captives who returned home often fulfilled important roles as cultural intermediaries, bridging Indian and European society with their linguistic skills, family ties, experiences, and attitudes. Still other individuals went into Indian communities on their own accord, sharing Indian lives and experiences, defending their interests, and mediating with outside powers. Individuals like Joseph Louis Gill, the Baron de St. Castin, and Phineas Stevens transcended cultural barriers and personified patterns of interaction common on dawnland frontiers.

The northern New England dawnland was an ethnic and national borderland plagued by war and treachery, distrust and destruction. As English settlers pushed into their lands, Abenakis died by the thousands from war, disease, famine, and dislocation, even as they waged deadly war against the invaders. Many sought refuge in French mission communities in Canada, where their descendants live today. Those who stayed in their homelands survived at tremendous cost, pushed into marginal areas by newcomers who took the best lands for themselves.[37]

But there is a brighter side to the story of Indian-European relations in northern New England, a side often obscured by dramatic instances of war and conquest. War was never constant; it never totally eradicated areas of peaceful encounter and never completely severed kinship ties and individual attachments that transcended ethnic lines. Many of the passages selected for this volume highlight instances of accommodation, interdependence, and peaceful interaction to demonstrate that the dawnland was not only a war zone but was also a middle ground of coexistence, cooperation, and mutual conversion. The lives that Indians and Europeans shared and made in the dawnland attest to the complexity and variety of human motivations and possibilities. Political, religious, military, and ethnic boundaries existed and sometimes became zones of bloody conflict; but, in a porous cultural borderland inhabited by Penobscots and West Country fishermen, Pigwackets and English Puritans, Pennacooks and Scotch-Irish Presbyterians, Kennebecs and Jesuit priests, Wawenocks and French noblemen, Missisquois and French soldiers, Sacos and French and English traders, Sokokis and Yankee settlers, Cowasucks and Scottish lowlanders, English captives in Indian villages, Indian soldiers in English armies, Indian converts in French missions, Indian students in English schools, and the offspring of various sexual unions, those boundaries sometimes took a back seat to individual ties, daily concerns, and the seasonal round of life in the dawnland.

Chapter One

First Encounters

The myth of discovery. In this statue on Isle La Motte in Lake Champlain, the French explorer Samuel de Champlain strikes a typical heroic pose while, equally typically, his anonymous Indian guide occupies a subordinate position. *Author's photograph.*

[European invasion of the dawnland did not begin as a bold and aggressive onslaught. European explorers relied for the success of their ventures upon good relations with the people they encountered. Indian guides showed them the way, drew maps for them on the ground or on birchbark, acted as intermediaries with more distant peoples, and sometimes served as interpreters of land and language. Indian villages fed and sheltered the newcomers, and Indian hunters and traders furnished them with the pelts and other products they sought. In this sense, the first Europeans to enter the dawnland were hardly "discoverers"; they came to a land inhabited by people who already knew it well. As the French historian Fernand Braudel observed, "Europeans often rediscovered the world using other peoples' eyes, legs and brains." Indeed, one of Samuel de Champlain's guides in 1604 was a Micmac chief named Messamouet, who spoke French because he had already been to France, where he stayed at the house of the governor of Bayonne.[1] The Pilgrims of New Plymouth likewise received invaluable information and assistance from well-traveled and bi-lingual Indians. In March 1621 a Pemaquid Abenaki named Samoset "came bouldly amongst them, and spoke to them in broken English." Samoset had learned the language from fishermen and had been captured by Englishmen who took him from Maine to Cape Cod, where he remained among the native Wampanoags. Samoset in turn introduced the Pilgrims to Squanto, a Patuxet Indian who had been abducted across the Atlantic, lived for a time in Cornhill, London, and returned home to find his tribe wiped out by disease.

But the Europeans were entering a world that was new to them, and they were encountering people of whom they had little or no previous knowledge. European sailors and explorers searched out the Indian inhabitants of the dawnland and endeavored to establish political and commercial ties. The Europeans came in relatively small numbers, their presence was not yet permanent, and they encountered Indians only briefly on the edges of their homeland. The first meetings between Indians and Europeans tended to be irregular and uncertain, geared toward the establishment of mutually beneficial relations. Cultural arrogance and misunderstandings contributed more than naked aggression to the deterioration of relations, and the French succeeded better than their English rivals in maintaining harmony.

Fish and furs attracted anonymous fishermen-turned-traders to the fringes of the dawnland by the early sixteenth century, and later explorers frequently encountered Indians who displayed clear evidence of previous contact. In 1602, Bartholomew Gosnold's crew met Indians in Casco Bay who "spake divers Christian words, and seemed to understand much more than we, for want of Language could comprehend."[2] Indians picked up more than simply vocabulary from these early encounters: diseases, trade goods, trading knowledge, and lessons in dealing with the strangers were all part of the exchanges that continued throughout the sixteenth and early seventeenth centuries. In return, Indians offered food, furs, hospitality, and information. They provided explorers with information on the land they saw—and on the lands and peoples they had not yet seen. European cartographers then interpreted this information to create maps that replaced Indian place-names with European ones, that obliterated Indian geography, and that effectively excluded Indians from large stretches of the charted territory.[3]

Around 1000 A.D., Norsemen attempted to colonize parts of Newfoundland and Labrador from Iceland and Greenland. They failed, but they established sailing routes that others would follow in centuries to come.[4] Englishman John Cabot sailed down the east coast of Newfoundland in 1497 and may have touched the coast of northern New England.[5] But the first clearly documented European voyage to the dawnland's shores occurred in 1524 when Florentine Giovanni da Verrazzano, sailing for the French king Francis I, visited the Maine coast. Estevan Gomez, a Portuguese pilot in the Spanish service, explored Penobscot Bay the following year. In the spring of 1580, Simon Ferdinando, a Portuguese navigator sailing for England's Sir Humphrey Gilbert, was in the area; Englishman John Walker acquired a haul of three hundred skins from Penobscot Bay later the same year. Frenchman Etienne Bellenger sailed along the coasts of Nova Scotia, New Brunswick, and Maine in 1583 and traded for furs with the Indians. John Brereton chronicled Bartholomew Gosnold's visit in 1602, and Englishman Martin Pring sailed into Casco Bay and traded along the coast in 1603. French explorer Samuel de Champlain visited Indian villages the length of the coast between Saco Bay and St. John River in 1604–1605. Champlain established a settlement at St. Croix on the present United States—

Canadian border, but half the colonists perished of hunger and disease. After the first winter, the survivors moved across the Bay of Fundy to Port Royal. In 1605, English voyagers under George Waymouth established relations with Abenakis on the coast, and, as will be seen, several Abenakis made the return journey to England as a result of the encounter. George Popham and a group of would-be settlers established a short-lived and ill-fated colony at Sagadahoc at the mouth of the Kennebec River in 1607. The French colony of St. Saveur on Mount Desert Island also failed; the English destroyed it in 1613. Captain John Smith, the hero of Jamestown, led the next venture in 1614 and renamed the whole region in 1616: It had previously been known as Norumbega, then as North Virginia, but now became New England. Christopher Levett sailed the Maine coast in 1623–1624, traded with the Abenakis, and tried to establish a colony at Casco Bay.

These adventures, explorers, and traders were not sufficiently numerous to threaten the Abenaki world, but they initiated changes, established precedents, and pulled the Abenakis into increasing contact with Europe. Some, like Champlain, dealt successfully with the Indians they met; others like Christopher Levett gave evidence of good intentions; and many, like Waymouth and Popham's men, failed to appreciate native ceremonial expectations, forms of greetings, and gift-exchange patterns and thus gave offense in their hurry to get down to hard bargaining.[6] Ethnocentrism frequently surfaced, mutual misunderstandings occurred, and animosities escalated. But as Europeans and Indians struggled to come to terms with new neighbors and new situations, each made genuine attempts at communication before sentiments hardened and hostility erupted.]

1. ANTICIPATING AND OBSERVING EUROPEANS

[Native American traditions from the dawnland recall ancient prophecies foretelling a time "when we must look for the coming of the white man from the direction of the rising sun" and warning that the new era would initiate a time of troubles for the Indians: "Knowing that a great change must follow his coming it made me weak and the weakness overcame me, because his coming will put a bar to our happiness, and our destiny will be at the mercy of events." Warnings foretold that "when he bring his women and children, he will come to stay, and he shall want all the land, because the land will be so sweet to him," and they

directed the Indians to take no part in the white man's wars that would follow,
"because the Great Spirit did not make the land for brothers to fight for." Similar
forebodings characterized Native American prophecies recalled and recorded
throughout North America.[7]

Some eastern tribes remembered European sailing ships as appearing like
floating islands or large white birds at their momentous first sighting of the
strangers.[8] Indian tradition recounted by Penobscot Joseph Nicolar of Old Town,
Maine, recalls one tribe's reaction "after the white man was seen sailing in his
strange craft along the coast."]

This long looked for event created such a stir that the noted
men were called to discuss the matter and to see what must be
done about it, and on their getting together it was decided that
there shall be some good spiritual men selected and sent on
along the coast to watch the strange people's movements. These
people were considered very strange because they were not
white as the snow, and not so white as the people expected them
to be, but were brown and hairy people. Whether they were
creatures with the speech or not, none knew because no one
had heard them talk. However it was determined to have them
watched and this watching to continue until his true description
and habits had been learned.

[But news of the Europeans' coming apparently did not always generate fear
and foreboding, as Joseph Nicolar recounted in this tradition.]

Just at this time an exciting news was brought from the extreme north to the effect that the white man's big canoe had
come again, and had landed its people who are still remaining
on the land on the north shore of the "Maquozz-bem-to-cook,
Lake River," and have planted some heavy blocks of wood in the
form of a cross. These people are white and the lower part of
the faces of the elder ones are covered with hair, and the hair
is in different colors, and the eyes are not alike, some have dark
while others have light colored eyes, some have eyes the color

of the blue sky. They have shown nothing only friendship, they take the red man's hands in their own and bow their heads down and make many signs in the direction of the stars; and their big canoe is filled with food which they eat and also give some to those that come to them and made signs of friendship. When this news spread, the people took it so quietly and talked about it in such a way, there was no excitement, but everybody took it as though it were an old affair, yet it had such effect upon them, that it was evident that the general desire was, that the habits of the strange people must be well learned, and all agree to wait and see what kind of a treatment they will extend to the red people. If the treatment they have already extended be continued, it was thought it will be the means of bringing happiness to both races. This was the conclusion reached, which after many years proved to be so wise, because it was upon this conclusion strictly lived up to, that the red man of the north never had any trouble with the white man.

(Joseph Nicolar, *The Life and Traditions of the Red Man* [Bangor, Me.: C. H. Glass & Co., 1893], 106–7, 128–29.)

2. VERRAZZANO MEETS THE ABENAKIS, 1524

[In 1524, French voyagers under the command of Florentine Giovanni da Verrazzano encountered their first Abenakis on the coast of Maine. The Indians' cautious and inhospitable behavior indicated they had already suffered bad experiences at the hands of European traders. Their behavior conditioned Verrazzano's attitude toward them; but the actions of Verrazzano and his crew did nothing to allay Abenaki suspicions of European sailors.]

The shore ran eastward. At a distance of fifty leagues, keeping more to the north, we found high country full of very dense forests, composed of pines, cypresses, and similar trees which grow in cold regions. The people were quite different from the others[9] for while the previous ones had been courteous in manner, these were full of crudity and vices, and were so barbarous that we could never make any communication with them, however many signs we made to them. They were clothed in skins of bear, lynx, sea-wolf and other animals. As far as we could judge from several visits to their houses, we think they live on game, fish, and several fruits which are a species of root which the earth produces itself. They have no pulse,[10] and we saw no sign of cultivation, nor would the land be suitable for producing any fruit or grain on account of its sterility. If we wanted to trade with them for some of their things, they would come to the seashore on some rocks where the breakers were most violent, while we remained in the little boat, and they sent us what they wanted to give on a rope, continually shouting to us not to approach the land. They gave us the barter quickly, and would take in exchange only knives, hooks for fishing, and sharp metal. We found no courtesy in them, and when we had nothing more to exchange and left them, the men made all the signs of scorn and shame that any brute creature would make.[11] Against their wishes, we penetrated two or three leagues inland with 25 armed men, and when we disembarked on the shore, they shot at us with their bows and uttered loud cries before fleeing into the woods. We did not find anything of great value in this land, except for the vast forests and some hills which could contain some metal: for we saw many natives with "paternostri" beads of copper in their ears. We departed, skirting the coast in a northeasterly direction.

(Lawrence C. Wroth, ed., *The Voyages of Giovanni da Verrazzano, 1524–1528* [New Haven: Yale University Press, 1970], 140–41; reproduced by courtesy of The Pierpont Morgan Library, New York, PML 61096.)

[Ten years later, when Jacques Cartier met Micmacs in the Bay of Chaleur, the Indians showed similar evidence of previous encounters with Europeans:

They held up furs on sticks and gestured for the French to come ashore, but took
care to hide their women in the woods.[12]]

3. BRERETON ENCOUNTERS INDIAN SAILORS, 1602

[In the spring of 1602 Bartholomew Gosnold's expedition encountered In-
dians off the coast of southern Maine who showed unmistakable evidence of
previous contact with Europeans. Early explorers in the Gulf of Maine found
European manufactured goods among the natives and naturally assumed that
the Indians got those goods direct from European sailors and traders, and
Basque fishermen may well have extended their voyages to the coast of Maine.
In fact, as Brereton's account of a meeting with Indian trader-sailors suggests,
many of the goods may have come via Micmac and other middlemen from the
eastern Gulf of Maine and Nova Scotia, who traded with Europeans in the
Gulf of St. Lawrence and then sailed southwest to trade with Abenakis. Seven
years later, Henry Hudson met Indians on the coast of Maine who sailed in two
shallops and brought beaver skins and other furs, "for the French trade with
them for red Cassocks, Knives, Hatchets, Copper, Kettles, Trevits, Beades, and
other trifles."[13]]

On Friday the fourteenth of May early in the morning, we
made the land, being full of faire trees, the land somewhat low,
certeine hummocks or hilles lying into the land, the shore ful of
white sand, but very stony or rocky. And standing faire alongst
by the shore, about twelve of the clocke the same day, we came
to an anker, where six Indians, in a Baske-shallop[14] with mast
and saile, an iron grapple, and a kettle of copper, came boldly
aboard us. One of them was apparelled with a waistcoat and
breeches of blacke serdge, made after our sea-fashion, hose and
shoes on his feet; all the rest (saving one that had a paire of
breeches of blue cloth) were all naked. These people are of tall
stature, broad and grim visage, of a blacke swart complexion,
their eiebrowes painted white. Their weapons are bowes and
arrowes. It seemed by some words and signes they made, that

some Basks or of S. John de Luz,[15] have fished or traded in this place, being in the latitude of 43 degrees.

(John Brereton, "Briefe and True Relation of the Discoverie of the North Part of Virginia, 1602," in Henry S. Burrage, ed., *Early English and French Voyages* [New York: Charles Scribner's Sons, 1932], 330–31.)

4. CHAMPLAIN ESTABLISHES PEACEFUL RELATIONS ON THE PENOBSCOT, 1604

[In September 1604, French explorer Samuel de Champlain reached the Penobscot River and opened negotiations with the inhabitants of the region. The following extract illustrates the tentative and cautious process of establishing relations, as well as the degree of ceremonial involved. The tact and diplomacy that Champlain displayed in the first French conference with these Indians initiated a period of Franco-Abenaki friendship that endured for a century and a half, until the fall of New France. Champlain's conduct sharply contrasts with the actions of some English explorers (see, for example, documents 6 and 7 of this chapter) that alienated the Abenakis and established a reputation for distrust. The account also shows that the Indian sagamores Bashaba[16] and Cabahis were eager to trade directly with the French and so bypass Indian middlemen such as Brereton encountered in 1602. The extract also illustrates the important role played by Indian guides as interpreters and intermediaries.]

The next day . . . we saw two canoes paddled by Indians, who came to observe us at a distance of a musket-shot. I sent our two Indians in a canoe to assure them of our friendship, but the fear they had of us made them turn back. The next morning they returned, and came alongside our pinnace, and held converse with our Indians. I had some biscuit, tobacco, and sundry other trifles given to them. These Indians had come to hunt beaver, and to catch fish, some of which they gave us. Having made friends with them, they guided us into their river Peimtegouet, as they call it, where they told us lived their chief named

Bessabez, headman of that river. I believe that this river is the one which several pilots and historians call Norumbega.

. . . .

On the sixteenth of the month, some thirty Indians came to us upon the assurance given to them by those who had acted as our guides. On the same day the above-mentioned Bessabez also came to see us with six canoes. As soon as the Indians on shore saw him arrive, they all began to sing, dance, and leap, until he had landed, after which they all seated themselves on the ground in a circle, according to their custom when they wish to make a speech or hold a festival. Cabahis, the other chief, also arrived a little later, with twenty or thirty of his companions, who kept by themselves; and they were much pleased to see us, inasmuch as it was the first time they had ever beheld Christians. Some time afterwards I landed with two of my companions and two of our Indians who acted as our interpreters. I ordered the crew of our pinnace to draw near the Indians, and to hold their weapons in readiness to do their duty in case they perceived any movement of these people against us. Bessabez, seeing us on shore, bade us sit down, and began with his companions to smoke, as they usually do before beginning their speeches. They made us a present of venison and waterfowl.

I directed our interpreter to tell our Indians that they were to make Bessabez, Cabahis, and their companions understand that the Sieur de Monts had sent me to them to see them, and also their country; that he wished to remain friends with them, and reconcile them with their enemies, the Souriquois and Canadians.[17] Moreover, that he desired to settle in their country and show them how to cultivate it, in order that they might no longer lead so miserable an existence as they were doing; and several other remarks on the same subject. This our Indians made them understand, whereat they signified that they were well satisfied, declaring that no greater benefit could come to them than to have our friendship; and that they desired us to settle in their country, and wished to live in peace with their enemies, in order that in future they might hunt the beaver more than they had ever done, and barter these beaver with us in exchange for things necessary for their usage. When he had finished his speech, I made them presents of hatchets, rosaries, caps, knives, and other little knick-knacks; then we separated. The rest of this day and the following night they did nothing but dance, sing, and make merry, awaiting the dawn, when we bartered a certain number of beaver-skins. Afterwards each returned, Bessabez with his companions in their direction and we in ours, well pleased to make acquaintance with these people.

(H. P. Biggar, ed., *The Works of Samuel De Champlain*, 6 vols. [Toronto: The Champlain Society, 1922–1936], 1:283–84, 294–96.)

5. CHAMPLAIN'S INDIAN GUIDES, 1605

[As Champlain sailed south past Cape Ann, which he called the Island Cape, in northern Massachusetts, he met half a dozen Indians in a canoe. Going ashore, he gave each one a knife and some biscuit and enlisted their help as guides. His account illustrated the reliance of European explorers upon the knowledge and goodwill of the native inhabitants.]

I made them understand as well as I could, that they should show me how the coast trended. After I had drawn for them with a charcoal the bay and the Island Cape, where we then were, they pictured for me with the same charcoal another bay which they represented as very large. Here they placed six pebbles at equal intervals, giving me thereby to understand that each one of these marks represented that number of chiefs and tribes. Next they represented within the said bay a river which we had passed, which is very long and has shoals. We found here quantities of vines on which the unripe grapes were a little larger than peas, and also many nut-trees, the nuts on which were no larger than musket-balls. These Indians informed us that all those who lived in this region cultivated the land and sowed seeds like the others we had previously seen. This place is in latitude 43 degrees and some minutes. Having gone half a league we perceived upon a rocky point several Indians who ran dancing along the shore towards their companions to inform them of our coming. Having indicated to us the direction of their home, they made signal-smokes to show us the site of their settlement. We came to anchor close to a little island, to which we sent our canoe with some knives and biscuits for the Indians, and observed from their numbers that these places are more populous than the others we had seen.

(Biggar, ed., *The Works of Samuel De Champlain*, 1:334–38.)

6. THE ENGLISH OPEN CONTACT WITH THE ABENAKIS, 1605

[Captain George Waymouth's encounter with Abenakis on the coast of Maine is the first recorded Anglo-Abenaki contact. James Rosier's account of the meeting provides one of the most detailed descriptions of the eastern Abenakis at the beginning of the seventeenth century and presents valuable insights into the coastal trade carried on between Indians and Europeans. The Abenakis were particularly interested in Waymouth's stock of trade goods and anxious to obtain metal cans and pots to supplement their own birchbark containers. These particular Abenakis may have had no previous contact with European traders, but, contrary to what the writer suggests, they were no strangers to trade. Native trade networks were extensive before Europeans arrived, and Indian trade took the form of reciprocal exchanges accompanied by formal gift-giving and ceremonial. Not surprisingly, Indians found European conceptions of trade as purely a business transaction both foreign and offensive. The Indian leader's oration was probably a form of greeting and his gestures meant to question whether the visitors came from the sea; but the English interpreted his behavior as unfriendly.

Other misunderstandings followed, and Rosier's account illustrates how relations soon deteriorated in an atmosphere of suspicion and distrust.[18]]

This day [May 30], about five a clocke in the afternoone, we in the shippe espied three canoas comming towards us, which went to the iland adjoining, where they went a shore, and very quickly had made a fire, about which they stood beholding our ships. We made signes with our hands and hats, weffing unto them to come unto us, because we had not seene any of the people yet. They sent one canoa with three men, one of which, when they came neere unto us, spake in his language very lowd and very boldly, seeming as though he would know why we were there, and by pointing with his oare towards the sea, we conjectured he ment we should be gone. But when we shewed them knives and their use, by cutting of stickes and other trifles, as combs and glasses, they came close aboard our ship, as desirous to entertaine our friendship. To these we gave such things as we perceived they liked, when wee shewed them the use: bracelets, rings, peacocke feathers, which they stucke in their haire, and tabacco pipes. After their departure to their company on the shore, presently came foure others in another canoa, to whom we gave as to the former, using them with as much kindness as we could.

The shape of their body is very proportionable, they are wel countenanced, not very tal nor big, but in stature like to us. They paint their bodies with blacke, their faces, some with red, some with blacke, and some with blew.

Their clothing is beavers skins, or deares skins, cast over them like a mantle, and hanging downe to their knees, made fast together upon the shoulder with leather. Some of them had sleeves, most had none; some had buskins [leggings] of such leather sewed. They have besides a peace of beavers skin betweene their legs, made fast about their waste, to cover their privities.

They suffer no haire to grow on their faces, but on their head very long and very blacke, which those that have wives, binde up behind with a leather string, in a long round knot.

They seemed all very civill and merrie, shewing tokens of much thankefulnesse, for those things we gave them. We found them then (as after) a people of exceedingly good invention, quicke understanding and readie capacitie.

Their canoas are made without any iron, of the bark of a birch tree, strengthened within with ribs and hoops of wood, in so good fashion, with such excellent ingenious art, as they are able to beare seven or eight persons, far exceeding any in the Indies.

One of their canoas came not to us, wherein we imagined their women were, of whom they are (as all salvages) very jealous.

When I signed unto them they should goe sleepe, because it was night, they understood presently, and pointed that at the shore, right against our ship, they would stay all night, as they did.

The next morning very early, came one canoa aboard us againe with three salvages, whom we easily then enticed into our ship, and under the decke, where we gave them porke, fish, bread and pease, all which they did eat; and this I noted, they would eat nothing raw, either fish or flesh. They marvelled much and much looked upon the making of our canne and kettle, so they did at a head-peece [helmet] and at our guns, of which they are most fearefull, and would fall flat downe at the report of them. At their departure I signed unto them, that if they would bring me such skins as they ware I would give them knives, and such things as I saw they most liked, which the chiefe of them promised to do by that time the sunne should be beyond the middest of the firmament. This I did to bring them to an understanding of exchange, and that they might conceive the intent of our comming to them to be for no other end.

. . . .

Thus because we found the land a place answereable to the intent of our discovery, viz. fit for any nation to inhabit, we used the people with as great kindnes as we could devise, or found them capable of.

The next day, being Saturday and the first of June, I traded with the salvages all the fore noone upon the shore, where were eight and twenty of them. Because our ship rode nigh, we were but five or sixe. For knives, glasses, combes and other trifles to the valew of foure or five shillings, we had 40 good beavers skins, otters skins, sables, and other small skins, which we knewe not how to call. Our trade being ended, many of them came abord us, and did eat by our fire, and would be verie merrie and bold, in regard of our kind usage of them. Towards night our captaine went on shore, to have a draught with the sein or net. And we carried two of them with us, who marvelled to see us catch fish with a net. Most of that we caught we gave them and their company. Then on the shore I learned the names of divers things of them; and when they perceived me to note them downe, they would of themselves, fetch fishes, and fruit bushes, and stand by me to see me write their names.

Our captaine shewed them a strange thing which they woondred at. His sword and mine having beene touched with the loadstone, tooke up a knife, and held it fast when they plucked it away, made the knife turne, being laid on a blocke, and touching it with his sword, made that take up a needle, whereat they much marvelled. This we did to cause them to imagine some great power in us, and for that to love and feare us.

. . . .

Our captaine had two of them at supper with us in his cabbin to see their demeanure, and had them in presence at service. They behaved themselves very civilly, neither laughing nor talking all the time, and at supper fed not like men of rude education; neither would they eat or drinke more than seemed to content nature. They desired pease to carry a shore to their women, which we gave them, with fish and bread, and lent them pewter dishes, which they carefully brought againe.

In the evening another boat came to them on the shore, and because they had some tabacco, which they brought for their owne use, the other came for us, making signe what they had, and offered to carry some of us in their boat, but foure or five of us went with them in our owne boat. When we came on shore they gave us the best welcome they could, spreading fallow deeres skins for us to sit on the ground by their fire, and gave us of their tabacco in our pipes, which was excellent, and so generally commended of us all to be as good as any we ever tooke, being the simple leafe without any composition, strong, and of sweet taste. They gave us some to carry to our captaine, whom they called our Bashabes; neither did they require any thing for it, but we would not receive any thing from them without remuneration.

[The Indians paid the English respect by giving Waymouth the name of their leader and offering gifts of tobacco. The trade-minded English refused to receive the tobacco as a gift, however, insisting on paying for it. Misunderstanding continued between the two parties despite frequent interchanges. Waymouth became alarmed at the growing numbers of Indians and, preconditioned to expect treachery, he became convinced that they were planning an attack. As Rosier's account goes on to show, it was the English who perpetrated the treachery.]

We came neere the point where we saw their fires, where they intended to land, and where they imagined some few of us would come on shore with our merchandize, as we had accustomed before. When they had often numbered our men very diligently, they scoured away to their company, not doubting we would have followed them. But when we perceived this, and knew not either their intents, or number of salvages on the shore, our captaine, after consultation, stood off, and wefted them to us, determining that I should go on shore first to take a view of them and what they had to traffique, if he, whom at our first sight of them seemed to be of most respect among them, and being then in the canoa, would stay as a pawne for me. When they came to us (not-withstanding all our former courtesies) he utterly refused; but would leave a yoong salvage; and for him our captaine sent Griffin[19] in their canoa, while we lay hulling a little off. Griffin at his returne reported, thay had there assembled together, as he numbered them, two hundred eighty three salvages, every one his bowe and arrowes, with their dogges, and wolves which they keepe tame at command, and not anything to exchange at all; but would have drawn us further up into a little narrow nooke of a river, for their furres, as they pretended.

These things considered, we began to joyne them in the ranke of other salvages, who have beene by travellers in most discoveries found very trecherous; never attempting mischife, untill by some remisnesse, fit opportunity affoordeth them certaine ability to execute the same. Wherefore after good advice taken, we determined so soone as we could to take some of them, least (being suspitious we had discovered their plots) they should absent themselves from us.

. . . .

About eight a clocke this day we went on shore with our boats, to fetch aboord water and wood, our captaine leaving word with the gunner in the shippe, by discharging a musket, to give notice if they espied any canoa comming; which they did about ten a clocke. He therefore being carefull they should be kindly entreated, requested me to go aboord, intending with dispatch to make what haste after he possibly could. When I came to the ship, there were two canoas, and in either of them three salvages. Two were below at the fire, the other staied in their canoas about the ship. Because we could not entice them abord, we gave them a canne of pease and bread, which they carried to the shore to eat. But one of them brought backe our canne presently and staid abord with the other two; for he being yoong, of a ready capacity, and one we most desired to bring with us into England, had received exceeding kinde usage at our hands, and was therefore much delighted in our company. When our captaine was come, we consulted how to catch the other three at shore which we performed thus.

We manned the light horseman [the ship's boat] with seven or eight men. One standing before carried our box of marchandise, as we were woont when I went to traffique with them, and a platter of pease, which meat they loved. But before we were landed, one of them (being too suspitiously fearefull of his owne good) withdrew himselfe into the wood. The other two met us on the shore side, to receive the pease, with whom we went up the cliffe to their fire and sate downe with them. Whiles we were discussing how to catch the third man who was gone, I opened the box, and shewed them trifles to exchange, thinking thereby to have banisht feare from the other, and drawen him to returne. But when we could not, we used little delay, but suddenly laid hands upon them. And it was as much as five or sixe of us could doe to get them into the light horseman. For they were strong and so naked as our best hold was by their long haire on their heads; and we would have beene very loath to have done them any hurt, which of necessity we had beene constrained to have done if we had attempted them in a multitude, which we must and would, rather than have wanted them, being a matter of great importance for the full accomplement of our voyage.

Thus we shipped five salvages, two canoas, with all their bowes and arrowes.

(James Rosier, "A True Relation of the Voyage of Captaine George Waymouth," in Henry S. Burrage, ed., *Early English and French Voyages* [New York: Charles Scribner's Sons, 1932] 367–69, 370–73, 377–79.)

[The capture of this group of Pemaquid Abenakis, including the sagamore Nahanda, was intended to provide the English with knowledge of the country and the Indians' language. It proved to be the first of many examples of English perfidy that alienated the Abenakis. The five captives were shipped across the Atlantic where they "discovered" England and caused a sensation. They were the first Abenakis to visit England, but not the last to visit Europe. Nor were the English the only ones to kidnap Indians: Estevan Gomez had carried off fifty-eight New England Indians in 1525, and Jacques Cartier had kidnapped two Indians to serve the French as guides and interpreters on future voyages.[20] As the next account shows, two of the Abenakis returned to play significant roles in subsequent Anglo-Abenaki encounters, which would henceforth be marked by distrust.]

7. THE VOYAGE TO SAGADAHOC, 1607

[Captain Robert Davies kept a journal of the expedition made in 1607 by Captain George Popham, with Captain Raleigh Gilbert as second in command, to establish a settlement at Sagadahoc on the Kennebec River. His account shows how, as during Waymouth's encounter two years before, Anglo-Abenaki relations deteriorated amid tension and distrust. Two of Waymouth's captives, Nahanda and Skidwarres figured prominently in this series of encounters. Nahanda, sagamore of the Pemaquid band, returned to his people in 1606 with the expedition led by Thomas Hanham and Martin Pring; Skidwarres acted as a reluctant guide and mediator for Popham and Gilbert. As the English approached Nahanda's village at the mouth of the Pemaquid, the Indians shouted the war cry, and there were tense moments until Skidwarres spoke to his people in their own tongue.]

This night followinge about myd nyght Capt. Gilbert caussed his ships bott to be maned and tooke to hemselffe 13 other my selffe beinge on, beinge 14 persons in all, and tooke the Indyan Skidwarres wth us. The weather beinge faier and the wynd calme we rowed to the weste in amongst many gallant illands and found the ryver of Pemaquyd to be but 4 leags weste from the illand we call St. Georges whear our ships remained still att anckor. Hear we landed in a lyttel cove by Skydwarres direction and marched over a necke of the land near three mills. So the Indyan Skidwarres brought us to the salvages housses whear they did inhabitt, although much against his will for that he told us that they wear all removed and gon from the place they wear wont to inhabitt. But we answered hem again that we wold nott retorn backe untill shutch time as we had spoken with som of them. At length he brought us whear they did inhabytt whear we found near a hundreth of them men wemen and children. And the cheeffe comander of them ys Nahanada. Att our fryste seight of them uppon a howlinge or cry that they mad they all presently isued forth towards us with thear bowes and arrows and we presently mad a stand and suffered them to com near unto us. Then our Indyan Skidwarres spoke unto them in thear language showinge them what we wear wch when Nahanada thear commander perseaved what we wear he caussed them all to laye assyd thear bowes and arrowes and cam unto us and imbrassed us and we did the lyke to them aggain. So we remained wth them near to howers and wear in thear housses. Then we tooke our leave of them and retorned wth our Indyan Skidwarres wth us towards our ships.

[Despite Skidwarres' presence, Nahanda remained cautious and was reluctant at first to allow more than a handful of the English to come ashore. When the Indians withdrew into the woods, Skidwarres went with them, rejoining his people after a two-year absence. The English built Fort. St. George on the Kennebec. Nahanda and Skidwarres kept in contact with them, and Popham and Gilbert hoped to employ them as intermediaries in opening trade with Bashaba on the Penobscot River. When arrangements fell through, they eagerly enlisted the services of another sagamore who claimed to be "Lord of the ryver of Sagadehock."[21] Again their attempts to trade faltered. Gilbert expected to

trade things of roughly equal value and refused Indian gifts he considered of little worth. The Abenakis interpreted his refusal as an act of bad faith, and by giving offense Gilbert missed the opportunity to establish good relations in the way Champlain had done several years previously. Instead, the encounter resulted in a tense stand-off similar to Lewis and Clark's confrontation with the Teton Sioux two hundred years later on the Missouri River.[22]

They entertayned him friendly, and tooke him into their boat and presented him with some triffling things, which he accepted. Howbeyt, he desired some one of our men to be put into his canoa as a pawne of his safety, whereupon Captain Gilbert sent in a man of his, when presently the canoa rowed away from them with all the speed they could make up the river. They followed with the shallop, having great care that the sagamo should not leape overbourd. The canoa quickly rowed from them and landed, and the men made to their howses, being neere a league on the land from the river's side, and carried our man with them. The shallop making good waye, at length came to another downefall, which was so shallowe and soe swift, that by noe meanes they could passe any further. Soe Captain Gilbert, with nine others, landed and tooke their fare, the salvadge sagamo, with them, and went in search after those other salvages, whose howses, the sagamo told Captain Gilber, were not farr off. And after a good tedious march, they came indeed at length unto those salvages' howses wheere found neere fifty able men very strong and tall, such as their like before they had not seene, all newly painted and armed with their bowes and arrowes. Howbeyt, after that the sagamo had talked with them, they delivered back again the man, and used all the rest very friendly, as did ours the like by them, who shewed them their comodities of beads, knives, and some copper, of which they seemed very fond; and by waye of trade, made shew that they would come downe to the boat and there bring such things as they had to exchange them for ours. Soe Captain Gilbert departed from them, and within half an howre after he had gotten to his boat, there came three canoas down unto them, and in them some sixteen salvages, and brought with them some tobacco and certayne small skynes, which were of no value, which Captain Gilbert perceaving, and that they had nothing ells wherewith to trade, he caused all his men to come abourd, and as he would have putt from the shore. The salvadges perceiving so much, subtilely devised how they might put out the fier in the shallop, by which meanes they sawe they should be free from the danger of our men's pieces. To performe the same, one of the salvadges came into the shallop and taking the fier brand which one of our company held in his hand thereby to light the matches, as if he would light a pipe of tobacco, as sone as he had gotten yt into his hand he presently threw it into the water and leapt out of the shallop. Captain Gilbert seeing that, suddenly commanded his men to betake them to their musketts and the targettiers too, from the head of the boat, and bad one of the men before, with his targett on his arme, to stepp on the shore for more fier. The salvages resisted him and would not suffer him to take any, and some others holding fast the boat roap that the shallop could not pott off. Captain Gilbert caused the musquettiers to present their peeces, the which, the salvages seeing, presently let go the boatroap and betooke them to their bowes and arrowes, and ran into the bushes, nocking their arrowes, but did not shoot, neither did ours at them. So the shallop departed from them to the further side of the river, where one of the canoas came unto them, and would have excused the fault of the others. Captain Gilbert made shew as if he were still friends, and enterayened them kindlye and soe left them, returning the place where he had lodged the night before, and there came to an anchor for that night.

("A Relation of a Voyage to Sagadahoc," in Burrage, ed., *Early English and French Voyages,* 406–8, 413–17.)

[Nahanda and Skidwarres returned and continued to act as intermediaries, bringing other Indians to trade at the fort, but the English never succeeded in restoring harmonious relations or establishing the trade connections they hoped for. After a harsh winter and Popham's death, the "Popham colony" was abandoned in 1608. Abenakis told the French that their shamans had used magic to drive the English away, in retaliation for their mistreatment of the Indians.²³]

8. SINGING WITH THE ARMOUCHIQUOIS AND ADMIRING THE ETCHEMINS: PIERRE BIARD, 1611–1612

[In 1611 Jesuit Father Pierre Biard accompanied an expedition under M. de Biancourt that brought him into contact with Indians living on the coast of Maine. These two extracts from the Jesuit Relations *record his experiences and impressions. The expedition arrived at Kennebec on October 28, 1611, and landed to see the site of the English colony at Sagadahoc. The French then began to ascend the Kennebec, when they met a group of Abenakis.]*

We had already advanced three good leagues, and had dropped anchor in the middle of the river waiting for the tide, when we suddenly discovered six Armouchiquois canoes coming towards us. There were twenty-four persons therein, all warriors. They went through a thousand maneuvers and ceremonies before accosting us, and might have been compared to a flock of birds which wanted to go into a hemp-field but feared the scarecrow. We were very much pleased at this, for our peple also needed to arm themselves and arrange the pavesade. In short, they continued to come and go; they reconnoitred; they carefully noted our numbers, our cannon, our arms, everything; and when night came they camped upon the other bank of the river, if not out of reach, at least beyond the aim of our cannon.

All night there was continual haranguing, singing and dancing, for such is the kind of life all these people lead when they are together. Now as we supposed that probably their songs and dances were invocations to the devil, to oppose the power of this cursed tyrant, I had our people sing some sacred hymns, as the *Salve,* the *Ave Maris Stells,* and others. But when they once got into the way of singing, the spiritual songs being exhausted, they took up others with which they were familiar. When they came to the end of these, as the French are natural mimics, they began to mimic the singing and dancing of the Armouchiquois who were upon the bank, succeeding in it so well that the Armouchiquois stopped to listen to them; and then our people stopped and the others immediately began again. It was really very comical, for you would have said that they were two choirs which had a thorough understanding with each other, and scarcely could you distinguish the real Armouchiquois from their imitators.

[The next morning the Indians accompanied the newcomers on their way upriver, but the French remained suspicious of their intentions. Europeans often found much to admire in the Indian inhabitants of the dawnland and sometimes attributed to them the qualities of "noble savages." Later, Father Biard traveled to the Penobscot River, where he met Indians to whom, in writing to his superior in Paris, he attributed some of these qualities. The Indians he met had recently been stricken by disease.]

At the confluence of these two rivers there was the finest assemblage of savages that I have yet seen. There were 80 canoes and a boat, 18 wigwams and about 300 people. The most prominent sagamore was called Betsabes, a man of great discretion and prudence; and I confess we often see in these savages natural and graceful qualities which will make anyone but a shameless person blush, when they compare them to the greater part of the French who come over here.

When they had recognized us they showed their great joy

during the evening by the usual demonstrations: dancing, singing and making speeches. And as for us, we were very glad to
be in a country of safety; for among the Etechemins, as these
are, and the Souriquois, as are those of Port Royal, we are no
more obliged to be on our guard than among our own servants,
and, thank God, we have never yet been deceived in them.

The next day I went to visit the savages, and followed my
usual custom, which I have described in speaking of Kinibequi.
But there was more to be done here, as they told me they had
some sick. I went to visit them, and as a priest, it being thus
ordained in the Ritual, I recited over them the holy Gospel and
Orisons, giving to each one a cross to wear around the neck.

(Reuben Gold Thwaites, ed., *The Jesuit Relations and Allied Documents*, 73 vols. [Cleve-
land: Burrows Bros., 1896–1901], 2:35–37, 49–51.)

9. INDIAN IMPRESSIONS OF EUROPEANS, 1616

*[When Indians and Europeans met, physical appearance naturally attracted
mutual curiosity. Europeans commented in lengthy and often derogatory terms
upon Indian physique, complexion, and looks. Written records of Indian impressions are much more rare, of course, but as Jesuit Pierre Biard discovered from
his experiences in Maine and Nova Scotia, Indians were often equally bewildered
by the newcomers' strange appearance. There is evidence to suggest that many
Indians traditionally regarded beards and hairiness as a sign of limited intelligence.[24]]*

They have often told me that at first we seemed to them very
ugly with hair both upon our mouths and heads; but gradually
they have become accustomed to it, and now we are beginning
to look less deformed.

(Thwaites, ed., *Jesuit Relations*, 3:73.)

10. THE COUNTRY OF MAWOOSHEN, 1623

[In 1623 Samuel Purchas wrote a description of the country between Mount Desert Island and the Saco River, "discovered by the English in the yeere 1602. 3. 4. 5. 6. 7. 8. 9." He described the area, which he called Mawooshen, as a series of nine river drainages and gave the names of the rivers, of the Indian towns situated on them, and of the Indian sagamores at each town. While precise identification of the Indian villages, tribes, and leaders is open to some debate, the details Purchas supplied make his work "the most important document on the Abenaki for the period," according to Dean Snow. Estimating total populations from warrior counts at a ratio of something like 5:1, it is clear that the dawnland as described by Purchas was certainly no empty wilderness. Even if the men enumerated in the account represented only 30 percent of the total population, the eastern Abenakis at the beginning of the seventeenth century numbered about ten thousand.[25]

Neere to the north of this River of Pemaquid are three townes: the first is Upsegon, where Bashabes their chief lord doth dwell. And in this towne are sixtie houses, and 250 men. It is three daies journey within the land. The second is Caiocame; the third Shasheekeing. These two last townes are opposite one to the other, the river dividing them both, and they are two daies journey from the towne of Bashabes. In Caiocame dwelleth Maiesquis, and in Shasheokeing Bowant, two sagamos, subjects to Bashabes. Upon both sides of this river up to the very lake, for a good distance the ground is plaine, without trees or bushes, but full of long grasse, like unto a pleasant meadow, which the inhabitants doe burne once a yeere to have fresh food for their deere.

. . . .

Upon this arme [of a river] there are four townes. The first is called Kenebeke, which hath eightie houses, and one hundred men. The lord whereof is Apomhamen. The second is Ketangheanycke, and the sagamos name is Octoworthe, who hath in his towne ninetie households, and three hundred and thirtie men. This towne is foure dayes journey from Kenebeke, and eight days journey from [blank]. To the northward is the third towne, which they call Naragooc; where there are fiftie households, and one hundred and fiftie men. The chief sagamo of that place is Cocockohamus. And on the small branch that runneth east standeth the fourth towne, named by Massakiga; where there are but eight households, and fortie men. Upon the northwest branch of the sound stand two townes more. The first is called Amereangan, and is distant from Kenebeke six dayes journey. In this place are ninetie housholdes, and two hundred and sixtie men, with two sagamoes; the one called Sasuoa, the other Scawas. Seven daies journey hence there is another sagamo, whose name is Octoworokin, and his townes name Namercante, wherein are fortie households, and one hundred and twentie men. A dayes journey above Namercante there is a downefall, where they cannot passe with their cannoes, but are inforced to carrie them by land for the space of a quarter of a mile, and then they put them into the river againe. And twelve dayes journey above this downfall there is another, where they carrie their boates as at the first. And six dayes journey more to the north is the head of this river, where is the lake that is of eight dayes journey long, and foure dayes broad before mentioned. In the lake there is one iland; and three dayes journey from this lake there is a towne which is called Buccawganecants, wherein are threescore households, and foure hundred men. And the sagamo thereof is called Baccatusshe. This man and his people are subjects to the Bashabez of Mawooshen, and in his countrey is the farthest limit of his dominion, where he hath any that doe him homage.

(Samuel Purchas, *Hakluytus Posthumus, or Purchas His Pilgrimes*, 20 vols. [Glasgow: James MacLehose and Sons, 1906], 19:400–404.)

11. CHRISTOPHER LEVETT CONTINUES THE "TRUCK," 1624

[Early bad experiences did not necessarily mar all subsequent encounters. Anglo-Abenaki contacts remained irregular in the early seventeenth century, and new meetings still could and did take place in friendship. Despite the cultural arrogance displayed by early English explorers and the continued sharp practices of English traders, Christopher Levett demonstrated that tactful and respectful conduct was the key to success, even as he adhered to strict English notions of trade.]

I then sent for the sagamores, who came, and after some compliments they told me I must be their cousin, and that Captain Gorges was so (which you may imagine I was not a little proud of, to be adopted cousin to so many great kings at one instant, but did willingly accept of it). And so passing away a little time very pleasantly, they desired to be gone, whereupon I told them that I understood they had some coats and beaver skins which I desired to truck for. But they were unwilling, and I seemed careless of it (as men must do if they require anything of them.) But at last Somerset swore that there should be none carried out of the harbor, but his cousin Levett should have all. And then they began to offer me some by way of gift, but I would take none but one pair of sleeves from Cogawesco, but told them it was not the fashion of English captains always to be taking, but sometimes to take and give, and continually to truck was very good.

(Christopher Levett, "A Voyage into New England, begun in 1623, and ended in 1624," [London, 1628], in *Collections of the Massachusetts Historical Society*, 3d ser., 8 [1843]: 170.)

12. AN EXPEDITION TO THE WHITE MOUNTAINS, 1642

[There are no first-hand accounts of English explorations into the interior of northern New England in the 1640s, but the following extracts from John Winthrop's journal record the first ascent of the White Mountains by a European in June 1642, which caused a flurry of excitement and prompted another journey the following October. As usual, the explorers made their way via Indian villages and used Indian trails, guides, and methods of travel, although in this case they ventured into territory where Pigwackets feared to tread.]

One Darby Field, an Irishman, living about Pascataquack, being accompanied with two Indians, went to the top of the White Hill. He made his journey in 18 days. His relation at his return was, that it was about one hundred miles from Saco, that after 40 miles travel he did, for the most part, ascend. Within 12 miles of the top was neither tree nor grass, but low savins, which they went upon the top of sometimes, but a continual ascent upon rocks, on a ridge between two valleys filled with snow, out of which came two branches of the Saco river, which met at the foot of the hill where was an Indian town of some 200 people. Some of them accompanied him within 8 miles of the top, but durst go no further, telling him that no Indian ever dared to go higher, and that he would die if he went. So they staid there till his return, and his two Indians took courage by his example and went with him [through thick clouds and cold to the tops of the mountains]. . . . When he came back to the Indians, he found them drying themselves by the fire, for they had a great tempest of wind and rain. About a month after he went again with five or six in his company. Then they had some wind on the top, and some clouds above them which hid the sun. They brought some stones which they supposed had been diamonds, but they were most crystal.

. . . .

Mention is made before the White Hills, discovered by one Darby Field. The report he brought of shining stones, etc., caused divers others to travel thither, but they found nothing worth their pains. Amongst others, Mr. Gorge and Mr. Vines, two of the magistrates of Sir Ferdinand Gorge's province, went thither about the end of this month. They went up Saco river in birch canoes, and that way, they found it 90 miles to Pegwagget, an Indian town,[26] but by land it is but 60. Upon Saco river, they found many thousand acres of rich meadow, but there are ten falls, which hinder boats, etc.

[From Pigwacket, they climbed through wooded terrain to the sources of the Connecticut, Kennebec, and Androscoggin rivers.]

(James Kendall Hosmer, ed., *Winthrop's Journal*, "*History of New England*," *1630–1649*, 2 vols. [New York: Barnes and Noble, 1906], 2:62–63, 85.)

13. PETER KALM MEETS LAKE CHAMPLAIN ABENAKIS, 1749

[By the mid-eighteenth century, the Abenakis had suffered much from war, disease, and other forces unleashed by European contact, but Swedish traveler Peter Kalm visiting Lake Champlain in 1749, like many other Europeans of his time, preferred to see simplicity and contentment in his Indians. The Abenakis he described were probably Missisquois.]

We often saw Indians in bark boats, close to the shore, which was, however, not inhabited, for the Indians came here only to catch sturgeons, wherewith this lake abounds, and which we often saw leaping up into the air. These Indians lead a very singular life. At one time of the year they live on the small store of corn, beans, and melons, which they have planted; during another period, or about this time, their food is fish, without bread or any other meat; and another season they eat nothing but game, such as stags, roes, beavers, etc., which they shoot in the woods and rivers. They, however, enjoy long life, perfect health, and are more able to undergo hardships than other people. They sing and dance, are joyful, and always content, and would not for a great deal exchange their manner of life for that which is preferred in Europe.

[Traveling north, Kalm later encountered more Abenakis about thirty miles from St. Jean. Although only a casual observer, Kalm noted indications of interaction between Abenakis, French, and Iroquois.]

Three native women also came in their canoe and took shelter for the night next to us. They had no man with them, yet each of them had a gun, for they had set out to shoot ducks. One was married, the other two were said to be single. They were Abenaquis Indians. The native who accompanied us during the whole journey was an Iroquois Indian. It is singular that an Abenaquis and an Iroquois rarely take lodgings together, yet now and then intermarry. The women who had come hither had their funnel shaped caps, trimmed on the outside with white glass beads. They also had on the French women's waists and jackets which I had never before seen natives wearing. Their evening meal consisted of corn and native Iroquois beans boiled together.

(Adolph B. Benson, ed., *Peter Kalm's Travels in North America,* 2 vols. [1770; reprint, New York: Wilson-Ericson, Inc., 1937], 2:394, 563.)

Chapter Two

Frontiers of Spirit and Soul

Abenaki residents of one of the French mission villages on the St. Lawrence. During the wars of the seventeenth and eighteenth centuries, many Abenakis from Maine, New Hampshire, and Vermont took refuge in French mission villages in Quebec. The French counted the Abenakis as among the most devout Catholics of all their Indian allies. *Gagnon Collection. Bibliothèque Municipale de la Ville de Montréal.*

[*As James Axtell's work demonstrates, the confluence of cultures in colonial North America witnessed a fascinating contest as French, English, and Indians endeavored to convert one another.[1] Nowhere was that contest more pronounced than along religious frontiers where Christian missionaries labored to reap a harvest of Indian souls while fighting to exclude rivals from the field. English Protestants and French Catholics reached into the dawnland with clear conviction that the religion and cosmology of the Abenakis and their neighbors was no more than pagan superstition, which should be eradicated and replaced by Christianity.*

The French enjoyed a clear advantage in the competition. Puritan English missionaries tried to congregate Indian converts into "praying towns" and rid them of their native hairstyle, dress, and language as prerequisites to instilling "civilized" Christian values. French Jesuit priests took up residence in Indian country and shared the lifestyle of their hosts. Unlike their gray-robed Recollect predecessors, the Jesuit Black Robes did not insist that Indians be remade into French persons before making them into Christians.[2] The contrast between English Puritans and French Jesuits was not lost on the Abenakis.

An Indian oral tradition suggests French missionaries may have been active in Abenaki villages on the shores of Lake Champlain as early as 1615. When the French built Fort St. Anne on Isle la Motte in 1666, they also established a mission there. They had a thriving mission on Lake Champlain by 1682 and, in 1700, built the first Catholic church in Vermont, overlooking the Missisquoi River.[3] There was a short-lived French mission at Mount Desert on the coast of Maine in 1614; Jesuits established a mission on the Kennebec in 1646; Capuchins began another at the mouth of the Penobscot in 1648; and one of the oldest Catholic cemeteries in New England, dating from 1688, is located in Penobscot country on Indian Island.[4] The French had a mission among the Cowasucks on the upper Connecticut before 1713. Jesuit teachings reached south across the dawnland to the villages of the Sokokis and Pennacooks, and French missions on the banks of the St. Lawrence attracted refugees and converts from New England in general and Abenaki country in particular.[5] Jesuit priests traveled into the heart of Abenaki country, built chapels and churches, and decorated them with the paraphernalia of their religion. They administered the sacraments in Indian villages across the dawnland and often functioned as military and political agents of the French Crown as well as servants of God (although the Penobscot chief, Loron, assured Governor Belcher of Massachusetts that the French priests "don't lead us to war, but show us the Way to Heaven"[6]*).*

French missionaries made heroic sacrifices in their campaign to win converts and save souls. Traveling alone into Indian country and making their abodes in Indian villages, they had to adapt to Indian ways. Some, like Father Sebastien Rasles, became almost totally immersed in Indian culture. They lived in Indian lodges, ate Indian food, and traveled the seasonal round by canoe and snowshoe. They learned the native language, adapted their messages to suit Indian oratorical styles, and behaved as much as possible according to Indian protocol and cultural expectations. Indifferent to the Indians' lands, women, and furs, they won respect by their poverty, their humility, their courage, and their apparent immunity to the devastating new diseases that left the shamans powerless. They shared the Indians' lives and earned their trust, even though their missionary calling required them to undermine Indian culture, promote divisions within the community, discredit established religious leaders, and initiate social and spiritual revolution. Father Jacques Bigot remarked that he functioned in a shamanistic role among the Abenakis. Arriving in times of cataclysmic change, Jesuit priests "helped the Abenakis to bridge the precontact and postcontact worlds." They functioned as intermediaries between Indian and European society, sometimes representing the Abenakis in conferences with the English. Men like Sebastien Rasles became pivotal figures in Abenaki history, and the Abenakis soon acquired a reputation as the most devout Catholics and staunchest of New France's Indian friends.[7]

The English did not give up the fight, but their efforts were too little and too late to match the zeal of the Jesuits and undermine their influence. By 1700, the English were sending missionaries to live among the eastern Abenakis and in villages on the Merrimack River. In 1717, the Reverend Joseph Baxter began an abortive effort to wean the Abenakis of the Kennebec Valley away from Catholicism and Father Rasles, and Cotton Mather looked forward to "having a considerable number of our eastern savages brought over from the popish to the Protestant religion." In 1735, the government of Massachusetts placed a minister at Fort Dummer to instruct the Indians who came down the Connecticut to trade there.[8] But the English were never able to duplicate the religious ties that bound Abenakis and French, nor were they able to destroy the network of Franco-Abenaki relations they feared and denounced with such passion.

French missionaries gloried in the results of their conversion campaigns, and English ministers shuddered at the thought of papist hands at work in dawnland villages. But both probably overestimated the success of the Jesuits, impressive though it was. When black-robed priests entered Abenaki villages with word of a new religion, the Indians faced a complex range of choices. Despite the un-doubted appeal of Catholic liturgy and Jesuit zeal, and despite the hammer blows European contact delivered to time-honored certainties, most Abenakis did not simply cast their old religion aside. Many hung back and awaited the outcome of the shaman-priest showdown; others quietly adhered to traditional beliefs and practices even as they considered the words and accepted the outward forms of the new religion. The selections in this chapter offer a sampling of the contest of beliefs waged in the dawnland. They suggest how missionaries and Abenakis accommodated to each other's presence and illustrate a vital arena of interaction between Indians and Europeans.]

1. DRUILLETTES AMONG THE ABENAKIS, 1646

[In 1646, Father Gabriel Druillettes established a mission among the Abe-nakis on the Kennebec River. The following extracts from the Jesuit "Relation of 1647" reveal the demands that missionaries like Druillettes made upon the Indians in their endeavors to achieve social transformation and spiritual revo-lution. It also shows how the conflict between Christianity and traditional beliefs often became a contest between the priests and the shamans or "jugglers." The priest's influence stemmed in part from demonstrations that he possessed greater power than his rivals, but as the account indicates, it also depended upon his characteristics of humility, generosity, and endurance, which the Indians ad-mired and which the Jesuits believed they displayed in their missionary work.

Shamans occupied a key position in Abenaki society, curing the sick, pre-dicting events, and functioning as intermediaries between the people and the spirit world. The missionaries sought to discredit the shamans and replace them as the spiritual leaders of the community.]

The Father went a league higher up than Kinibeki, where the savages assembled to the number of fifteen great cabins. They built him a little chapel of boards, made in their manner. It was here that the Father, having sufficient command of their language, efficiently instructed them. He enabled them to understand the object which kept him with them, and the importance of acknowledging him who created them and who will punish them or bless them, according to their works. Seeing that a great part of them showed a liking for the good news of the Gospel, he asks them three things in token of their good-will, and their desire to receive the Faith of Jesus Christ.

The first was, to give up the liquors of Europe, whence ensues great intoxication among the savages. The Abnaquiois promised to avoid these excesses, and have fairly well kept their word.[10]

The Father asked them, in the second place, to live peaceably with one another, and to stop the jealousies and the quarrels which occur among those little nations. It is incredible how much the savages of the same region are united together; but, as one sees in France, between two cities or hamlets, I know not what cavilings, there may be seen also in this part of our America small envies between the various districts of the savages. Men are men everywhere, just as much so at the end of the world as at the middle of it. There were with the Father some savages from various places: on this account there arose, from time to time, disputes, which were much easier to end when they had promised to love one another. So, when their lips had been too widely opened—to speak in their fashion—and when their tongues had not walked straight, they came to ask pardon of one another in the chapel; indeed, there was one of them who, impelled by his fervor, beat himself in the presence of his companion, asking him who has made all to pardon them both their offenses.

The third evidence that the Father secured was, that they

should throw away their Manitou—or, rather, their demons, or fantastic charms. There are few young men among the savages, who have not some stone, or other thing, which they keep as a token of dependence upon the demon, in order to be happy in the hunt, or in play, or in war. It is either given them by some sorcerer, or they dream that they will find it in some place, or their imagination makes them believe that the Manitou presents to them what they encounter. I doubt not that the demon slips into these follies; but I can hardly believe that he communicates with them perceptibly, as he does with the sorcerers and magicians of Europe, and with some peoples of this America. Be this as it may, those who had some of these charms, or Manitous, drew them from their pouches; some cast them away, others brought them to the Father. There were even some sorcerers or jugglers who burned their drums and other instruments of their trades; so that one no longer heard in their cabins those howlings, those cries, those commotions which they raised about their sick, because most of the people loudly protested that they would have recourse to God. I say the most part, and not all; some did not relish this change, and brought it about that a sick man was blown upon and sung over by those insulters. But this poor man, being well prepared for Heaven, would never consent to their superstitions, saying plainly that, if he recovered health, he would regard it as a gift proceeding from him who alone can give and take it away when he pleases. . . .

At the beginning of the year, when these good people were preparing themselves for their great hunt, the sorcerers or jugglers, taking occasion by the hair, acted as soothsayers. They published through the cabins that all those who prayed, and who denounced what these had preached to them would be wretched and would soon die; that the Patriarch—thus they named the Father—and all those who should keep his path, would be taken by the Hiroquois [Iroquois], who molest this nation as well as the others. The savages, who had begun to relish the words of eternal life, were not awed by these threats. They continued their prayers as usual, and the majority placed themselves upon the side of the Father, in order to have the consolation of lodging near his cabin, that they might hear him, and confirm themselves more and more in the truths which they admire. So there they all were in the field; they ascend eight or ten days' journey along the river of Kinibeki. They enter a great lake, where they appoint their rendezvous after their hunt. Having separated into several bands, they declared war on the deer, the elks, the beavers, and other wild beasts.[11]

The Father constantly instructed his band, following it in all its expeditions, with labors too great to buy kingdoms of the earth, but very small for securing the Kingdom of Heaven to souls whose price and value must be estimated in the blood of Jesus Christ.

Their hunt finished, they all met on the shores of that great lake, at the place which they had appointed. It was here that the sorcerers lost their credit—for not only did those who prayed to God incur no disaster, not only did the Father and his people not fall into the ambushes of the Hiroquois, but God further favored them with a successful hunt; and some sick people, at a distance from the Father, having had recourse to God in their sufferings, had received the blessing of very unexpected health. . . .

In conclusion, these peoples have manifested a great affection for the Father. They also said that his life was very different from the lives of their sorcerers, and that the God whom he adored had indeed another power than their Manitou. "It must surely be," they said, "that the God whom this Father announces to us, is powerful, since he so perfectly cures the greatest and the most contagious diseases, which the Manitou or Genii, whom our sorcerers invoke, cannot do. It must surely be that this God is great, and that he has a great spirit, since he causes this stranger to understand and speak our language in two or three months; and the Algonquins, after having remained a whole year with us, cannot speak it. It must certainly be that this God is good and very powerful, since he has taken from this Patriarch the fear of the most contagious diseases, and has given him safety against the threats of our sorcerers and the malice of their charms, at which he mocks. This man is very different from our jugglers. The latter are always asking, and the former never asks anything; the latter are almost entirely absent from our sick, but the former spends days and nights with them. The latter seek nothing but robes of otter, of beaver, and other animals; the former does not so much as look at them from the corner of his eye. Our sorcerers live as well as means allow; the Father fasts often, and has spent fifty days with a little Indian corn, without desiring to taste meat. If one offer him anything that is at all delicate, he straightway carries it to our sick. Certainly it must be that his God very greatly sustains him. We see plainly that he is of a rather delicate constitution; he is not accustomed to our expeditions and to our fatigues; he has led a wholly sedentary life; he is influential among his people, and yet he endures even more than we. He is joyful in the dangers and the hardships of a long journey and an iron road. He is always active about us and our children and our sick; he is welcome everywhere. The French of Pentagouet have cherished him; and, what is much more astonishing, the English, who have neither the same country nor the same language, have respected him. All that shows that his God is good and very powerful."

(Thwaites, ed., *Jesuit Relations,* 31:189–205.)

2. DRUILLETTES RETURNS TO THE ABENAKIS

[Several years later, Father Druillettes returned to Maine. Jesuit enthusiasm for their work aside, Druillette's reception testified to the strength of the ties that developed between French missionaries and Abenaki converts.]

As soon as the news of the Father's return was carried to the other villages of the Abnaquiois, people came from all sides to invite him, with earnest and pressing entreaties, to instruct all the country. He visited first the 12 or 13 settlements or villages of Kenebec, which the French commonly call Quinibequi, and partly along the coast of Acadia, which the English occupy. He was everywhere received like an Angel descended from Heaven. If the years have their Winter, they also have their Spring. If these missions have their griefs, they are not deprived of their joys and consolations. "These latter," says the Father, "I have felt in such intensity as to be beyond the power of expression, upon seeing the Gospel seed that I had, four years previously, planted in ground which had for so many centuries produced only brambles and thorns, bear fruits worthy of God's table.

(Thwaites, ed., *Jesuit Relations*, 37:257.)

3. THE CONVERSION OF WANALANCET, 1674

[Puritans battled to save Indian souls from what they saw as the twin evils of heathen ignorance and Catholic corruption. For three years running, missionary John Eliot journeyed to the spring fishing camps of the Pennacooks on the Merrimack River. There he worked diligently to convert the Pennacook chief, Passaconaway, and then his son, Wanalancet. Wanalancet had serious misgivings and recognized that his actions would divide his people, but he finally agreed to embrace the new religion. Daniel Gookin was present at the historic meeting.[12]]

May 5th 1674, according to our usual custom, Mr. Eliot and myself took our journey to Wamesit, or Pawtuckett, and arriving there that evening, Mr. Eliot preached to as many of them as could be got together out of Matthew xxii. 1–14, the parable of the marriage of the king's son. We met at the wigwam of one called Wannalancet, about two miles from the town, near Pawtuckett falls, and bordering upon Merrimak river. This person, Wannalancet, is the eldest son of old Pasaconaway, the chiefest sachem of Pawtuckett. He is a sober and grave person, and of years, between fifty and sixty. He hath been always loving and friendly to the English. Many endeavors have been used several years to gain this sachem to embrace the Christian religion; but he hath stood off from time to time, and not yielded up himself personally, though for four years past he hath been willing to hear the word of God preached, and to keep the sabbath. A great reason that hath kept him off, I conceive, hath been the indisposition and averseness of sundry of his chief men and relations to pray to God; which he foresaw would desert him, in case he turned Christian. But at this time, May 6th, 1674, it pleased God so to influence and overcome his heart, that it being proposed to him to give his answer concerning praying to God, after some deliberation and serious pause, he stood up, and made a speech to this effect.

Sirs you have been pleased for four years last past, in your abundant love, to apply yourselves particularly unto me and my people, to exhort, press, and persuade us to pray to God. I am very thankful to you for your pains. I must acknowledge, said he, I have, all my days, used to pass in an old canoe (alluding to his frequent custom to pass in a canoe upon the river) and now you exhort me to change and leave my old canoe, and embark in a new canoe, to which I have hitherto been unwilling. But now I yield up myself to your advice, and enter into a new canoe, and do engage to pray to God hereafter.

This his professed subjection was well pleasing to all that were present, of which there were some English persons of quality; as Mr. Richard Daniel, a gentleman that lived in Billerica, about six miles off, and Lieutenant Henchman, a neighbour at Chelmsford, besides brother Eliot and myself, with sundry others, English and Indians. Mr. Daniel before named desired brother Eliot to tell this sachem from him, that it may be, while he went in his old canoe, he passed in a quiet stream, but the end thereof was death and destruction to soul and body. But now he went into a new canoe, perhaps he would meet with storms and trials; but yet he should be encouraged to persevere, for the end of his voyage would be everlasting rest. Moreover he and his people were exhorted by brother Eliot and myself, to go on and sanctify the sabbath, to hear the word, and use the means that God hath appointed, and encourage their hearts in the Lord their God. Since that time, I hear that sachem doth persevere and is a constant and diligent hearer of God's word, and sanctifieth the sabbath. Though the doth travel to Wamesit meeting every sabbath, which is above two miles, and though sundry of his people have deserted him since he subjected to the gospel, yet he continues and persists.

(*Collections of the Massachusetts Historical Society* 1 [1792]: 187.)

4. ABENAKIS FLEE TO THE FRENCH MISSION, 1676–1677

[The French established a mission at Sillery near Quebec in 1630 as an experimental community of Christianized Indians; but alcoholism, diseases, war, lack of funds, and cultural resistance from the local Algonquin and Montagnais Indians led to its rapid decline. The outbreak of King Philip's War in New England revived the mission as Abenakis fled north, seeking refuge from the conflict. The French viewed this migration as providential and seized upon the refugees to continue God's work. Sokokis and Abenakis continued to migrate

north to the mission villages, and Sillery soon had more occupants than it could handle. Father Thiery Beschefer, Superior of the Missions of the Society of Jesus in Canada, described the Abenaki influx in his report to the Reverend Father Provincial of the Provence in France in October 1683.¹³]

We have here also another mission, which is among the Abnaquis settled at Sillery, a league and a half from Quebec. It was the last one begun, and nevertheless it is in no wise behind the others, as regards the fervor of the Christians who compose it. Sillery is the home of the Algonquins, where they formerly had one of the most flourishing missions in Canada; but drunkenness caused such disastrous ravages among them that there is only a wretched remnant of that nation, scattered through the woods and in places where, as they no longer have any missionaries to reproach them with their misconduct, they can indulge in their vice with greater freedom. It seems as if God's providence had brought the Abnaquis hither, with the view of substituting them for the Algonquins.

These tribes inhabit the country that borders on Acadia and New England on the seashore, 60 leagues from here. The war in which they were engaged with the English, to whom they caused much trouble, at the outset compelled about thirty of them to leave their country; for they dreaded everything from a war which, however it might have been to their advantage until then, always threatened them with unpleasant consequences. They thought that they could not better provide for their safety than by taking refuge among the French. They were gladly received at Sillery, where they were adopted by the Algonquins, a few of whom still remained. The missionary who then had charge of the mission soon learned their language, and at once set to work to instruct them, although drunkenness, to which they were unusually addicted, seemed to remove all hope of producing any great result among them. But the charity that was displayed toward them in providing them with everything they needed—for they had come destitute of everything—and, above all, grace, soon won their hearts; and they were found to possess a docility surpassing anything that could be hoped for. These propitious beginnings were soon followed by still more favorable results. For no sooner were they convinced of the truth of our religion than their only thought was to make their kindred who were still in Acadia participate in their happiness; for they could not bear, without profound grief, to see the persons most dear to them separated from them for all eternity. This soon made these neophytes New Apostles. Several returned to Acadia: some to bring hither their fathers and mothers; some their brethren; others their best friends, and even all their countrymen, if they could, and with such eagerness for their salvation that, on their arrival, the missionary found them already instructed in most of our mysteries—our zealous neophytes thus returning, as if in triumph at having snatched these spoils from the demon. As the missionary who was then at Sillery had been sent elsewhere, Father Jacques Bigot, who had been studying their language for only three months, during which he had made great progress, took charge of that mission. By his gentleness in not being repelled by their savage temper, or even by their faults, and by his condescension in taking an interest in the details of all their trivial affairs, he soon became master of their hearts.

(Thwaites, ed., *Jesuit Relations*, 62:259–61.)

5. A CONFERENCE WITH AN INDIAN SAGAMORE, 1696

[In November 1694, the Abenaki chief Bomaseen, "a Commander of prime Quality among the Indians," and two companions came to Pemaquid under a flag of truce. The English seized them and sent Bomaseen to Boston "that he

*might in a close Imprisonment there, have Time to consider of his Treacheries,
and his Cruelties, for which the Justice of Heaven had thus delivered him up."
During his Bostonian captivity, in 1696, Bomaseen was visited by the Puritan
minister Cotton Mather. The following discourse, in which Mather refers to
himself in the third person, reveals little of the realities of Indian beliefs or of
the Indians' true responses to Mather's words; but it does illustrate the intense
rivalry that existed between English Protestants and French Catholics for Indian
allegiance, spiritual as well as political, and the nature of Puritan attitudes
towards both French and Indians.]*

Bommaseen was, with some other Indians, now a prisoner, in
Boston. He desired a conference with a minister of Boston,[14]
which was granted him. Bommaseen, with the other Indians
assenting and asserting to it, then told the minister, that he
prayed his instruction in the Christian religion; inasmuch as he
was afraid, that the French, in the Christian religion, which they
taught the Indians, had abused them. The minister enquired of
him, what of the things taught them by the French, appeared
most suspicious to them? He said, the French taught them, that
the Lord Jesus Christ was of the French nation; that His Mother,
the Virgin Mary, was a French lady; that they were the English
who had murdered Him; and, that whereas He rose from the
dead, and went up to the Heavens, all that would recommend
themselves unto His favour, must revenge His quarrel upon the
English, as far as they can. He asked the minister, whether these
things were so, and prayed the minister to instruct him in the
True Christian Religion. The minister considering that the hu-
mour and manner of the Indians was to have their discourses
managed with much of similitude in them, looked about for
some agreeable object, from whence he might with apt resem-
blances convey the ideas of Truth unto the minds of salvages.
And he thought none would be more agreeable to them than a

tankard of drink, which happened then to be standing on the table. So he proceeded in this method with them.

He told them (still with proper actions painting and pointing out the signs unto them,) that our Lord Jesus Christ had given us a Good Religion, which might be resembled unto the good drink in the cup upon the table.

That if we take this Good Religion, (even that good drink,) into our hearts, it will do us good, and preserve us from death.

That God's book, the Bible, is the cup wherein that good drink of religion is offered unto us.

That the French, having the cup of good drink in their hands, had put poison into it, and then made the Indians to drink that poisoned liquor, whereupon they run mad, and fell to killing of the English, though they could not but know it must unavoidably issue in their own destruction at the last.

That it was plain the English had put no poison into the good drink; for they set the cup wide open, and invited all men to come and see before they taste, even the very Indians themselves; for we translated the Bible into Indian. That they might gather from hence that the French had put poison into the good drink, inasmuch as the French kept the cup fast shut, (the Bible in an unknown tongue) and kept their hands upon the eyes of the Indians, when they put it unto their mouths.

The Indians expressing themselves to be well satisfied with what the minister had hitherto said, prayed him to go on, with showing them, what was the good drink, and what was the poison which the French had put into it.

He then set before them distinctly the chief articles of the Christian Religion, with all the simplicity and sincerity of a Protestant, adding upon each, "This is the good drink, in the Lord's Cup of Life." And they still professed that they liked it all.

Whereupon he demonstrated unto them how the Papists had

in their Idolatrous Popery, some way or other depraved and altered every one of these articles, with scandalous ingredients of their own invention, adding upon each, "This is the poison which the French have put into the cup."

At last, he mentioned this article.

"To obtain the pardon of your sins, you must confess your sins to God, and pray to God that He would pardon your sins, for the sake of Jesus Christ, who died for the sins of His people. God loves Jesus Christ infinitely, and if you place your eye on Jesus Christ only when you beg the pardon of your sins, God will pardon them. You need confess your sins to none but God, except in cases when men have known your sins or have been hurt by your sins; and then those men should know that you confess your sins. But after all, none but God can pardon them."

He then added, "The French have put poison into this good drink. They tell you that you must confess your sins to a priest, and carry skins to a priest, and submit unto a penance enjoined by a priest, and this priest is to give you a pardon. There is no need of all this. 'Tis nothing but French poison, all of it."

The wretches appearing astonished to meet with one who would so fairly put them into a glorious way to obtain the pardon of their sins, and yet take no bever-skins for it, in a rapture of astonishment they fell down on their knees, and got his hand into theirs, and fell to kissing of it with an extream show of affection.

He shaking them off, with dislike of their posture, Bommaseen, with the rest of them, stood up; and first lifting up his eyes and hands to Heaven, declaring that God should be judge of his heart in what he said, he then said, "Sir, I thank you for these things; I resolve to spit up all the French poison; you shall be my Father; I will be your son; I beseech you, to continue to instruct me in that religion, which may bring me to the salvation of my soul!" Now God knows, what heart this Indian had, when he so expressed himself: to Him let us leave it.

But so much for this digression.

(Cotton Mather, "Decennium Luctuosum," in Charles M. Lincoln, ed., *Narratives of the Indian Wars 1675–1699* [New York: Charles Scribner's Sons, 1913], 255–58.)

6. THE LIMITS OF CONVERSION

[The conversion of Wanalancet did not guarantee that the Pennacooks would follow in his footsteps. As the following extract shows, they were neither totally converted to Protestantism nor completely weaned away from the French. In 1700, the English were alarmed by rumors of a multitribal insurrection fomenting in Pennacock country in the Merrimack Valley. As usual, as this letter from M. Laborie to Lord Bellomont of June 17, 1700, shows, they saw Jesuit hands at work.]

The four Indians who returned here are departing to-day for Penikook with 25 others whom they have persuaded, in spite of all my efforts, to accompany them. They gave as a reason that the inhabitants of New Roxbury continually annoyed them, and when I was not satisfied, they said that the religion of the Penikook Indians was more beautiful than ours, for the French gave them silver crosses to wear on their necks. And they added that there was another strong reason which they could not tell but would soon be known. In all they say I can see the activity of the priests and the concealment of some design.

(*Calendar of State Papers, Colonial Series, America and the West Indies* [London: Her Majesty's Stationery Office, 1910; reprint, Krauz Reprint Ltd., 1964], 1700:401.)

[Just four days later, the government of Massachusetts resolved to act with speed and send a minister to the Indians on the Merrimack River "to Instruct them in the true Christian Religion."[15]]

7. CATHOLIC ABENAKIS DECLINE PROTESTANT MISSIONARIES, 1701

[English attempts to counteract Catholic influence among the Abenakis were often too little and too late to make any serious inroads, as illustrated by this extract from a conference between Commissioners from Massachusetts Bay and the eastern Indians in June 1701.]

The Commissioners: We are in an especial manner directed to invite you unto a union with us in the true Christian Religion, separated from those foolish superstitious and plain idolatries with which the Roman Catholicks and especially the Jesuits and missionarys have corrupted it. To which intent we are to offer you the assistance of teachers for your instruction in like manner as is practised amongst those Indians who live amongst us, of whom great numbers have happily received, and live in the faith of our Lord Jesus Christ, in which great undertaking we shall expect nothing more on your parts than your good treatment of those ministers whom we shall at any time send amongst you. *The Indians' answer:* It much surprizeth us that you should propose any thing of religion to us, for we did not think any thing of that nature would have been mentioned.

Furthermore nothing of that nature was mentioned when the peace was concluded between all nations. Furthermore the English formerly neglected to instruct us in religion which if they had then offered it to us, we should have embraced it and detested the religion which we now profess. But now being instructed by the French, we have promised to be true to God in our religion, and it is this we profess to stand by.

(*Collections of the Maine Historical Society*, 2d ser., 10 [1907]: 94.)

8. FATHER RASLES DESCRIBES HIS MINISTRY, 1722

[In English eyes, Sebastien Rasles personified the sinister influence of Catholicism in the dawnland. Born in Besançon, France, in 1652, Rasles joined

the Society of Jesus in 1675. On arriving in New France, he was despatched to the mission at the Falls of the Chaudière, where he learned to speak Abenaki, and then spent two years at the Kaskaskia mission in the Illinois country. After being transferred to Maine in 1694, Rasles devoted his life to the Abenakis, working out of the mission village of Norridgewock [Nanrantsouak] on the Kennebec River. The following extracts from a letter written to his nephew in the fall of 1722 illustrate Rasles' dedication and the degree to which missionaries like him were able to secure Abenaki attachment to the French. Rasles' work won him the trust of the Indians—even to the extent of being permitted to speak in their councils—and earned him the bitter hostility of the English.[16]

During the more than thirty years that I have spent in the midst of forests with the savages, I have been so occupied in instructing them and training them in Christian virtues that I have scarcely had leisure to write frequent letters, even to the persons who are dearest to me. Nevertheless, I cannot refuse you the little account that you ask of my occupations. I owe it in gratitude for the friendship which makes you so much interested in what concerns me.

I am in a district of this vast extent of territory which lies between Acadia and New England. Two other missionaries are, like myself, busy among the *Abnakis* savages; but we are far distant from one another. The *Abnakis* savages, besides the two villages which they have in the midst of the French colony, have also three other important ones, each situated on the bank of a river. These three rivers empty into the sea to the south of Canada, between New England and Acadia.

The village in which I dwell is called *Nanrantsouak*. It is situated on the bank of a river, which empties into the sea thirty leagues below. I have built here a church which is commodious and well adorned. I thought it my duty to spare nothing, either for its decoration or for the beauty of the vestments that are used in our holy ceremonies: altar-cloths, chasubles, copes, sacred vessels, everything is suitable, and would be esteemed in the churches of Europe. I have trained a minor clergy of about forty young savages, who, in cassocks and surplices, assist at divine service. Each one has his duty, not only in serving at the holy Sacrifice of the Mass, but in chanting the divine office at the Benediction of the blessed Sacrament, and in the processions—which are made with a great concourse of savages, who often come from a great distance in order to be present at them. You would be edified with the good order which they observe, and with the reverence which they show.

. . . .

After Mass, I catechize the children and the young people. A great number of older persons are present, and answer with docility to the questions which I ask them. The remainder of the morning, until noon, is devoted to all those who have anything to tell me. At that time they come in crowds, to reveal to me their griefs and anxieties, or to tell me the causes of complaint which they have against their tribesmen, or to consult me about their marriages or their other private affairs. I must instruct some, and console others; reestablish peace in disunited families, and calm troubled consciences; and correct a few others with reprimands, mingled with gentleness and charity—in fine, send them all away content, as far as I can.

In the afternoon, I visit the sick and go to the cabins of those who have need of special instruction. If they are holding a council, which often happens among the savages, they send one of the chiefs of the meeting, who begs me to be present at their deliberations. I go immediately to the place where the council is in session. If I think that they are taking a wise course, I approve it; if, on the contrary, I find anything amiss in their decision, I declare my own opinion, which I support with a few sound reasons and they conform to it. My advice always determines their decisions. I am invited even to their feasts.

. . . .

When the savages go the sea to spend some months hunting ducks, bustards, and other birds that are found there in great numbers, they build on some island a church which they cover with bark, near which they set up a little cabin for my dwelling. I take care to transport thither a part of the ornaments, and the service is performed there with the same propriety and the same throng of people as in the village.

. . . .

The whole Abnakis Nation is Christian and is very zealous in preserving its religion. This attachment to the Catholic Faith has made it thus far prefer an alliance with us to the advantages that it would have obtained from an alliance with its English neighbors. These advantages are very attractive to our savages; the readiness with which they can engage in trade with the English, from whom they are distant only two or three days' journey, the convenience of the route, the great bargains they find in the purchase of goods which suit them—nothing would be more likely to attract them. Whereas in going to Quebec they must travel more than fifteen days to reach it; they must be supplied with provisions for the journey, and there are several rivers to cross and frequent portages to make. They feel these inconveniences, and they are not indifferent to their own interests. But their faith is infinitely dearer to them, and they believe that if they were to break off their connection with us they would very soon be without a missionary, without sacraments, without the sacrifice, almost without any service of religion, and in manifest danger of being plunged back into their former belief. This is the bond which unites them to the French. There have been vain endeavors to break this bond—both by snares that have been laid for their simplicity, and by violence, which could not fail to irritate a tribe so infinitely jealous as is this of its rights and liberty. These beginnings of misunderstanding continue to alarm me, and make me fear the dispersion of the flock which

Providence has confided to my care for so many years, and for which I would willingly sacrifice all that remains to me of life. See the various artifices to which the English have resorted to detach them from the alliance with us.

. . . .

A missionary can scarcely fail to be an object of hate to these gentlemen. Love for the religion which he endeavors to impress upon the hearts of these savages holds these neophytes firmly in union with us, and separates them from the English. The latter therefore regard me as an invincible obstacle to their plan of spreading themselves over the territory of the *Abnakis,* and of gradually seizing this mainland which is between New England and Acadia. They have often attempted to remove me from my flock and more than once a price has been set on my head. It was about the end of January in the year 1722 when they made a new attempt, which had no other success than to manifest their ill will toward me.

(Thwaites, ed., *Jesuit Relations,* 67:85–97, 113.)

9. THE POWER OF LANGUAGE, 1723

[Jesuit missionaries like Sebastien Rasles sometimes spent more of their lives among the Indians than they did living in European society. Rasles studied with an Abenaki family band and baptized one of their children with his own name. He wrote to his brother, "As for what concerns me personally, I assure you that I see, that I hear, that I speak, only as a savage."[17] In this extract of a letter to his brother, Rasles depicts the process of acquiring competence in an Indian language. Rasles produced an Abenaki-French dictionary, which is preserved at Harvard University.[18]]

It was in the midst of these tribes, which are considered the least rude of all our savages, that I served my missionary apprenticeship. My chief occupation was the study of their language; it is very difficult to learn, especially when one has no other masters than savages. They have several sounds which are uttered only by the throat, without making any motion of the lips; *ou,* for instance, is of this number, and that is why in writing we indicate it by the figure 8, in order to distinguish it from other letters. I spent part of the day in their cabins, hearing them talk. I was obliged to give the utmost attention, in order to connect what they said, and to conjecture its meaning. Sometimes I caught it exactly, but more often I was deceived because, not being accustomed to the trick of their guttural sounds, I repeated only half the word, and thereby gave them cause for laughter.

At last, after five months of continual application, I succeeded in understanding all their terms; but that did not enable me to express myself to their satisfaction. I had still much progress to make before catching the form of expression and the spirit of the language, which are entirely different from the spirit and form of our European languages. In order to shorten the time, and thus enable me sooner to perform my duties, I selected a few savages who had most intelligence, and who used the best language. I repeated to them in a clumsy manner some passages from the catechism, and they gave them to me again, with all the nicety of their language. I immediately wrote these down, and by this means, in a reasonably short time I had made a dictionary, and also a catechism which contained the precepts and mysteries of religion.

It cannot be denied that the language of the savages has real beauties, and there is an indescribable force in their style and manner of expression.

(Thwaites, ed., *Jesuit Relations,* 67:143–45.)

10. THE DEATH OF FATHER RASLES, 1724

[Regarding the presence of Jesuit missionaries in Abenaki villages as a sinister threat to their own religion and settlements, the English tried repeatedly to destroy Rasles' mission and seize the notorious priest. In 1705, Colonel Hilton and 275 men marched to Norridgewock and, though Rasles escaped, burned his church. In 1720, the Massachusetts Council offered one hundred pounds for Rasles' arrest. Colonel Thomas Westbrook attacked Norridgewock with one hundred men in 1722, pillaged the church, and carried off Rasles' papers, including his Abenaki dictionary. Westbrook tried again to capture Rasles the following year. Finally, in 1724, Johnson Harmon and Jeremiah Moulton led an English expedition accompanied by Indian auxiliaries in a successful attack on the village. Father de la Chasse, Superior-General of the Missions in New France, reported Rasles' martyrdom in a letter from Quebec, October 29, 1724.[10]]

Father Rasles, the missionary of the *Abnakis,* had become very odious to the English. As they were convinced that his endeavors to confirm the savages in the Faith constituted the greatest obstacle to their plan of usurping the territory of the savages, they put a price on his head; and more than once they had attempted to abduct him, or to take his life. At last they have succeeded in gratifying their passion of hatred, and in ridding themselves of the apostolic man; but, at the same time, they have procured for him a glorious death, which was ever the object of his desire—for we know that long ago he aspired to the happiness of sacrificing his life for his flock. I will describe to you in few words the circumstances of that event.

After many acts of hostility had been committed on both sides by the two nations, a little army of Englishmen and their savage allies, numbering eleven hundred men, unexpectedly came to attack the village of *Nanrantsouak.* The dense thickets with which that village is surrounded helped them to conceal their movements, and as, besides, it was not enclosed with palisades, the savages were taken by surprise, and became aware of the enemy's approach only by a volley from their muskets, which riddled all the cabins. At that time there were only fifty warriors in the village. At the first noise of the muskets, they tumultuously seized their weapons, and went out of their cabins to oppose the enemy. Their design was not rashly to meet the onset of so many combatants, but to further the flight of the women and children, and give them time to gain the other side of the river, which was not yet occupied by the English.

Father Rasles, warned by the clamor and the tumult of the danger which was menacing his neophytes, promptly left his house and fearlessly appeared before the enemy. He expected by his presence either to stop their first efforts, or at least to draw their attention to himself alone, and at the expense of his life to procure the safety of his flock.

As soon as they perceived the missionary, a general shout was raised which was followed by a storm of musket-shots that was poured upon him. He dropped dead at the foot of a large cross that he had erected in the midst of the village, in order to announce the public profession that was made therein of adoring a crucified God. Seven savages who were around him, and were exposing their lives to guard that of their father, were killed by his side.

The death of the shepherd dismayed the flock. The savages took to flight and crossed the river, part of them by fording, and part by swimming. They were exposed to all the fury of their enemies, until the moment when they retreated into the woods which are on the other side of the river. There they were gathered, to the number of a hundred and fifty. From more than two thousand gunshots that had been fired at them only thirty persons were killed, including the women and children, and fourteen were wounded. The English did not attempt to pursue the fugitives; they were content with pillaging and burning the village. They set fire to the church, after a base profanation of the sacred vessels and of the adorable Body of Jesus Christ.

The precipitate retreat of the enemy permitted the return of the Nanrantsouakians to the village. The very next day they visited the wreck of their cabins, while the women, on their part, sought for roots and plants suitable for treating the wounded. Their first care was to weep over the body of their holy missionary. They found it pierced by hundreds of bullets, the scalp torn off, the skull broken by blows from a hatchet, the mouth and the eyes filled with mud, the bones of the legs broken, and all the members mutilated. This sort of inhumanity, practiced on a body deprived of feeling and of life, can scarcely be attributed to any one but to the savage allies of the English.

After these devout Christians had washed and kissed many times the honored remains of their father, they buried him in the very place where, the night before, he had celebrated the holy Sacrifice of the Mass—that is, in the place where the altar had stood before the burning of the church.

By such a precious death did the apostolic man finish, on the 23rd of August in this year, a course of thirty-seven years spent in the arduous labors of this mission.

(Thwaites, ed., *Jesuit Relations*, 67:231–37.)

[Following the destruction of their village, some 150 Norridgewocks took refuge in French mission villages in Canada, although many returned when the war was over.20]

11. BAPTISMS AND BURIALS: EXTRACTS FROM THE REGISTERS AT FORT ST. FREDERIC

[French forts in the dawnland functioned as trade centers, military outposts, and meeting grounds for Gallic and Indian culture. In some cases, they also

*afforded spiritual solace and services for resident Frenchmen and visiting In-
dians alike. The registers at Fort St. Frederic on the southern edge of Lake
Champlain give hints of the extent of Franco-Abenaki interaction in such places.
Abenakis from St. Francis, Missisquoi, and other communities in the Champlain
Valley journeyed to the fort and took advantage of the chaplain's services to get
married, baptize their children, and bury their dead. French officers and interpreters regularly acted as sponsors or god-parents.]*

Baptisms

Charles-Jerome, son of François and Catherine, Abenaki Indians . . . 1733. Godfather, Charles Monarque, godmother,
Marie Monarque.

Marie-Françoise and Marie-Madeleine, daughters of Pierre
Nicolas and Suzanne, Abenaki Indians, 24 July 1735. Godfather
Dominique Janson Lapalme and Nicolas Moran; godmother,
Madeleine Renaudot.

Michel, son of André Mantoch and Dorothée, Abenakis from
Missisquoi, 10 October 1737. Godfather, Michel Denis; godmother, Charlotte Legrain, called Lavallée.

Charlotte, daughter of Pierre-Thomas and Anne, Abenaki
Indians from Missisquoi, 23 February 1738. Godfather, François
Janis; godmother, Charlotte Legrain, called Lavallée.

Catherine-Antoine, daughter of Pierre and Agnes, Abenaki
Indians from Saint Francis, 1 March 1738. Godfather, Pierre
Hertel de Beaubassin; godmother, Anne-Madeleine, an Abe-
naki.

Jean-Baptiste, son of Pierre-Jean, called the White Head[21] and
Hélène, Abenaki Indians from Missisquoi, 19 April 1740. Godfather, Jean-Baptiste de Montigny, an officer, godmother, Mar-
guerite-Rosalie de Chevigny.

Joseph-Louis, son of Robert and Marie-Marthe, Missisquoi

Abenakis, 19 March 1741. Godfather, Louis Ostiquaien; godmother, Catherine, wife of the godfather.

Catherine-Antoine, daughter of Gabriel and Anne Thérèse, Abenaki Indians from Missisquoi, 21 February 1745. Godfather, Pierre Hertel de Beaubassin.

Marie-Catherine, daughter of Charlot and Marguerite, Abenakis from Missisquoi, 14 October 1745. Godfather, Pierre Hertel de Beaubassin; godmother, Marie Monique, an Abenaki.

Étienne-Joseph, son of Louis and Marie, Missisquoi Abenakis, 14 December 1748. Godfather, cadet Étienne Hertel; godmother, Anne-Marie, an Abenaki.

François-Joseph, son of Jean-Baptiste and Marie-Anne, Abenaki Indians from Missisquoi, 3 March 1750. Godfather, Jean-Baptiste; godmother, Marie, both Abenakis.

Jean Baptiste, son of Ignace and Thérèse. Abenaki Indians from Saint Francis, 6 February 1751. Godfather, Jean-Baptiste, a Missisquoi Indian.

Marie-Josephe, natural daughter of Hélène, an Abenaki woman from Missisquoi, 4 November 1753. Godfather, Michel Boileau; godmother, Anne-Madeleine, an Abenaki.

Robert, son of François and Marie-Esther, Abenaki Indians from Missisquoi, 8 March 1754. Godfather, Joseph, an Abenaki.

Marie-Catherine, daughter of Pierre and Agnes, Abenakis from Missisquoi, 1 July 1755. Godfather, Joseph Courval; godmother, Marie-Catherine Leriger La plante, wife of J. B. Payan (baptized at Fort St. Jean).

Burials

Pierre Jean, son of Nespa8it and Marguerite Malhonnete, Indians from Saint Francis, 27 April 1733. Age, about one year.

Jacques, a Saint Francis Indian, 28 April 1733. Age, about 17 years.

Madeleine-Monique, daughter of Pierre-Thomas Cadenait and Aimée, Missisquoi Abenakis, 23 February 1738. Age, 5 years.

Marie-Catherine, widow of Pierre, an Abenaki, 9 January 1745. Age, 100 years.

Marie-Anne, daughter of Joseph and Marguerite, Missisquoi Abenakis, 2 March 1745. Age, 7 months.

Louis, son of Marguerite, an Abenaki woman from Saint Francis, 16 April 1745. Age, 2 years.

François Mantok, an Abenaki from Missisquoi, 4 April 1748. Age, about 40.

Marie-Françoise, wife of Joseph Portneuf, an Indian from Saint Francis, 23 June 1751.

An Abenaki Indian from Saint Francis, 21 July 1756. Age, about 6 years.

(Pierre-Georges, Roy, *Hommes et Choses du Fort Saint-Frédéric* [Montreal: Les Editions Des Dix, 1946], 268–312; editor's translation.)

12. ABENAKIS RESIST REMOVAL, 1757

[Abenaki ties to the French did not rob them of their independence of thought or action. In 1757, delegates from the mission villages of St. Francis and Becancour went to Governor Vaudreuil and forcefully protested Jesuit plans to remove their mission to the Ohio River where it would cater to "Loup"—probably displaced Delaware—Indians. When the Abenakis refused to go, the Jesuits retaliated by refusing them the sacraments and even denying them access to church. But the Abenakis were not easily cowed.]

Well and good, say the Indians to their missionary, you are the father of prayer. The prayers, the sacraments, and the church all belong to you, but it is we who have built your house, it is ours, and we are going to close its door to you. Jerome, the chief of the village, also presented a note to M. de Vaudreuil, conceived in these terms: "I, Jerome,[22] chief of the villages of the Abnakis, say to you, my father, that the black robes wish to make us leave our native hearthstones and carry our council fire elsewhere. This land we inhabit is ours. What it produces is the fruit of our labor. Dig into it and you will find the bones of our ancestors. Thus, it is necessary that our ancestors' bones rise up from the ground and follow us into a foreign land." The Jesuits finally renounced, at least for the present, this enterprise.

[About twenty Abenaki apostles accompanied Father Virot to the Ohio, but they met a cold reception from the Indians there and were back at St. Francis three years later.]

(Edward P. Hamilton, ed., Adventure in the Wilderness: The American Journals of Louis Antoine de Bougainville 1756–1760 [Norman: University of Oklahoma Press, 1964], 83–84.)

13. THE CONTEST CONTINUES, 1764

[The English victory in the Seven Years' War did not extinguish French influence among the dawnland tribes, nor did it shake the Indians' attachment to their Catholic religion. The following extracts from a conference with the Penobscots and from Governor Bernard's letter voicing his concerns to the Earl of Halifax demonstrate the continuing importance of the Catholic religion in the lives of the Indians, as well as the continuing threat of French Catholicism in the minds of the English.]

A Conference between his Excellency Governor Bernard and Aleser a chief and others of the Penobscot Indians held at Fort Pownall September 26, 1764.

Aleser. All the young men that you wanted to go to Canada and Norridgewalk immediately went at your desire, and now we hope you'll mind what we desire and assist us. We are poor.

There is one God, and we have a religion among us that we

cannot part with, and we want a Father to baptize our children, and marry us, and administer the sacrament to us, and confess us, and shew us the way to Heaven; that is, to keep us from what is bad, correct our lives, and absolve our sins. It is a few years since Canada was taken, and since we have had no father among us, our people grow loose and disorderly, drink too hard, and run into many bad practices, which a Father (if we had one among us) would remind us of and correct. It is usual to help the poor. We are poor, and therefore help us in the matter of religion.

I am a young man and therefore would not talk too much, lest the old men should dislike it. I would say no more upon this.

Governor Bernard to the Earl of Halifax, Sept. 29, 1764.

The Indians must have a priest of some kind or other. If he be a true Romish priest, he will keep them estranged from and inimical to Great Britain, flatter them with the expectation of a French revolution, and have them ready to rise upon the least foreign invasion or internal Canadian commotion; and all this by means of their religion. On the other hand a missionary of the Church of England will meet with great difficulties; but I am far from thinking they will be insurmountable. He will have a safe and convenient residence at Fort Pownall. And by exercising his functions in the chapple there (which I have had built there this year) with as much show and form as our religion will admit of, I am satisfyed that the Indians would by degrees be reconciled to it. I mentioned before that a French Protestant in English orders would be most suitable upon account of his language (which is generally understood by the Penobscot Indians and universally by the Passamaquoddies) as well as of his nation.

But one who has been a Romish priest and has conformed to the Church of England, if he was sincere and discrete would be more suitable. Canada must afford many such persons, but in general the priests there are very ignorant and illiterate. Ireland must have such; but he must be master of the French tongue if not a Frenchman.

(*Collections of the Maine Historical Society*, 2d ser., 13 [1909]: 368, 372.)

[*The French were not the only ones to exert pressure on the tribes through religion, and the United States soon took up the tradition. Busy trying to enlist Penobscot and Passamaquoddy support for the impending expedition against the British at Penobscot in July 1779, Colonel John Allan sent the Penobscots a war belt of wampum and "the priest to push them along to Business."*[23]]

Chapter 3

Dawnland
Diplomacy

Signatures of the Abenakis and their allies in a letter from the "Eastern Indians" to the governor of Massachusetts, July 27, 1721. *Massachusetts Archives.*

[Relations between Abenakis and English frequently broke down into petty violence and open warfare. But resorting to arms was not always a knee-jerk response to any problem that arose. Diplomatic negotiations were a principal means by which Europeans and Indians settled or avoided disputes, reaffirmed friendships and terminated hostilities, and, of course, transferred land.[1] They approached these negotiations from different perspectives, engaged in them for different purposes, and often left them with different understandings of what had occurred. Nevertheless, both saw diplomacy as an avenue of communication and a means of reaching agreement in a world of interethnic and international contact. Europeans in Indian country regularly adapted their procedures to suit native protocol; Indians regularly tried to initiate dialogue as a means of resolving issues that arose from interaction with the newcomers.

The French were careful to conduct relations with proper regard for Indian rights and concerns; they did not establish posts and settlements on Abenaki land without first obtaining the Abenakis' consent in open meetings. The Gallic reputation for generally harmonious relations with Indians is well known, but their respect for Indian rights was based on practical realities. As a memorandum to Versailles pointed out, the Abenakis were the sole bulwark of New France against the English and Iroquois, and "if we do not agree or do not pretend to agree to their rights over the country which they occupy, never will we be able to engage them in any war for the defense of this same country which is the first line of defence of Canada." With few demands on Abenaki lands and relying upon ties of religion and reciprocity for Abenaki allegiance, the French had little reason to resort to treaty-making to secure their ends.[2]

French and English ministers disagreed over the boundaries between New France and New England and about sovereignty over the Abenaki inhabitants of the territories they claimed.[3] The French were able to justify their claims by pointing out that they were there with the Indians' consent. Much more concerned with acquiring land, the English tried to formalize their relations with the Indians and legitimize their occupation of Abenaki territory by right of conquest. They repeatedly entitled their treaties, "Acts of Submission," and demanded that the Indians submit to the crown and acknowledge their own wrong-

doings. Abenakis resorted to council just as often to reassert that they were free and independent and subject to no foreign power. Abenaki diplomats consistently strived to preserve their land and independence, even as they recognized their increasing weakness and vulnerability. Their efforts frequently aggravated existing divisions and generated new factions within the tribes.⁴ Even when English power and arrogance increased, Abenakis continued to "go through channels" and voice their complaints in formal protest and petition. Indians often expressed the importance of meeting European officials face-to-face to air concerns and resolve misunderstandings: The Pennacook war chief, Kancamagus, went in person to the governor of New Hampshire in an effort to avoid conflict.⁵

Matters of local importance received attention as well as issues of peace and war. A small band of Presumpscots living near Sebago Lake sent delegates to Boston in 1739 to express their grievances against the English settlers of New Marblehead who, among other things and contrary to agreement, had built a dam that blocked the upriver passage of salmon. The governor and council ordered the passage reopened and promised to look into the Presumpscots' other complaints.⁶ The incident offers a marked contrast to the infamous affair at Old Marblehead in 1677 when outraged townswomen literally tore apart two Abenaki prisoners.⁷

The first formal arrangement between the English and Abenakis occurred in the 1660s, when it was agreed that Abenaki sachems and English courts should each deal with their own offenders. Such arrangements rarely functioned effectively, and in subsequent years, colonial officials and Indian delegates met regularly in councils to iron out their differences. The English also increased their demands in a string of formal treaties with the Abenakis or "Eastern Indians," often demanding that the tribes subject themselves to English jurisdiction. Many of these treaties were dictated at the end of wars. There were major Anglo-Abenaki conferences in 1698 after King William's War, in 1713 after Queen Anne's War, in 1725–1727 at the end of Dummer's War, in 1749 after King George's War, and so on. The Treaty of Falmouth in 1749, like many other English treaties, was based on Dummer's Treaty of 1725.⁸ Anxious to ensure that all the tribes comply with its terms, the English met in 1752 and 1754 with the Norridgewocks and Penobscots who had been absent at Falmouth and secured their agreement to the 1749 treaty. This chapter reproduces several of these early treaties to illustrate the pattern of demands and expectations that developed in English diplomatic dealings with the Abenakis.⁹

How *something was said often was as important as* what *was said, and dawnland diplomats sprinkled their speeches with Indian metaphors of kinship and friendship. Presents played a significant role in negotiations as tangible testimony of sincerity and goodwill. Speakers marked their words with gifts, and colonial officials gave handsome presents to visiting Indian delegations. But the diplomatic formalities did not guarantee smooth proceedings. At the George-town council on Arrowsick Island at the mouth of the Kennebec in August 1717, the Abenaki sachem Wiwurna and Governor Shute of Massachusetts exchanged heated words over the issue of Indian lands and English forts. The Abenakis stalked angrily from the conference "in a hasty abrupt manner without taking leave, and left behind them their English Colours." The Abenakis later re-turned—without Wiwurna—and agreed to ratify the treaty made at Portsmouth four years earlier.[10] In July 1732, delegates from the Penobscots, Norridgwocks, Pigwackets, and Androscoggins at Falmouth had to remind Governor Belcher of some diplomatic etiquette: The governor had pressed the Indians for immediate answers and failed to mark his own answers with presents. The Abenakis re-minded him that they did things only after deliberating among themselves.[11] And, as the selections from meetings in 1752–1753 in this chapter demonstrate, Abenakis continued to voice in council their anger over English trespass on their land.*

Limits in authority and in understanding nullified the effectiveness of many treaties. Abenakis were unfamiliar with written laws and English courts; the English were unfamiliar with the workings of tribal politics. Frontiersmen be-yond the effective reach of English law felt free to act as they liked; Abenaki warriors retaliated despite the admonitions of their sachems. The English as-sumed Abenaki delegates could speak and make binding decisions for their whole tribe, but, as Kenneth Morrison points out, "when Abenaki sachems declared that they could not restrain their young men, they frankly admitted the limits of tribal law, politics, and diplomacy." Translation difficulties and conflicting in-terpretations of agreements created distrust, and the English tendency to mis-interpret Indian silence as acquiescence in their demands caused additional problems and resentment. Moreover, like their Puritan counterparts in southern New England, English commissioners on the Maine frontier proved adept at abusing the treaty process and resorting to duplicitious tactics to get their way, especially when it came to negotiations over land. As James H. Merrell observes in a southern context, "We must remember that the hearty handshakes, the friendly words, and the piles of presents concealed contempt and a manipulative, even exploitative instinct."[12]

Nevertheless, preoccupation with the violence and warfare that erupted with grim regularity in the dawnland should not blind us to the importance of diplomatic encounters between Indians and Europeans. Diplomacy provided a forum for negotiations and public meetings, offered a mechanism for airing grievances and resolving issues, and presented a means of formalizing relations and legitimizing transactions. It also functioned as an effective instrument in the dispossession and defeat of the Indian participants.]

1. LETTERS OR PETITIONS FROM JOHN HOGKINS, COMMONLY CALLED HAWKINS, ONE OF THE SACHEMS OF THE PENACOOK INDIANS, 1685

[In 1685, the English became alarmed by a gathering of Indians at Pennacook. Reports in Indian country said that Lieutenant Governor Edward Cranfield of New Hampshire planned to unleash the Mohawks against the Pennacooks in a preemptive strike. Such a plan was not without precedent: Governor Andros of New York had instigated a Mohawk attack on King Philip's forces a decade before.[13] Many Pennacooks fled their village in fear of the impending attack, but their war chief, Kancamagus—known to the English as John Hogkins or Hawkins—headed a delegation to see Governor Cranfield in person and, in a series of letters "all Indian hand," petitioned him to call off the Mohawks.[14] The first two letters appear below.]

May 15th, 1685.

Honour Governor my friend, you my friend I desire your worship and your power because I hope you can do som great matters this once. I am poor and naked and I have no men at my place because I afraid allways Mohogs he will kill me every day and night. If your worship when please pray help me you no let Mohogs kill me at my place at Malamake Revir called Panukkog and Natukkog, I will submit [to] your worship and your power. And now I want powder and such allminishon shott and guns because I have forth at my hom and I plant theare.

This all Indian hand but pray you do consider

your humble Servant

John Hogkins.

May 15th, 1685.

Honour Mr. Governor, now this day I com your house I want se you and I bring my hand at before you. I want shake hand to you; if your worship when please then you receve my hand then shake your hand and my hand. You my friend because I remember at old time when live my grant father and grant mother then Englishmen com this country then my grant father and Englishmen they make a good govenant. They friend all wayes, my grant father leving at place called Malamake Rever other name chef Natukkog and Panukkog, that one rever great many names, and I bring you this few skins at this first time I will give you my friend

This all Indian hand

John + hawkins Sagomor	peter x Robin
Simon Betogkom	Gorge x Roddunnonukgus
Joseph + traske	Hope x hoth
king + hary his	John x Toneh
Sama + linis	John + Canowa
wapeguanat x Taguachuashat	John + owamosimmin
old Robin +	Natonill x Indian
mamanosques x andwa	

(Nathaniel Bouton, ed., *New Hampshire Provincial Papers*, vol. 1 [Concord, 1867], 583–84.)

2. ARTICLES OF PEACE WITH
THE INDIANS INHABITING NEW HAMPSHIRE AND
MAINE, 1685

[Kancamagus got little satisfaction from the governor and led his people out of harm's way until the English made a treaty with the Indians of Maine and New Hampshire that provided protection for his people.]

Articles of Peace, agreed upon the 8th day of September, in the year of our Lord 1685, between the subjects of his Majesty, King James the Second, inhabiting the Provinces of New Hampshire and Maine, and the Indians inhabiting the said Provinces:

It is agreed there shall be for the future a lasting peace, friendship and kindness, between the English and the Indians, and that no injury shall be offered by the one to the other.

That if any Englishman doth any injury to an Indian, upon complaint made to any justice of peace the Englishman shall be punished, and the Indian shall have present satisfaction made him. And if any Indian doth an injury to the English, or threaten to do any injury, the sagamore to whom that Indian doth belong shall punish him in presence of one of the king's justices of the peace.

That if any other Indian shall design any mischief or harm to the English, the Indians inhabiting the aforesaid province shall give present notice thereof to the English, and shall assist the English.

That so long as the aforesaid Indians shall continue in friendship with the English, they shall be protected against the Mohawks, or any others, and may freely and peaceably set down by the English near any of their plantations.

Robert Mason	Walter Barefoot
Robert Elliot	Henry Green
John Davis	Francis Hooke

The mark (of Mesandowit
The mark X of Wahowah, *alias* Hopehood
The mark B of Tecamorisick, *alias* Josias
The mark ∽ of John Nomony, *alias* Upsawah
The mark W of Umbesnowah, *alias* Robin.

We, whose names are hereunto written, do freely consent and engage to comply and perform the within written articles, as our neighbors have done, and do further engage as followeth:

Lastly—That the Indians shall not at any time hereafter remove from any of the English plantations, with their wives and children, before they have given fair and timely notice thereof unto the English, from whence they do so remove. And in case the said Indians shall remove with their wives and children, without such fair and timely notice given to the English, that then it shall be taken, *pro confesso,* that the Indians do intend and design war with the English, and do hereby declare that the peace is broken. And it shall and may be lawful to and for the English, or any on their behalf, to apprehend the said Indians, with their wives and children, and to use acts of hostility against them, until the sagamores shall make full satisfaction for all charge and damage that may arise thereby.

John Davis
Francis Hooke.

The mark of Netambomet, sagam of Saco
The mark X of Wahowah, *alias* Hopehood

The mark) of Ned Higgon

The mark ⊃ of Newcome

Kancamagus, *alias* John Hawkins, sagamon

Signed this instrument, 19 September, 1685; his C mark;

Bagesson, *alias* Joseph Traske, his O mark;

And agreed to all within written.

Teste:

Jos.Rayn.

(Nathaniel Bouton, ed., *New Hampshire Provincial Papers*, vol. 1 [Concord, 1867], 588–89.)

3. TREATY WITH THE "EASTERN INDIANS," 1693

[When King William's War broke out in 1689, the English began diplomatic initiatives to neutralize the Abenaki threat. In 1693, Governor William Phips negotiated the following treaty with the eastern Abenakis. In contrast with the treaties concluded in 1665 and 1685, the 1693 treaty contained provision that Indians should be subject to English justice and authorities when disputes arose. It also required that the Indians return any captives and allow the English to settle and improve Abenaki lands. But, as Kenneth Morrison observes, the agreement "only formalized misunderstandings."¹⁵ The treaty had to be renewed five years later.]

The Submission and Agreement of the Eastern Indians at Fort William Henry in Pemmaquid, the 11th day of August, in the Fifth year of the Reign of our Soveraign Lord and Lady, William and Mary, by the Grace of God, of England, Scotland, France, and Ireland, King and Queen, Defenders of the Faith, etc. 1693

Whereas a Bloody War has for some years now past been made and carried on by the Indians within the Eastern parts of the said Province, against Their Majesties Subjects the English, through the instigation and influences of the French; and being sensible of the miseries which we and our people are reduced unto, by adhering to their ill council: We whose names are hereunto subscribed, being Sagamores and Chief Captains of all the Indians belonging to the several rivers of Penobscote and Kennebeck, Amarascogin, and Saco, parts of the said Province of the Massachusets Bay, within Their said Majesties Soveraignty, having made application unto his Excellency Sir William Phips, Captain General and Governour in Chief in and over the said Province, that the war may be put to an end; Do lay down our arms, and cast our selves upon Their said Majesties grace and favour. And each of us respectively for our selves, and in the name and with the free consent of all the Indians belonging unto the several rivers aforesaid, and of all other Indians within the said Province of and from Merrimack River, unto the most Easterly bounds of the said Province, hereby acknowledge our hearty subjection and obedience unto the Crown of England, and do solemnly covenant, promise and agree, to and with the said Sir William Phips, and his successors, in the place of Captain General and Governour in Chief of the aforesaid Province or territory, on Their said Majesties behalf, in manner following, *viz.*

That at all time and times for ever, from and after the date of these presents, we will cease and forbear all acts of hostility towards the subjects of the Crown of England, and not offer the least hurt or violence to them or any of them in their persons or estate; but will henceforward hold and maintain a firm and constant amity and friendship with all the English.

We abandon and forsake the French interest, and will not in any wise adhere to, join with, aid or assist them in their wars, or designs against the English, nor countenance, succour, or conceal any of the enemy Indians of Canada or other places, that shall happen to come to any of our plantations within the English territory, but secure them if in our power, and deliver them up unto the English.

That all English captives in the hands or power of any of the Indians within the limits aforesaid, shall with all possible speed be set at liberty, and returned home without any ransom or payment to be made or given for them or any of them.

That Their Majesties subjects the English, shall and may peaceably and quietly enter upon, improve, and for ever enjoy, all and singular their rights of lands, and former settlements and possessions within the eastern parts of the said Province of the Massachusets Bay, without any pretensions or claims by us, or any other Indians, and be in no wise molested, interrupted, or disturbed therein.

That all trade and commerce, which hereafter may be allowed between the English and Indians, shall be under such management and regulation as may be stated by an act of the General Assembly, or as the Governour of the said Province for the time being, with the advice and consent of the Council, shall see cause to direct and limit.

If any controversie, or difference, at any time hereafter happen to arise between any of the English and Indians for any real or supposed wrong or injury done on one side or the other, no private revenge shall be taken by the Indians for the same, but proper application be made to Their Majesties Government, upon the place, for remedy thereof in a due course of justice, we hereby submitting ourselves to be ruled and governed by Their Majesties laws, and desire to have the benefit of the same.

For the more full manifestation of our sincerity and integrity in all that which we have herein before covenanted and promised, we do deliver unto Sir William Phips, their Majesties Governour as aforesaid, Ahassombamett, brother to Edgeremett,

Wenongahewitt, cousin to Madockawando, and Edgeremett, and Bagatawawongon, alias[16] Sheepscoat John, to abide and remain in the custody of the English, where the Governour shall direct, as hostages or pledges, for our fidelity, and true performance of all and every the foregoing articles, reserving liberty to exchange them in some reasonable time for a like number, to the acceptance of the Governour and Council of the said Province, so they be persons of as good account, and esteem amongst the Indians, as those which are to be exchanged. In testimony whereof, we have hereunto set our several marks and seals, the day and year first above-written.

The above-written instrument was deliberately read over, and the several articles and clauses thereof interpreted unto the Indians, who said they well understood, and consented thereunto, and was then signed, sealed, and delivered in the presence of us.

John Wing
Nicholas Manning
Benjamin Jackson.

Edgeremett
Madockawando
Wassambomet of Navidgwock
Wenobson of Teconnet in
  behalf of Moxus
Ketterramogis of Narridgwock
Ahanquit of Penobscot
  John Hornybrook
  John Bagatawawongo, *alias,*
  Sheepscoat John   Interpreters
  Phill. Ounsakis, Squaw.

Bomaseen
Nitamemet
Webenes
Awansomeck
Robin Doney
Madaumbis
Paquaharet, *alias,* Nathaniel

(Charles H. Lincoln, ed., *Narratives of the Indian Wars 1675–1699* [New York: Charles Scribners' Sons, 1913], 249–51.)

4. "THE EPILOGUE OF A LONG TRAGEDY," 1698

[The 1693 treaty did not put an end to Anglo-Abenaki hostilities, and, after the Treaty of Ryswick terminated the Anglo-French war, the Indians and the English met to renew the original treaty. The treaty proceedings revealed the continuing influence of French priests as military agents in French villages, the sufferings the war brought to Abenaki villages, and the recurrent controversy surrounding the return of captives, some of whom preferred to remain with the Indians.]

Major Converse, and Captain Alden, in pursuance of instructions received from the Lieutenant Governour and Council, arriving at Penobscot on October 14, 1698, were there informed, that Madockawando, the noted sagamore, with several other sachims of the east, were lately dead. And six days after this, the chief sachims now living, with a great body of Indians, entertained them with a friendly discourse, wherein they said that the Earl of Frontenac has went them word, there was a peace concluded between the Kings of France and England, and that one of the articles in the peace was for prisoners on both sides to be returned, and they were resolved to obey the Earl of Frontenac as their Father. And accordingly such prisoners of ours, as they had now at hand, might immediately return, if we could perswade them, for they would not compel them. When our English messengers argued with them, upon the perfidiousness of their making a new war, after their submission, the Indians replied that they were instigated by the French to do what they did, against their own inclinations, adding, that there were two Jesuits, one toward Amonoscoggin, the other at Narridgaway,[17] both of which, they desired the Earl of Bellomont, and the Earl of Frontenac, to procure to be removed; otherwise it could not be expected that any peace would continue long. The Indians also, and the English prisoners, gave them to understand, that the last winter, many, both Indians and English prisoners, were starved to death. Particularly, nine Indians in one company went a hunting, but met with such hard circumstances, that after they had eat up their dogs and their cats, they dyed horribly famished. And since the last winter, a grievous and unknown disease is got among them, which consumed them wonderfully. The sagamore Saquadock further told them that the Kennebeck Indians would fain have gone to war again this summer, but the other refused, whereupon they likewise desisted. And they resolved now to fight no more; but if any ill accident or action should happen on either side, he did in the name of the Indians desire, that we would not presently make a war upon it, but in a more amicable way compose the differences.

That the Indian affayrs might come to be yet more exactly understood, the General Assembly of the Province employed Colonel John Phillips, and Major Convers, to settle them. These gentlemen took a difficult and dangerous voyage, in the depth of winter, unto the eastern parts, in the province-galley, then under the Command of Captain Cyprian Southack. And the principal sagamores of the Indians there coming to them, did again renew and subscribe the submission, which they had formerly made in the year 1693, with this addition unto it.

And whereas, notwithstanding the aforesaid submission and agreement, the said Indians belonging to the rivers aforesaid, or some of them through the ill counsel and instigation of the French, have perpetrated sundry hostilities His Majesties subjects, the English, and have not delivered and returned home several English captives in their hands, as in the said submission they covenanted.

Wherefore, we whose names are hereunto subscribed, sagamores, captains, and principal men of the Indians belonging unto the rivers of Kennebeck, Ammonoscoggin, and Saco, and parts adjacent, being sensible of our great offence and folly, in not complying with the aforesaid submission and agreement, and also of the sufferings and mischiefs that we have hereby exposed our selves unto, do in all humble and most submissive manner cast our selves upon His Majesties mercy, for the pardon of all our rebellions, hostilities, and violations of our promises, praying to be received into His Majesties grace and protection; and for, and on behalf of our selves, and of all other the Indians, belonging to the several rivers and places aforesaid, within the Soveraignty of His Majesty of Great-Britain, do again acknowledge and profess our hearty and sincere obedience, unto the Crown of England, and do solemnly renew, ratify and confirm all and every of the articles and agreements, contained in the aforesaid recited commission. And in testimony thereof, we, the said sagamores, captains, and principal men, have hereunto set our several marks and seals at Casco-Bay, near MaresPoint, the seventh day of January, in the tenth year of the Reign of his Majesty, King William the Third, Annoque Domini, 1698,9.

Subscribed by

Moxus,—and a Great Number more.

In the presence of

James Converse   John Gills, Interpreter,

Cyprian Southack   And Scodook, *alias* Sampson.

At this time also, the Indians restored as many of the English captives, in their hands, as were able to travel above an hundred miles in this terrible season of the year, from their headquarters, down to the sea-side, giving all possible satisfaction for the restoration of the rest as early in the spring as there could be any travelling.

(Lincoln, ed., *Narratives of the Indian Wars 1675–1699*, 273–75.)

5. THE TREATY OF PORTSMOUTH, 1713

[By the end of Queen Anne's War, Abenakis, and French were exhausted from years of conflict and welcomed a restoration of peace. The Abenakis came to terms with Governor Dudley at Portsmouth in 1713, in a treaty that shows the English pattern of terming treaties as acts of submission and portraying the Abenakis as the guilty party in the recent war. They repeatedly demanded that the Abenakis declare their submission to the Crown and depicted any subsequent acts of hostility as tantamount to treason. The Abenakis consistently rejected the notion that they were subject to any power, and the terms of the treaty reflected English wishes more accurately than dawnland diplomatic realities. Increasing English settlement in the wake of Queen Anne's War caused the Kennebec Abenakis considerable concern and prompted the Georgetown Treaty in 1717, where, after some heated debate, the Treaty of Portsmouth was reaffirmed.]

At Portsmouth, in Her Majesty's Province of New Hampshire, in New England, the thirteenth day of July, in the twelfth year of the Reign of our Sovereign Lady Anne, by the Grace of God, of Great Britain, France, and Ireland, Queen, Defender of the Faith, &c.
THE SUBMISSION AND AGREEMENT OF THE EASTERN INDIANS

Whereas for some years last past we have made a breach of our fidelity and loyalty to the Crowns of Great Britain, and have made open rebellion against Her Majesty's subjects, the English inhabitants in the Massachusetts, New Hampshire, and other of her Majesty's territories in New England, and being now sensible of the myseries which We and our people are reduced thereunto thereby, we whose names are here subscribed, being delegates of all the Indians belonging to Norrigawake, Narrakamegock, Amascontoog, Pigwocket, Penecook, and to all other Indian plantations situated on the Rivers of St. Johns, Penobscot, Kenybeck, Amascogon, Saco, and Merimack, and all other Indian plantations lying between the said Rivers of St. Johns and Merrimack, parts of Her Majesty's Provinces of the Massachusetts Bay and New Hampshire, within Her Majesty's Sovereignty, having made application to his Excellency, Joseph Dudley, Esq., Captain General and Governor in Chief in and over the said Provinces, that the troubles which we have unhappily raised or occasioned against Her Majesty's subjects, the English, and ourselves, may cease and have an end, and that we may enjoy Her Majesty's grace and favor, and each of us respectively, for ourselves and in the name and with the free consent of all the Indians belonging to the several rivers and places aforesaid, and all other Indians within the said Provinces of the Massachusetts Bay and New Hampshire, hereby acknowledging ourselves the lawfull subjects of our Sovereign Lady, Queen Anne, and promising our hearty subjection and obedience unto the Crown of Great Britain, doe solemnly covenant, promise, and agree to and with the said Joseph Dudley, Esq., Governor, and all such as shall hereafter be in the place of Captain, General and Governor in Chief of the aforesaid Provinces or territories on Her Majesty's behalf, in manner following. That is to say:

That at all times forever, from and after the date of these presents, we will cease and forebear all acts of hostility toward all the subjects of the Crown of Great Britain, and not to offer the least hurt or violence to them or any of them in their persons or estates, but will honor, forward, hold, and maintain a firm and constant amity and friendship with all the English, and will not entertain any treasonable conspiracy with any other nation to their disturbance.

That Her Majesty's subjects, the English, shall and may peaceably and quietly enter upon, improve, and forever enjoy, all and singular their rights of land and former settlements, properties and possessions, within the eastern parts of said Provinces of

Massachusetts Bay and New Hampshire, together with all the islands, islets, shoars, beaches, and fisheries within the same, without any molestation or claims by us or any other Indians and be in no wais molested, interrupted, or disturbed therein. Saving unto the said Indians their own grounds, and free liberty for hunting, fishing, fowling, and all other their lawful liberties and privileges, as on the eleventh day of August, in the year of our Lord God one thousand six hundred and ninety-three.

That for mutual safety and benefit, all trade and commerce which hereafter may be allowed betwixt the English and Indians shall be in such places and under such management and regulations as shall be stated by Her Majesty's Governments of the said provinces respectively. And to prevent mischiefs and inconveniences the Indians shall not be allowed, for the present, and until they have liberty from the respective Governments, to come near to any of English plantations or settlements on this side of Saco River.

That if any controversy or difference at any time hereafter happen to arise betwixt any of the English or Indians, for any real or supposed wrong or injury done on the one side or the other, no private revenge shall be taken by the Indians for the same, but proper application shall be made to Her Majesty's Government, upon the place, for remedy thereof, in our course of justice, we hereby submitting ourselves to be ruled and governed by Her Majesty's laws, and desire to have the protection and benefit of same.

We confess that we have, contrary to all faith and justice, broken our articles with Sir William Phipps, Governor, made in the year of our Lord God 1693, and with the Earl of Bellomont, Governor, made in the year of our Lord God 1699, and the assurance we gave to his Excellency, Joseph Dudley, Esq., Governor, in the years of our Lord God 1702, in the month of August, and 1703, in the month of July, notwithstanding we have been well treted by the said Governors. And we resolve for the future not to be drawn into any perfidious treaty or correspondence, to the hurt of any of the subjects of Her Majesty the Queen of Great Britain, and if we know of any such we will seasonably reveal it to the English.

Wherefore, we whose names are hereunto subscribed, delegates for the several tribes of the Indians, belonging unto the River of Kenybeck, Amarascogen, St. Johns, Saco, Merrimac, and parts adjacent, being sensible of our great offence and folly in not complying with the aforsaid submission and agreements, and also of the sufferings and mischiefs that we have thereby exposed ourselves unto, do, in humble and submissive manner, cast ourselves upon Her Majesty's mercy for the pardon of our past rebellions, hostilities, and violations of our promises, praying to be received unto Her Majesty's grace and protections. And for and on behalfe of ourselves, and of all other the Indians belonging to the several rivers and places aforesaid, within the sovereignty of Her Majesty of Great Britain, do again acknowledge and profess our hearty and sinceer obedience unto the Crown of Great Britain, and do solemnly renew, ratify, and confirm all and every of the articles and agreements contained in the former and present submission.

This treaty to be humbly laid before Her Majesty, for her ratification and further orders. In witness whereof, we, the delegates aforesaid, by name Kireberuit, Iteansis, and Jackoit for Penobscot, Joseph and Eneas for St. Johns, Waracansit, Wedaranaquin, and Bomoseen for Kennebeck, have hereunto set our hands and seals, the day and year first above written.

(Frederic Kidder, "The Abenaki Indians, Their Treaties of 1713 and 1717 . . . ," *Collections of the Maine Historical Society*, 1st ser., 6 [1859]: 250–53.)

6. DUMMER'S TREATY, 1725–1727

[The English regarded Dummer's Treaty, negotiated at three conferences between 1725 and 1727, as the basis of their diplomatic relations with the Abenakis. As David Ghere has shown, the treaty involved considerable misunderstandings and probable deception, but it illustrates the issues the English regarded as fundamental in treaty-making. The treaty repeated many of the requirements of the Treaty of Portsmouth, and the English obliged the Abenakis to renew it at every subsequent conference for the next thirty years, paying particular attention to questions of land and sovereignty. Dummer's Treaty also required Abenaki allegiance against hostile tribes and endeavored to undermine Abenaki unity.[18]]

The SUBMISSION and AGREEMENT of the Delegates of the Eastern Indians

Whereas the several Tribes of the Eastern Indians viz. The Penobscot, Nerridgawock, St. Johns, Cape Sables, and other tribes inhabiting within His Majesties Territories of *New England* and *Nova Scotia,* who have been engaged in the present war, from whom we, Saguaarum alias Loron, Arexis, Francois Xavier, and Meganumbee, are delegated and fully impowered to enter into articles of pacification with His Majesties Governments of *Massachusetts-Bay, New-Hampshire,* and *Nova Scotia,* have contrary to the several treaties they have solemnly entered into with the said Governments, made an open rupture, and have continued some years in acts of hostility against the subjects of His Majesty King GEORGE within the said Governments.

They being noe sensible of the miseries and troubles they have involved themselves in, and being desirous to be restored to His Majesties grace and favour, and to live in peace with all His Majesties Subjects of the said Three Governments, and the Province of *New York* and Colonies of *Connecticut* and *Rhode Island* and that all former acts of injury be forgotten, have concluded to make, and we do by these presents in the name and behalf of the said tribes, make our submission unto his most Excellent Majesty GEORGE by the Grace of GOD of *Great Britain, France* and *Ireland,* KING, Defender of the Faith, &c. in as full and ample manner, as any of our predecessors have heretofore done.

And we do hereby promise and engage with the Honourable WILLIAM DUMMER Esq., as he is Lieutenant Governour and Commander in Chief of His Majesties Province of the *Massachusetts Bay* and with the Governors or Commanders in Chief of the said Province for the time being, *That is to say.*

We the said delegates for and in behalf of the several tribes abovesaid, do promise and engage, that at all times for ever, from and after the date of these presents, we and they will cease and forbear all acts of hostility, injuries and discords towards all the subjects of the Crown of *Great Britain,* and not offer the least hurt, violence or molestation to them or any of them in their persons or estates, but will hence forward hold and maintain a firm and constant amity and friendship with all the English, and will never confederate or combine with any other nation to their prejudice.

That all the captives taken in this present war, shall at or before the time of the further ratification of this treaty be restored without any ransom or payment to be made by them or any of them.

That His Majesty's Subjects the English shall and may peaceably and quietly enter upon, improve and for ever enjoy all and singular their rights of land and former settlements, properties and possessions within the eastern parts of the said Province of the *Massachusetts Bay,* together with all Islands, isletts, shoars, beaches and fishery within the same, without any molestation or claims by us or any other Indians, and be in no ways molested, interrupted or disturbed therein. Saving unto the *Penobscot, Nerridgawock,* and other tribes within His Majesties Province aforesaid, and their natural descendants respectively, all their lands, liberties and properties not by them conveyed or sold to or possessed by any of the English subjects as aforesaid, as also the priviledge of fishing, hunting, and fowling as formerly.

That all trade and commerce which hereafter may be allowed betwixt the English and Indians, shall be under such management and regulation as the Government of the *Massachusetts* Province shall direct.

If any controversie or difference at any time hereafter happen to arise between any of the English and Indians for any real or supposed wrong or injury done on either side, no private revenge shall be taken for the same but proper application shall be made to His Majesties Government upon the place for remedy or redress thereof in a due course of justice.

We submitting our selves to be ruled and governed by His Majesty's laws, and desiring to have the benefit of the same.

We also the said delegates, in behalf of the tribes of Indians, inhabiting within the French territories, who have assisted us in this war, for whom we are fully impowered to act in this present treaty, do hereby promise and engage, that they and every of them shall henceforth cease and forbear all acts of hostility force and violence towards us all and every the subjects of His Majesty the King of Great Britain.

We do further in behalf of the Tribe of the *Penobscot* Indians, promise and engage, that if any of the other tribes intended to be included in this treaty, shall notwithstanding refuse to confirm and ratifie this present treaty entred into on their behalf and continue or renew acts of hostility against the English, in such case the said *Penobscot* Tribe shall joine their young men with the English in reducing them to reason.

In the next place we the aforementioned delegates do promise and engage with the Honourable JOHN WENTWORTH Esq., as he is Lieutenant Governor and Commander in Chief of His

Majesties Province of *New Hampshire,* and with the Governors and Commander in Chief of the said Province for the time being, that we and the tribes we are deputed from will henceforth cease and forebear all acts of hostility, injuries and discords towards all the subjects of His Majesty King GEORGE within the said Province. And we do understand and take it that the said Government of *New Hampshire* is also included and comprehended in all and every the articles aforegoing excepting that respecting the regulating the trade with us.

And further we the aforenamed delegates do promise and engage with the Honourable LAWRENCE ARMSTRONG Esq., Lieutenant Governor and Commander in Chief of His Majesties Province of *Nova Scotia* or *L'Acadie* to live in peace with His Majesties good subjects and their dependants in that Government according to the articles agreed on with Major Paul Mascarene commissioned for that purpose, and further to be ratified as mentioned in the said articles.

That this present treaty shall be accepted, ratified and confirmed in a publick and solemn manner by the Chiefs of the several Eastern Tribes of Indians included therein at *Falmouth* in *Casco Bay* some time in the month of *May* next. *In testimony* whereof we have signed these presents, and affixed our seals. Dated at the Council Chamber in *Boston* in *New England,* this fifteenth day of December, Anno Domini, one thousand seven hundred and twenty-five, Annoque Regni Regis GEORGIJ, Magnae Britanniae, &c Duodecimo.

("Indian Treaties," *Collections of the Maine Historical Society,* 1st ser., 3 [1853]` 416–19.)

[One by one, the Abenaki tribes fell in line with Dummer's Treaty, although Grey Lock's Missisquois never succumbed. Dummer's Treaty initiated some seventeen years of peace on the Maine frontier, but it was a fragile truce based on misunderstanding rather than a mutually satisfactory settlement of differences.]

7. INDIAN EXPLANATION OF THE TREATY OF CASCO BAY, 1727

[The Norridgewocks, Wawenocks and Arasagunticooks who were not present in 1726 ratified Dummer's Treaty at Casco Bay in July 1727, but, as the following document indicates, there was more than a suspicion of misunderstanding about what actually went on. The texts of treaties as reported and preserved by Europeans constituted only the summary of lengthy proceedings with Indian delegates in council. Mistranslation, misunderstanding, and deliberate distortion often marred the texts. This testimony by a Penobscot participant at the Treaty of Casco Bay shows there was often considerable difference between what the English recorded as having happened, and what Indian delegates remembered had happened. There were also significant distinctions in the ways Indians and European approached the business of treaty-making.[19]]

I Panaouamskeyen, do inform ye—ye who are scattered all over the earth take notice—of what has passed between me and the English in negotiating the peace that I have just concluded with them. It is from the bottom of my heart that I inform you; and, as a proof that I tell you nothing but the truth, I wish to speak to you in my own tongue.

My reason for informing you, myself, is the diversity and contrariety of the interpretations I receive of the English writing in which the articles of peace are drawn up that we have just mutually agreed to. These writings appear to contain things that are not, so that the Englishman himself disavows them in my presence, when he reads and interprets them to me himself.

I begin then by informing you; and shall speak to you only of the principal and most important matter.

First, that I did not commence the negotiation for a peace, or settlement, but he, it was, who first spoke to me on the subject, and I did not give him any answer until he addressed me a third time. I first went to Fort St. George to hear his propositions, and afterwards to Boston, whither he invited me on the same business.

We were two that went Boston: I, Laurance Sagourrab, and John Ehennekouit. On arriving there I did indeed salute him in the usual mode at the first interview, but I was not the first to speak to him. I only answered what he said to me, and such was the course I observed throughout the whole of our interview.

He began by asking me, what brought me hither? I did not give him for answer—I am come to ask your pardon; nor, I come to acknowledge you as my conqueror; nor, I come to make my submission to you; nor, I come to receive your commands. All the answer I made was that I was come on his invitation to me to hear the propositions for a settlement that he wished to submit to me.

Wherefore do we kill one another? he again asked me. 'Tis true that, in reply, I said to him—You are right. But I did not say to him, I acknowledge myself the cause of it, nor I condemn myself for having made war on him.

He next said to me—Propose what must be done to make us friends. 'Tis true that thereupon I answered him—It is rather for you to do that. And my reason for giving him that answer is, that having himself spoken to me of an arrangement, I did not doubt but he would make me some advantageous proposals. But I did not tell him that I would submit in every respect to his orders.

Thereupon, he said to me—Let us observe the treaties concluded by our Fathers, and renew the ancient friendship which existed between us. I made him no answer thereunto. Much less, I repeat, did I, become his subject, or give him my land, or acknowledge his King as my King. This I never did, and he never proposed it to me. I say, he never said to me—Give thyself and thy land to me, nor acknowledge my King for thy King, as thy ancestors formerly did.

He again said to me—But do you not recognize the King of England as King over all his states? To which I answered—Yes, I recognize him King of all his lands; but I rejoined, do not hence infer that I acknowledge thy King as my King, and King of my lands. Here lies my distinction—my Indian distinction. God hath willed that I have no King, and that I be master of my lands in common.

He again asked me—Do you not admit that I am at least master of the lands I have purchased? I answered him thereupon, that I admit nothing, and that I knew not what he had reference to.

He again said to me—If, hereafter, any one desire to disturb the negotiation of the peace we are at present engaged about, we will join together to arrest him. I again consented to that. But I did not say to him, and do not understand that he said to me, that we should go in company to attack such person, or that we should form a joint league, offensive and defensive, or that I should unite my brethren to his. I said to him only, and I understand him to say to me, that if any one wished to disturb our negotiation of peace, we would both endeavor to pacify him by fair words, and to that end would direct all our efforts.

He again said to me—In order that the peace we would negotiate be permanent, should any private quarrel arise hereafter between Indians and Englishmen, they must not take justice into their own hands, nor do any thing, the one to the other. It shall be the business of us chiefs to decide. I again agreed with him on that article, but I did not understand that he alone should be judge. I understood only that he should judge his people, and that I would judge mine.

Finally he said to me—There's our peace concluded; we have regulated every thing.

I replied that nothing had been yet concluded, and that it was necessary that our acts should be approved in a general assembly. For the present, an armistice is sufficient. I again said to him—I now go to inform all my relatives of what has passed between us, and will afterwards come and report to you what they'll say to me. Then he agreed in opinion with me.

Such was my negotiation on my first visit to Boston.

As for any act of grace, or amnesty, accorded to me by the Englishman, on the part of his King, it is what I have no knowledge of, and what the Englishman never spoke to me about, and what I never asked him for.

On my second visit to Boston we were four: I, Laurence Sagourrab, Alexis, Francois Xavier and Migounambe. I went there merely to tell the English that all my nation approved the cessation of hostilities, and the negotiation of peace, and even then we agreed on the time and place of meeting to discuss it. That place was Caskebay, and the time after Corpus Christi.

Two conferences were held at Caskebay. Nothing was done at these two conferences except to read the articles above reported. Every thing I agreed to was approved and ratified, and on these conditions was the peace concluded.

One point only did I regulate at Caskebay. This was to permit the Englishman to keep a store at St. Georges; but a store only, and not to build any other house, nor erect a fort there, and I did not give him the land.

These are the principal matters that I wished to communicate to you who are spread all over the earth. What I tell you now is the truth. If, then, any one should produce any writing that makes me speak otherwise, pay no attention to it, for I know not what I am made to say in another language, but I know well what I say in my own. And in testimony that I say things as they are, I have signed the present minute which I wish to be authentic and to remain for ever.

(E. B. O'Callaghan, ed., *Documents Relative to the Colonial History of the State of New York*, 15 vols. [Albany: Weed, Parsons & Co., 1855], 9:966–67.)

8. CONFERENCE HELD AT DEERFIELD, 1735

[In 1735, Governor Jonathan Belcher of Massachusetts Bay appointed a minister to Fort Dummer and met at Deerfield with Ountaussoogoe and other Caughnawaga chiefs to explain the appointment. Some St. Francis Abenakis also attended the meeting. Since the majority of the Indians present were Iroquois, the conference preliminaries involved more formalities than was often the case in meetings with the Abenakis and other tribes farther east and included characteristic Iroquoian expressions of condolence. Nonetheless, it illustrates the importance of protocol in the diplomacy of the dawnland and the extent to which Europeans observed Indian etiquette, symbolism, idioms, and customs.]

His Excellency first received the Cagnawaga tribe of the Indians, with the St. Francois, who were placed on seats at a suitable distance over against His Excellency; they having first made their compliments to the Governor by shaking hands, &c.

Joseph Kellogg, Esq., being a sworn Interpreter,

Governour—to the Interpreter—Inform the chiefs I shall speak.

My good friends and brethren, I am glad to see you: I give thanks to the great God who has safely conducted you through a long and tedious journey. It is a great pleasure to me that we have the opportunity of refreshing our faces with the sight of each other—Holding out one string of *wampum,* proceeds, and says,—My good friends and brethren, this is to wipe away all tears from your eyes. Then holding out a second—This is to open your throats that you may speak with all freedom. Then a third—This is to wipe away all blood, and to comfort you under all your past difficulties. And then His Excellency delivered them the three strings in one.

Auouantauresaunkee, Indian speaker—We that are deputed from our tribes are come at your Excellency's call—at your desire—and are glad we are got safe here, after a long and tedious travel over hills and high mountains, and join with the Governour in our thanks to God that we see the faces of each other in health and peace. As your Excellency has done to us, we do the same in answer to you—holding a string of *Wampum,* proceeds and says,—Our desire is that all tears may be wiped away from your Excellency's eyes. Then holding out a second string— That your throat may be open, that all freedom of speech may be had, we desire the path may be clear and open, and no difficulty in the way. Then holding out a third string—We desire the place where the Governour stands may be clean from all filth of blood. And then he delivered the three strings to the Governour.

The Governour sent for three of us, but usually more of us come than are sent for. We are eight instead of three. We have brought our wives who we always want with us. (Then delivers a belt of wampum, being in answer to one the Governour sent them by the messenger that called them.)

We incline to be short lest we should be troublesome to the Governour. We are here the representatives of the three families of Cagnawaga tribe, Ountaussoogoe and three others, one of the families having sent two delegates.

We desire that nothing may be taken amiss by your Excellency; if a wrong word should happen to fall from us, we desire it may be taken up and rectified; it is what has been usual and we desire it may be so now.

The way is now clear, and the door open for freedom of speech; but we have nothing to say at present. We were sent for, and it is not customary for those that are drawn by the hand to speak first, and therefore wait to hear what your Excellency has to say, and desire you would please to appoint the time, when we shall be ready to attend.

(*Collections of the Maine Historical Society,* 1st ser., 4 [1856]: 124–25 [full text of conference is on pp. 123–44].)

9. ABENAKIS AND PHINEAS STEVENS, 1752–1753

[Meetings between Europeans and Indians did not always follow a pattern in which arrogant and powerful Englishmen dictated terms to defeated and dispirited Indians, as the following exchanges between Abenaki delegates and Captain Phineas Stevens illustrate. In 1752–1753, as Anglo-French tensions simmered, the English wanted to build a fort at Cowass on the upper Connecticut River. Abenaki delegates, in a series of meetings with Stevens, made it clear that they would not be browbeaten, that they still possessed the power to defend their homelands. The English recognized that the Abenakis were not making empty threats, and they soon abandoned their plans to occupy the Cowass country.

In July 1752, Stevens met with St. Francis Abenakis in council at Montreal, as an emissary from the governor of Massachusetts. In the presence of the Baron de Longueuil, governor of Montreal, Iroquois from Caughnawaga, and Indians from the Lake of the Two Mountains, the Abenakis were quick to voice their concerns and to stress their sovereignty.]

Atiwaneto, Chief Speaker

Brother, We speak to you as if we spoke to your Governor of Boston.

We hear on all sides that this Governor and the Bostonians say that the Abenakis are bad people. 'Tis in vain that we are taxed with having a bad heart. It is you, brother, that always attack us; your mouth is of sugar but your heart of gall. In truth, the moment you begin we are on our guard.

Brothers, We tell you that we seek not war, we ask nothing better than to be quiet, and it depends, brothers, only on you English, to have peace with us.

We have not yet sold the lands we inhabit, we wish to keep the possession of them. Our elders have been willing to tolerate you, brothers Englishmen, on the seabord as far as Sawakwato, as that has been so decided, we wish it to be so.

But we will not cede one single inch of the lands we inhabit beyond what has been decided formerly by our fathers.

You have the sea for your share from the place where you reside; you can trade there. But we expressly forbid you to kill a single beaver, or to take a single stick of timber on the lands we inhabit. If you want timber we'll sell you some, but you shall not take it without our permission.

Brothers, Who hath authorized you to have those lands surveyed? We request our brother, the Governor of Boston, to have those surveyors punished, as we cannot imagine that they have acted by his authority.

Brother, You are therefore masters of the peace that we are to have with you. On condition that you will not encroach on those lands we will be at peace, as the King of France is with the King of Great Britain.

By a Belt.

I repeat to you Brothers, by this belt, that it depends on yourselves to be at peace with the Abenakis.

Our Father who is here present[20] has nothing to do with what we say to you; we speak to you of our own accord, and in the name of all our allies. We regard our Father, in this instance, only as a witness of our words.

We acknowledge no other boundaries of yours than your settlements whereon you have built, and we will not, under any pretext whatsoever, that you pass beyond them. The lands we possess have been given us by the Master of Life. We acknowledge to hold only from him.

We are entirely free. We are allies of the King of France, from whom we have received the Faith and all sorts of assistance in our necessities. We love that monarch, and we are strongly attached to his interests.

Let us have an answer to the propositions we address you, as soon as possible. Take this message in writing to give to your Governor. We also shall keep a copy of it to use in case of need.

Without stirring a step it is easy for you Governor to transmit his answer to us; he will have merely to address it to our Father who will have the goodness to send it to us.

(O'Callaghan, ed., *Documents Relating to the Colonial History of New York*, 10 [1858]: 252–54.)

[Diplomatic encounters did not always take the form of orchestrated meetings in formal assemblages. Sometimes, individual Abenakis and colonial officers conveyed the intent of their people. In the following two passages, Abenakis came to Phineas Stevens at Fort Number Four, as an individual they trusted to act as an intermediary in communicating their concerns to the government.]

Ye beginning of January last six Indians of the St. Francois Tribe, came to No. 4 Fort under a flagg of truce. The first thing they asked after, was whether it was all well, to which he answered yes, and asked whether they had not heard of the late treaty at the eastward.[21] Their answer was no, they knew of no such thing. He told them there was no doubt, but some of their tribe was present at the treaty. They said none of their chiefs—for if they had any treaty with the English it would be at Albany or in some of these parts. They further said to ye captain, you well know what you heard from our chief men last summer at Montreal, and what they say is always strong. In the most of ye conversation he had with them he told me, they manifested great uneasiness at our people's going to take a view of Cowass meadows last spring, but never fully declared their minds till the morning they took their departure, when with a great deal of deliberation (as he expressed it) they told him, for the English to settle Cowass was what they could not agree to. And as the English had no need of that land, but had enough without it, they must think the English had a mind for war, if they should go there, and said, if you do we will endeavour, that you shall have a strong war, that they should have the Mohawks and Ottawas to help them.[22] That there was four hundred Indians now a hunting on this side St. Francois River, and that the owners of the land at Cowass would be all there this spring, and that they at No. 4 might expect that if the affair of settling Cowass went forward, to have all their houses burnt. They told him further, they had no mind for war and desired him to use his interest to prevent ye English going to Cowass, and said again if they go there must be a war, and it would be a war of the English making.

(Massachusetts State Archives, Boston, Mass. Archives 32:336–37.)

[The following letter from Ebenezer Hinsdale to Governor Benning Wentworth, November 26, 1753, is of interest for a number of reasons. Despite deteriorating Anglo-Abenaki relations, which were soon to erupt into full-scale warfare, elder Abenaki chiefs endeavored to restrain their warriors in the face of provocation. Gathering war clouds did not bring trade to a complete halt or eradicate cooperative relations. The final part of the document shows that the French, conscious of the Abenakis' value as allies, took care to ascertain their wishes before building a trading post at the north end of Lake Memphremagog.]

Last week two Indians of the Fransoway tribe came into No. 4, alias Charlestown, one of them a Cape Cod Indian taken out of Captain Gorham's company at Annapolis last war now incorporated with the St. Fransoways, the other a lad who speaks good English, being kept in the Massachusetts Province last war, and upon ye peace returned home.

Upon Captain Stevens enquiring of them after two Indians vis. Is-battis alias Sabbaday and Prun-so-way alias Teransoway, who went eastward from Charles Town in their hunt last spring and have not returned according to appointment.

They answer: These Indians are supposed dead, for they hear from Indians by the way of Albany, that they went into ye English settlements. That the English gave them rum with poison which destroyed them. That is was said among themselves, it may be the English killed them, because one of them stole a Negro from them.

However, they say, *ten smart* fellows fixed out and were coming down to revenge their death, but were stayed by ye old men, who said it may be these reports are not true; many times such stories prove false, and if they should prove so, you would do what you will be sorry for. It is best you stay your hand for the year: go to your hunting and visit all the trading-houses east and west in that country, where you may find the certainty of the matter.

They inform that there are four sachems or chiefs in the St. Fransoway tribe, whose names as follows viz.

1. An-won-noo-co.
2. Nun-nau-wa-so.
3. Toh-qua-so-mit.
4. Paul-per-wa-so-mit.

That ye last mentioned whose name signifies the smallest overseer or inspector is up Connecticut River hunting and purposes to come down to Charles Town with ten others next Christmas or when the travailing is good on the ice in Connecticut River.

They inform that the large armament of French and Indians who last went against the Tweetwa Indians are returned home, have made peace with the Tweetwas and done some spoil on the Flatheads,[23] have brought home between 20 and 30 captives and expect intirely to extirpate that nation.

Further that the new Governour of Canada is arrived, that he is very earnest to build a trading house on the hither end of the Lake called Main-pow-be-gag which is about halfway between Connecticut River (above Coo-os) and St. Fransoway.

That ye French and Indians have held a consultation on this

affair almost all last summer. The Indians who claim the land are loth to consent to it, inasmuch as they think it will spoil their hunting ground. That they have not as yet determined to build it.

(Bouton, ed., *New Hampshire Provincial Papers*, 6 [1872], 236.)

10. THE ALTERNATIVE TO ACQUIESCENCE, 1754

[While the St. Francis Abenakis asserted their independence and remained confident of their strength, most eastern Abenakis who lived closer to the English had suffered badly from English power. English treaty makers often dictated terms with the arrogance of military superiority. They sometimes gave Abenaki diplomats clear warning that if they rejected the gloved hand of peace on English terms they could expect the metal fist of war. In June and July 1754, Massachusetts Governor William Shirley met in two conferences with chiefs of the Norridgewocks and Penobscots, securing their ratification of Dummer's Treaty and the Falmouth Treaty of 1749 and demanding explanations for recent disturbances on the frontier. Shirley closed his conference with the Norridgewocks with a clear reminder and a thinly veiled threat that illustrated the relative positions from which the English and Abenakis were negotiating by this time.]

If you live in peace with the *English,* your tribe may increase and multiply; but if you should be unfortunately led into a war with us, your whole tribe will in the end probably be destroyed, and not a man of it left to enjoy any of your lands.

You well know that the number of your tribe does not now consist of more than one third part, it did of before the war with us in 1723 and 1724.

(*A Journal of the Proceedings at Two Conferences begun to be held at Falmouth in Casco Bay, . . . between His Excellency William Shirley, Esq. . . . and the Chiefs of the Norridgwalk . . . and Penobscot Indians* [Boston: John Draper, 1754], 21–22.)

[In September 1766, Governor Guy Carleton of Quebec and Governor Harry Moore of New York met on Isle La Motte at the north end of Lake Champlain to settle the boundary between their colonies. Mohawks from the mission village of Caughnawaga and Abenakis from Missisquoi also attended. Only a partial record of the meeting survives, but the Caughnawagas made generous concessions to the English of the rights they claimed to lands around the lake. The lands on the east side of the lake belonged to the Abenakis, and the Missisquoi delegates were quick to register their protest: Abenakis had inhabited these lands since time immemorial, and the only concessions they had made were to the French who, in 1748, had assembled the people in open council and obtained permission to build a sawmill.]

The Speech of the Misiskoui Indians to the Governor of Quebec in the North End of Lake Champlain 8th Sept. 1766.

Brother

We the Misiskoui Indians of the St. Francis or Abenaki Tribe have inhabited that part of Lake Champlain known by the name of Misiskoui [since a] time unknown to any of us here present, without being molested or any one's claiming right to it, to our knowledge, except about eighteen years ago, the French Governor Mr. Vaudreuil and Intendant came there, and viewed a spot convenient for a saw-mill to facilitate the building of vessels and batteaus at St. Johns, as well as for the use of the navy at Quebec; and on the occasion convened our people to ask this approbation, when they consented and marked out a spot large enough for that purpose, as well as for the cutting of the saw-timbers, about half a league square, with the condition to have what boards they wanted for their use gratis. But at the commencement of last war, said mill was deserted, and the iron work buried; after which we expected every thing of the kind would subside. But soon after peace was made, some English people came there to rebuild the mill, and now claim three leagues in breadth and six in depth, which takes in our village and plantations by far.

We therefore request of you, brother, to enquire into this affair, that we obtain justice as it is of great concern to us.

We also beg you will not allow any traders to come and bring spirituous liquors among us, being near enough to bring peltries of skins to Montreal market.

A belt and strings

(National Archives of Canada C-11, 888, vol. 3:328–29.)

12. REPORT OF COMMITTEE ON PENOBSCOT INDIANS,
1786

[For the most part, the Penobscots and other "Eastern Indians" supported the American cause during the Revolution, but the independence won by the United States brought the Penobscots little protection from the land hunger of their former allies. In the years between the end of the Revolution and the admission of Maine as a state in 1820, the Massachusetts government steadily increased the pressure on Indian lands, until the native inhabitants of Maine were confined to reservations. In 1786, Massachusetts pressed the Penobscots to give up their lands. The Indians resisted, but in years following, as it became increasingly difficult to make a living, the Penobscots found themselves compelled to sell off more and more of their lands. In 1796, they signed a treaty yielding almost 200,000 acres in the Penobscot Valley. Other cessions followed, until the tribe was virtually denuded of land and confined to Indian Island at Old Town and other islands on the Penobscot River. These land cessions transgressed the Indian Trade and Non-Intercourse Act of 1790, which required congressional approval for any land transfers from Indian tribes, and formed the basis for the Penobscot and Passamaquoddy land claims of the 1970s and the landmark settlement of 1980.[24] This report from the Massachusetts commissioners in 1786 shows the kind of arguments and artifices employed to induce the Indians to hand over their lands and suggests that the new Americans, like their colonial forebears, regarded treaty negotiations primarily as a land-grabbing device.]

Commonwealth of Massachusetts
To his Excellency the Governor and the
Honorable the Council

May it please your Excellency and Honors

In virtue of a resolve of the General Court, by which the under signers were on the 6th of July last authorized, to treat with the Penobscot Tribe of Indians, respecting their claims to land, on the River Penobscot; to make full enquiry into the nature and extent of their said claims, and by an amicable treaty to adjust and ascertain the same so far as may be practicable; and in behalf of this Commonwealth, by the use of all fair, open, and honorable methods to endeavor to obtain from the said Indians, an acquittal and relinquishment of their possessions, and a release of all their claims and pretensions of title to the said lands; and in case the same cannot be obtained, to agree upon and limit the boundaries of their said claims and possessions on terms mutually advantageous and satisfactory to the parties.

We met on the 28th instant about sixty five of the said tribe, with four of their sachems, or heads, who appeared as representatives of the whole, viz, Orino, Ossang, called Esquire Ossang, Colonel John Neptune, and Victor Barvett.

We represented to them in the first place that by the termination of the war, a favorable opportunity offered for settling all the lands, in this part of the Commonwealth. Therefore it was that the General Court, equally attentive to the interest of the Penobscot Tribe, as to that of their other inhabitants, had directed us to inquire into the nature and extent of their claims, lest in executing their designs of settling their lands, they should infringe on those claims. This drew from the tribe a declaration that they would limit their claims to a small river about six miles above the head of the tide, (which head of the tide was the boundary of their former claim) thence to the head of the river. This claim they founded on the doings of the Provincial Congress at Watertown on the 21st of June 1775. We then explained to them the nature of that resolve, and that if they held all the lands mentioned therein, which was 6 miles on each side of the river from the head of the tide it would be of little use, if the state should settle the other lands, the strip left, would be no hunting ground for them. That it was therefore much for their interest, to quit all pretensions to lands below for more extended limits above. After much time being spent on the subject and in leading them into a belief that the state really wished to promote their happiness it was agreed by the said Indians on their part that they would relinquish all their claims and interest to all the lands on the west side of Penobscot River, from the head of the tide, up to the River Pasquataquiss being about forty three miles, and all their claims and interests on the east side of the river from the head of the tide aforesaid up to the River Mantanomkeektook being about 85 miles—reserving only to themselves the island on which the Old Town stands, about 10 miles above the head of the tide, and those islands on which they now have actual improvements in the said river, lying from Sunkhaze River, about 3 miles above the said Old Town to Passadunkee Island, inclusively, on which Island their new town so called, now stands.

In consideration hereof we in the name and in behalf of the Commonwealth engage that the Indians should hold and enjoy in fee the islands reserved as aforesaid and the fee of two islands in the bay called and known by the name of White Island, and Black Island, near Naskeeg point. And we further agreed that the lands on the west side of the River Penobscot, to the head of all the waters thereof, above the said river, Pasquataquiss and the lands on the east side of the river to the head of all the waters thereof, above the said River Montanomkeektook, should ly as hunting ground for the Indians and should not be laid out or settled by the state or engrossed by individuals thereof. And we further agreed as aforesaid to make the Indians a present of three hundred and fifty blankets, two hundred pounds of powder with a proportion of shott and flints!

We further report that prior to a termination of the above agreement and very early in the conference we discovered a total aversion in the Indians to surrender all their claims agreeably to a wish of the General Court expressed in the resolve aforesaid. The Indians were so far from doing this, that when they were urged to relinquish as far north as the west side of the river as on the east side they absolutely refused on any terms whatever, to comply with the proposition. We then discovered that this could not be further insisted on, and we preserve that line of conduct which would give satisfaction to the Indians, a circumstance which we desired to effect, as thereby we should at once gratify our own feelings, and we trust evidence our attention to the wishes of our constituents, and the spirit of their resolve. The Indians further agreed and engaged that as soon as the agreement should be confirmed on the part of the Commonwealth, and the blankets, powder, shott and flints, should be delivered that they would sign a relinquishment of all their right and interest to the lands agreeably to the above contract.

Matters being thus agreed, the tribe took leave of us with evident marks of satisfaction in what had been done, and of esteem and love to the Commonwealth.

B. Lincoln
Thos Rice
Rufus Putnam

Penobscot River, August 30, 1786

(*Collections of the Maine Historical Society*, 2d ser. 21 [1916]: 239–42.)

Chapter Four

War in the Dawnland

Powder horn of Jonathan Hobart, a soldier stationed at Fort Number Four on the Connecticut River during the French and Indian Wars. See Entry no. 24. *Courtesy of William H. Guthman, Guthman Americana.*

[The coming of Europeans transformed northern New England into a war zone. Indian warriors fought for hunting territories, revenge, and prestige long before European soldiers set foot on their land, although there is little evidence that Abenakis fought for other than defensive reasons before the arrival of Europeans. Native conflicts were ritualistic, intermittent, seasonal, and far less bloody than was common in Europe. Europeans brought their Old World rivalries to the dawnland; they also brought devastating new methods of waging war. From the earliest conflicts generated by competition for pelts and trade, through the Anglo-French contests for empire, and again during the American Revolution, dawnland inhabitants saw their lives disrupted by recurrent outbreaks of interethnic and international warfare.

English expansion, escalating interethnic tensions, imperial rivalry, and the colonists' competition for Indian allies made war a way of life for many tribes. Warfare came to assume a disproportionate amount of importance in Indian society, even as firearms and metal weapons rendered that warfare more deadly and English "total war" tactics brought destruction to Abenaki villages and noncombatants.

King Philip's War (1675–1676) saw Puritan English forces defeat and disperse the Algonquian tribes of southern and central New England. Abenakis got their first taste of fighting Englishmen as the conflict spilled over into the dawnland. Refugees from shattered tribes fled to the dawnland—or crossed it on their way to French mission villages—where they regrouped to fight another day. Major European conflicts had their counterparts in North America. During King William's War (1689–1697), Franco-Indian raids in 1690 on Schenectady, New York, Salmon Falls, New Hampshire, and Casco Bay initiated a pattern of warfare that threatened New England's northern frontier for half a century. Conflict erupted again in Queen Anne's War (1702–1713), until, exhausted from the fray, New England and New France welcomed an uneasy peace established by the Treaty of Utrecht.

But European treaties did not remove the root causes of Anglo-Abenaki hostility, nor did French and English ministers dictate peace and war in Abenaki villages. From 1723 to 1727, Abenaki warriors carried guerilla warfare to the

English frontier as France watched from the sidelines. Grey Lock, a Woronoke refugee operating from Missisquoi, hit the Massachusetts frontier in a series of lightning raids and played cat and mouse with pursuing English militia companies. In Maine, English counteroffensives were more effective, and they destroyed Penobscot in 1723, Norridgewock in 1724.

Anglo-French conflict resumed with inconclusive results in King George's War (1744–1748) and climaxed in the Seven Years' War (1756–1763). After a half century of conflict, English arms won smashing victories on a global scale, leaving France demoralized and denuded of territories. The surrender of New France marked the end of the North American phase of a world war. Abenakis who had fought in and beyond the dawnland alongside their French allies now found themselves with no protection against the flood of settlers the English victory unleashed into the dawnland. Just as Abenakis were adjusting to the fact that they now had to deal with King George instead of King Louis, the victors fell to fighting among themselves in the American Revolution. Many other Indian tribes aligned themselves with the redcoats, but, as always, the situation in the dawnland was far from clear. Most Abenakis tried to remain neutral, many lent their support to the American colonists, and some fought for the British.

Fighting in the forests of northern New England was very different from the wars on the battlefields of contemporary Europe: Guerilla tactics and petty skirmishes decided things more often than mass offensives by well-drilled troops. Indian war parties filtered through the forests to raid enemy tribes or attack colonial settlements. Colonial armies adopted Indian methods of fighting as they tramped through the dawnland to strike at Indian or European adversaries and British officers who had earned considerable experience of guerilla warfare in Austria, Flanders, and the Scottish Highlands adapted their soldiering to Indian warfare in North America. Europeans and Indians were uprooted from their villages and families to serve with French and English armies, and former neighbors sometimes sighted one another down the barrel of a flintlock. Moreover, although it is usual to contrast the hierarchy and discipline of European armies with the egalitarianism and individualism of Indian war parties, New England provincial armies displayed characteristics and attitudes that British officers abhorred but that Indian enemies and neighbors would have recognized. "Rather than a uniform hierarchy of officers and men," concludes Fred Ander-

son, "*a provincial army was in fact a confederation of tiny war bands, bound together less by the formal relationships of command than by an organic network of kinship and personal loyalties.*"[1]

The war for North American supremacy was a titanic struggle between two imperial powers and between the European and Indian worlds, but Indian commitments were never unanimous. In the dawnland, the struggle usually translated into vicious intercolonial, intertribal, and interracial petite guerre, *complicated by a frequent lack of colonial cooperation and a common absence of tribal unity. As some of the selections in their chapter illustrate, it was also war fought by human individuals with their own hopes and fears.]*

1. CHAMPLAIN TRANSFORMS DAWNLAND WARFARE, 1609

[In 1609, accompanied by allies from the Montagnais and Algonquin tribes, Samuel de Champlain traveled down the Richelieu River into the lake that bears his name. Intertribal conflicts had already taken their toll in the area, and the French explorer noted the Abenaki strategy of withdrawing from their villages that was to become standard practice in time of war for the next 150 years.[2] Lake Champlain formed the boundary between the dawnland and the Iroquois territory in the west, and Champlain came with every expectation of encountering the Mohawks, who were rivals in the fur trade and enemies of France's Indian allies. When Champlain's party met a large party of Mohawks near Crown Point, the Indians engaged in a long-range exchange of insults, lined up for battle in traditional fashion, and, in normal circumstances, the affair would have been settled with minimal casualties. It is possible that the Mohawks were in fact a diplomatic embassy and that Champlain's Indian allies lured them into range of the French guns while telling Champlain that they were out for war.[3] The decisive intervention of Champlain and his gunmen not only won the battle and marked the beginning of long-lasting Franco-Iroquois hostilities, it also changed forever the face of Indian warfare in northern New England. Traditional rituals, defensive tactics, and woven shields were forgotten as mobile war parties of gunmen waged a deadly new form of guerilla warfare.]

This region although pleasant is not inhabited by Indians, on account of their wars; for they withdraw from the rivers as far as they can into the interior, in order not to be easily surprised.

On the following day we entered the lake which is some 80 or 100 leagues in length, in which I saw four beautiful islands about ten, twelve and fifteen leagues in length, which, like the Iroquois river, were formerly inhabited by Indians, but have been abandoned, since they have been at war with one another.

. . . .

Towards ten or eleven o'clock, after walking around our camp, I went to take a rest, and while asleep I dreamed that I saw in the lake near a mountain our enemies, the Iroquois, drowning before our eyes. I wanted to succor them, but our Indian allies said to me that we should let them all perish, for they were bad men. When I awoke they did not fail to ask me as usual whether I had dreamed anything. I told them what I had seen in my dream. This gave them such confidence that they no longer had any doubt as to the good fortune awaiting them.

Evening having come, we embarked in our canoes in order to proceed on our way, and as we were paddling along very quietly, and without making any noise, about ten o'clock at night on the twenty-ninth of the month, at the extremity of a cape which projects into the lake on the west side, we met the Iroquois on the war-path. Both they and we began to utter loud shouts and each got his arms ready. We drew out into the lake and the Iroquois landed and arranged all their canoes near one another. Then they began to fell trees with the poor axes which they sometimes win in war, or with stone axes; and they barricaded themselves well.

Our Indians all night long also kept their canoes close to one another and tied to poles in order not to get separated, but to fight all together in case of need. We were on the water within bowshot of their barricades. And when they were armed, and everything in order, they sent two canoes which they had separated from the rest, to learn from their enemies whether they wished to fight. And these replied that they had no other desire, but that for the moment nothing could be seen and that it was necessary to wait for daylight in order to distinguish one another. They said that as soon as the sun should rise, they would attack us, and to this our Indians agreed. Meanwhile the whole night was spent in dances and songs on both sides, with many insults and other remarks, such as the lack of courage of our side, how little we could resist or do against them, and that when daylight came our people would learn all this to their ruin. Our side too was not lacking in retort, telling the enemy that they would see such deeds of arms as they had never seen, and a great deal of other talk, such as is usual at the siege of a city. Having sung, danced, and flung words at one another for some time, when daylight came, my companions and I were still hidden, lest the enemy should see us, getting our fire-arms ready as best we could, being however still separated, each in a canoe of the Montagnais Indians. After we were armed with light weapons, we took, each of us, an arquebus and went ashore. I saw the enemy come out of their barricade to the number of two hundred, in appearance strong, robust men. They came slowly to meet us with a gravity and calm which I admired; and at their head were three chiefs. Our Indians likewise advanced in similar order, and told me that those who had the three big plumes were the chiefs, and that there were only these three, whom you could recognize by these plumes, which were larger than those of their companions; and I was to do what I could to kill them. I promised them to do all in my power, and told them that I was very sorry they could not understand me, so that I might direct their method of attacking the enemy, all of whom undoubtedly we should thus defeat; but that there was no help for it, and that I was very glad to show them, as soon as the engagement began, the courage and readiness which were in me.

As soon as we landed, our Indians began to run some two hundred yards towards their enemies, who stood firm and had not yet noticed my white companions who went off into the woods with some Indians. Our Indians began to call to me with loud cries; and to make way for me they divided into two groups, and put me ahead some twenty yards, and I marched on until I was within some thirty yards of the enemy, who as soon as they caught sight of me halted and gazed at me and I at them. When I saw them make a move to draw their bows upon us, I took aim with my arquebus and shot straight at one of the three chiefs, and with this shot two fell to the ground and one of their companions was wounded who died thereof a little later. I had put four bullets into my arquebus. As soon as our people saw this shot so favourable for them, they began to shout so loudly that one could not have heard it thunder, and meanwhile the arrows flew thick on both sides. The Iroquois were much astonished that two men should have been killed so quickly, although they were provided with shields made of cotton thread woven together and wood, which were proof against their arrows. This frightened them greatly. As I was reloading my arquebus, one of my companions fired a shot from within the woods, which astonished them again so much that, seeing their chiefs dead, they lost courage and took to flight, abandoning the field and their fort, and fleeing into the depth of the forest, whither I pursued them and laid low still more of them. Our Indians also killed several and took ten or twelve prisoners. The remainder fled with the wounded. Of our Indians fifteen or sixteen were wounded with arrows, but these were quickly healed.

After we had gained the victory, our Indians wasted time in taking a large quantity of Indian corn and meal belonging to the enemy, as well as their shields, which they had left behind, the better to run. Having feasted, danced, and sung, we three hours later set off for home with the prisoners. The place where this attack took place is in 43 degrees and some minutes of latitude, and was named Lake Champlain.

(Biggar, ed., *The Works of Samuel De Champlain*, 2:90–101.)

2. ALLIANCE AGAINST THE IROQUOIS, 1651

[Economically motivated Mohawk raids caused considerable upheaval in the dawnland. Mohawk wolf packs waylaid Indian canoe brigades carrying furs to Albany and Montreal, Mohawk diplomats levied tribute in wampum from New England tribes, and Mohawk power threatened the missions, commerce, and settlements of New France. In 1628, the Mohawks defeated the Mahicans on the Hudson River after a four-year war, and in subsequent years, they stepped up the tempo of their incursions into and across the dawnland.[4] In 1650, Father Gabriel Druillettes traveled to New England with a proposal for a joint Franco/Anglo/Algonquian alliance against the Iroquois. He was accompanied by Noel Tekwarimat, chief of the Christianized Indians at Sillery, and seven or eight canoes of Abenakis. The dawnland tribes responded favorably to the idea, agreeing to set aside their own differences in the common cause, but the New England colonies suffered little from Mohawk raids and saw no reason to get involved. The projected alliance proved abortive, but Algonquian-Iroquois hostilities continued. In 1669, the New England tribes launched a multitribal expedition into Iroquois territory, where they met with a heavy defeat.[5] Eventually, the English replaced the Iroquois as the major threat to the Indians of the dawnland and their French allies. The following extract is from the journal that Druillettes kept of his tour.]

On the twenty-fourth of April, the Sokouckiois [Sokoki] arrives, bringing a message on the part of four villages,—to wit, of the Sokouckiois, of the Pagamptagwe [Pocumtuck], of the Penagouc [Pennacook], and of the Mahingans [Mahicans], situated on the river of Manate. He answers the propositions that

I had made to him by word of mouth, last autumn, the eighteenth of November. (The Abnaquiois, joining me, had made a present to the Sokouckiois, of fifteen collars, and ten or twelve porcelain bracelets, which might be valued at seven or eight bundles of beaver skins, in order to say to them: "Do what Onontio and Tekwirimaeth tell you.")[6] He said that those four villages, having held a council during three months of the past winter, had resolved to take the risks against the Irocquois with Onontio and Noel, whether the English did or did not undertake the war against the Irocquois; and, when the Irocquois shall be exterminated, they will oppose every other nation whatsoever that may wish to make war toward Quebecq. 2nd. He adds that several other nations, which are allied to these, will accompany them to war, especially, one called Noutchihuict, very numerous and dreaded by the Irocquois. It is situated between the Mahingans and Manathe.[7]

He offers to Nouel Takwirimath either now to wipe away the blood of the Algonquins and of the Sokouckiois who have killed one another inadvertently, or for lack of recognizing one another; or, else, to wait until after the death of the Irocquois, in order to give each other the satisfaction which they are accustomed to render mutually in such a case. . . .

It is certain that all the nations of savages which are in New England hate the Irocquois, and fear lest, after the Hurons and the Algonquains, he will exterminate them. Indeed, he has broken the heads of many of their men, finding them hunting beaver, without making any satisfaction.

Moreover, it is certain that the Sokouckiois have been closely allied to the Algonquains, and are very glad to deliver themselves from the annual tribute of porcelain which the Irocquois exact—nay, even, to revenge themselves for the death of many of their fellow-countrymen, killed by the Irocquois. Besides that, they hope for the beaver hunt about Quebecq, after the destruction of the Irocquois.

(Thwaites, ed., *Jesuit Relations,* 36:101–5.)

3. ABENAKI RAIDS, 1677

[The Abenakis became involved in the northern phases of King Philip's War and, in what developed into a separate conflict, carried their raids to the coastal settlements of Maine. The following extract of a letter from Richard Waldron in April 1677 presents a view of Abenaki warfare from the perspective of their English victims.]

11th Inst: 2 men more killed at Wells. 12th: 2 men, one woman and 4 children killed at York and 2 houses burnt. 13th: a house burnt at Kittery and 2 old people taken captiue by Simon and 3 more, but they gaue ym their liberty again without any damage to their persons. 14th: a house surprized on south side Piscataq between Portsmouth and Bloody Point, a young man killed and 2 young women carried away thence. 16th: a man killed at Greenland and his house burnt; another sett on fire but ye enemy was beaten off and ye ffire put out by some of our men who then recouered alsoe one of ye young women taken 2 days before who states there was but 4 Indians. They run sculking about in small parties like wolues. Wee haue had parties of men after ym in all quarters which haue sometimes recouered something they haue stoln but can't certainly say they haue killed any of ym. . . .

(*Collections of the Maine Historical Society,* 2d ser., 6 [1900]: 163.)

4. PENOBSCOT WOMEN AND CHILDREN KEEP A VIGIL, 1689

[Rarely in the history of Indian wars do we get a glimpse into life on the Indians' "home front." Abenaki warriors have traditionally been portrayed as

faceless killers rather than as husbands, brothers, fathers, and sons, with families of their own. In 1689, Father Pierre Thury, who had lived with the Penobscots since 1687, described the Abenaki raids on the Maine frontier, including their capture of the English fort at Pemaquid. His picture of Penobscot women and children kneeling in the chapel, keeping a rosary for the safe return of their men, contradicts the traditional ethnocentric view of the Abenakis, as does the fact that once Fort Pemaquid surrendered, the Indians took it without further bloodshed.]

Almost all our warriors, who numbered about one hundred, took confession before they left, as if they were going to die on this expedition. They also resolved to fight in the open if the need arose.

The women and children also followed their example and took confession, after which the women recited an endless rosary in the chapel, taking turns one after another from the first light of dawn until night, asking God, through the intervention of the Sainted Virgin, to take pity on them and protect them during this war.

(*Collection de Manuscrits . . . Rélatifs à la Nouvelle-France,* 4 vols. [Quebec: Imprimérie à Côté et Cie, 1883–1885], 1:464–65; editor's translation.)

5. INDIAN AUXILIARIES, 1689

[Dawnland warriors did not align themselves along strictly racial lines. European colonists enlisted Indian auxiliaries and scouts to help them wage war in Indian country; Indian tribes valued European support in their wars against enemy tribes, and in the epic struggle for mastery of the continent, English and French armies each had substantial contingents of Indian allies. English colonists confronting Abenaki warriors fighting in their own territory found it "very necessary to maintain a number of southern Indians for soldiers, who are best acquainted with the manner of these Indians' skulking fight."[8] On July 2, 1689, Massachusetts passed the following orders for enlisting Indian aid.]

That the Maquas bee improued for the destruction of our enemy Indians and for their incouragement to pay them eight pounds for every fighting man's head or scalpe they shall bring in. And that vpon our treating with them wee present them with fifty pounds for renewing and confirming our former friendship with them. And that forthwith a meet person bee dispatched to Connecticut to joyne with those in that collony whome they see meet to send to the Maquas for that purpose.

It is ordered by the Representatives yt Captain Benjamin Church of New Bristoll be sent unto and intreated to use his endeavor, to procure a hundred Indians inhabiting ye Colony of New Plimouth of such as he may think fit for service against or Indian enemies to be under the command of said Captain Church.

It is ordered that Mr. Jno Stanton be Intreated to procure a hundred or more of fighting men of the Mohegans and Pequots to be improved against our common Indian enemie, to be under the command of said Mr. Stanton.

(*Collections of the Maine Historical Society*, 2d ser., 9 [1907]: 4–5.)

[Indians not only served with the English, they also complained when their enlistment money was not paid in full and, on occasion, deserted.⁹]

6. DAWNLAND WARFARE FOR ENGLISH SOLDIERS, 1691

[The guerilla warfare of the forests required a particular kind of response from the English and taxed the militia to the full. As these instructions to Captain John Marsh and Daniel King in June 1691 indicate, the English struggled to contain mobile Indian war parties who knew every inch of the terrain.]

Yor soldiers being mustered and furnished with armes and ammunition fit for service, you are forthwith to advance in search of the said enemy Ffrench or Indians, first ranging the woods about the ffrontier on the north of Merrimack to clear off an[y] sculking parties of them, and then march further east in pursuit and prosecution of the said enemy according as you may receive intelligence of their motions, or the most likely places where to find them, and make what spoiles you can upon them. Also give necessary releife and succor as you have opportunity to any towns, plantations or persons of the English that may be endangered or distressed by the Enemy.

In all yor marchings and encampings be sure to keep out good scouts and watches, that you be not ambuscadoed, surprized or overpowred by the enemy.

(*Collections of the Maine Historical Society*, 2d ser., 5 [1897]: 262.)

7. DIVIDED LOYALTIES, 1700

[In 1700, the English became alarmed by rumors of a multitribal insurrection brewing in Pennacook country. Indians from throughout New England gravitated to Pennacook in anticipation of hostilities, but, as the following extract shows, choosing sides was not always an easy matter. In an area where peaceful cooperation was also a fact of life, individual attachments often transcended ethnic lines, and many Indians regarded accommodation and adjustment as the best strategies for dealing with the English.]

He is sorry for trouble arising in a streight what to do, his family gon to Pennecook already yet unresolved what to do, thinks best for him to be English side. The Indians disgusted at him. English and Indians all say Governour very cunning man but Indians can, for all that, and will blind his eyes, for he can't see they'll speak him fair and he little thinks how near trouble is.

To his cousin Eben: Sabin Menequabben with tears in his eyes said he was in a great streight his family was gone to Pennecook to the other side, and he thought he must go too; and if he did he must fight against the English and that lookt hard.

(*Collections of the Maine Historical Society,* 2d ser., 10 [1907]: 64–65.)

8. GUERILLA WARFARE, DAWNLAND STYLE, 1704

[Queen Anne's War saw the pattern of raid, counter-raid, and forest skirmishing reenacted on dawnland frontiers. Early in 1704, French and Indian raiders surprised and destroyed Deerfield on the middle Connecticut River; about the same time, Major Winthrop Hilton led a futile expedition against Pigwacket. Later that year, Caleb Lyman led an Anglo-Indian expedition from Northampton against the Abenaki village at Cowass on the upper Connecticut. Lyman did not reach his objective, but he did surprise a small Abenaki encampment some twenty miles from Cowass. These accounts furnish good examples of the kind of tedious marching and small-scale fighting that was typical in the dawnland as English militia tried to retaliate against elusive foes by striking at their home bases.]

February 1703/4

Journal of the March and Proceedings with the Forces under my Command lately sent forth against the Indian Enemy and Rebels

We bagan our march from Newiche wanock and set forth from thence the ninth of February instant, following Your Excellencys instructions as near as possibly could. vizt:

Feb. 9th We marched this day sixteen miles, discovered nothing. Encamped.

10th Marched by breake of day, discovered two of the enemy's camps, judged they might hold betwixt forty or fifty Indians. We travailed twenty one miles this day and encamped.

11th Marched by breake of day, discovered two more of the enemyes camps, much of the same bigness with the former. We travailed about thirty miles this day and encamped.

12th Marched very earley, still upon the enemuies track, and came to Saco River about eight in the morning. Judged by the pilots to have fallen upon the river about Fifty Miles upwards, haveing before we came to the river travailed about eighteen miles, where we found the greatest part of the enemy had left the river to the southward. We set out a scout to discover further after them.

13th We found they altered their course again, and came upon the track of the Indians they left (when departed to the southward) that had kept the river and then marched all to the eastward. We left the eastern track and made the best of our way to Pegwockit Fort. We travailed this day twenty miles and encamped.

14th Bad weather, did nothing but secure our provisions and armes.

15th Marched before day, met with several old tracks of the enemy. We travailed till sunset, judged about twenty five miles, then encamped.

16th Marched before day, and about ten a clock in the forenoon our pilots were discouraged, lest they might not find Pegwockit. I then encamped and drew forth one hundred choice men, ordering every man a bisket, with a designe to march them directly up the river in order to find Pegwockit (leaving the rest to guard all our provisions, knapsacks etc.). We found Pegwockit Fort about sunset, so we returned again to our encamped men which we left behind, being eight miles back. Judged we travailed this day thirty two miles. When we came to the fort, we found it a large place of about an acre of ground taken in with timber set in the ground in a circular form with posts, and about one hundred wigwams therein; but had been deserted about six weekes as we judged by the opening their barnes where their corn was lodged, and that they deserted it in hast upon some alarm, because we found their corn scattered about the mouthes of their barnes.

17th Marched homewards upon the River Saco about thirty miles, saw nothing remarkable.

18th Marched homewards about eighteen miles.

19th Being very stormey could not travail.

20th Marched homewards about twenty five miles.

21st Marched about twenty three miles, and came to Saco Fort.

22nd Marched to Wells, being twenty miles.

23rd Marched to the Banke, being twenty five miles. All our men well in health thanks to Almighty God.

May it please your Excellency.

This is what offers upon this expedition and I humbly conceive that the winter time is the onely time ever to march against the Indian enemy—both for their discovery and the health and least danger of our people. And [I] shall always be ready to serve Her Majesty under Yor Excellcys commands, and for my country's sake.

     I am

Your Excellcys humble servant
Winthrop Hilton.

(*Collections of the Maine Historical Society*, 2d ser., 9 [1907]: 140–42.)

Mr. Caleb Lyman's Account of Eight Enemy Indians Killed by Himself and Five Friend Indians.

Sometime in the month of May, 1704, there came intelligence from *Albany*, of a number of enemy *Indians* up *Connecticut* River, who had built a fort and planted corn, at a place called *Cowassuck*. On the fifth of *June* following, we let out (by order of authority) from *Northampton*, and went nine days journey into the wilderness, (through much difficulty, by reason of the enemy's hunting and scouting in the woods, as we perceived by their tracks and firing) and then came across some fresh tracks, which we followed till we came in sight of the abovesaid river. Supposing there might be a number of *Indians* at hand, we being not far from the place where the fort was said to be built, here we made a halt, to consult what methods to take. And soon concluded to send out a spy, with green leaves for a *cap* and *veste*, to prevent his own discovery, and to find out the enemy. But before our spy was gone out of sight, we saw two *Indians*, at a considerable distance from us, in a *canoo*, and so immediately recalled him. And soon after we heard the firing of a gun up the river. Upon which we concluded to keep close till sunset; and then if we could make any further discovery of the enemy, to attack them, if possible, in the night. And accordingly, when the evening came on, we moved towards the river, and soon perceived a *smoke*, at about half a miles distance, as we thought, where we (afterwards) found they had taken up their lodging. But so great was the difficulty, that (though we used our utmost care and diligence in it) we were not able to make the approach till about *two* a clock in the morning, when we came within twelve rods of the *wigwam*, where they lay. But here we met with a new difficulty, which we feared would have ruined the whole design: for the ground was so covered over with dry sticks and brush, for the space of five rods, that we could not pass without making such a *crackling*, as we thought would alarm the enemy and give them time to escape. But while we were contriving to compass our design, God in his good Providence so ordered, that a very small cloud arose, which gave a smart *clap of thunder*, and a sudden shower of rain. And this opportunity we embraced, to run thorow the thicket; and so came undiscovered within sight of the *wigwam*; and perceived by their noise, that the enemy were awake. But however, being unwilling to lose any time, we crept on our hands and knees till we were within three or four rods of them. Then we arose, and ran to the side of the *wigwam,* and fired in upon them. And flinging down our *guns,* we surrounded them with our *clubs* and *hatchets,* and knockt down several we met with. But after all our diligence, *two* of their number made their escape from us: one *mortally* wounded, and the other not hurt; as we afterwards heard.

When we came to look over the slain, we found seven dead upon the spot: *six* of whom we *scalpt,* and left the other unscalpt. (Our *Indians* saying, They would give one to the country, since we had each of us one; and so concluded we should all be rich enough.) When the action was thus over, we took our *scalps* and *plunder,* such as *guns, skins,* etc. and the enemies *canoos*; in which we came down the river about twelve miles, by break of day. And then thought it prudence to dismiss and break the *canoos,* knowing there were some of the enemy betwixt us and home.

(Samuel Penhallow, *The History of the Wars of New England, With the Eastern Indians* [Boston, 1726], 20–22.)

[News of the attack alarmed the community at Cowass and, according to Samuel Penhallow, the Abenakis "immediately forsook their Fort and Corn at Cowassuck, and never returned to this Day, that we could hear of, to renew their Settlement in that place." Cowasucks did in fact return at the end of the war. More often, English expeditions shared Hilton's experience, coming up empty-handed as Indian communities evaporated into the forest at their approach. Following an Indian raid on Cocheco, or Dover, New Hampshire, in the spring of 1711,[10] for example, an English retaliatory force went in pursuit "to Ossipe and Winnepisseocay Ponds, being places of general resort for fishing, fowling and hunting; but saw none, only a few deserted wigwams; for being so closely pursued from one place to another, they removed to other nations, leaving only a few cut-throats behind, which kept the country in a constant alarm."[11]]

9. THE COWASUCKS REFUSE REFUGE, 1704

[Withdrawal, and even migration, was a common Abenaki response to military danger and the disruption of war. Many Abenakis followed well-worn paths

to mission villages in Canada, where the French welcomed them with open arms. In 1704, Governor Vaudreuil invited several tribes to resettle on the St. Lawrence where they could enjoy French protection against the English. Some bands accepted, but the Cowasucks preferred to stay and fight in their homeland. The same month that the Cowasuck delegates were declining Vaudreuil's offer, Caleb Lyman was leading his expedition against their village.]

Speech of the Abenaki Indians of Cowasuck to the Governor-General, 13 June 1704.

Father, to tell the truth you have shown great care for me in inviting me to come and settle on your lands. However, I cannot bring myself to come there because the English have already struck me too hard. I believe, therefore, that the only place where I can strike back against the English is the place I come from, which is called Cowasuck. I could not do that easily if I was in your country. [Presented a wampum belt.]

Father, hear me, I wish to remain at Cowasuck. It is true you have acted well in offering me a fort on your lands, and that would have been good if we had been at peace as we used to be, and we could have done it easily. But hear me, I am a warrior. I offer you my village which is like a fort thrust towards the enemy, so that your lands on this side can be protected, and so that you can think of me as "my child who is at Cowasuck to carry on the war and protect me, serving as a palisade against my enemies."

(National Archives of Canada, MG1 F3, vol. 2:407–10; editor's translation.)

10. PIGWACKETS RETURN HOME, 1715

[Indians who migrated to Canada in wartime did not always remain there and often returned home once peace was restored. Despite French efforts to discourage him, the Pigwacket chief, Athurnando, or Atecuando, led his people

back to their village on the headwaters of the Saco River after Queen Anne's War.]

Messieurs de Ramezay and Begon write on November 7, 1715, that Father Aubry, the Jesuit missionary of the Abenakis, has informed them that Athurnando—one of the principal chiefs of that nation, who has resided for eight years at St. Francois, whither Monsieur de Vaudreuil and Monsieur de Beauharnois had induced him to settle with all his village, to the number of 60 warriors, so that he might remain there at least during the war—came back to St. Francois in the month of August last from Pegouaki, where his former village was situated. He had gone thither to hunt during the winter, and began last spring to sow corn there. He told Monsieur Begon that he intended to speak to Monsieur de Vaudreuil—who he supposed had returned from France—to ask him, in fulfillment of the promise that he had given, for permission to reestablish his former village, since peace was declared; and to take there with him the savages of St. Francois and of Becancourt, who might wish to follow him, hoping that some Loup savages from Orange[12] would join him. The chief also intended to ask that Father Aubry might go with him. . . .

(Thwaites, ed., *Jesuit Relations*, 67:31.)

11. ABENAKI WARFARE, 1723

[The English accused Jesuit priests of instigating Abenaki attacks on their settlements and even, on occasion, of leading raids themselves.[13] Jesuit missionaries who lived most of their lives with the Abenakis certainly had plenty of opportunity for first-hand knowledge of Abenaki warfare. In the following extract from a letter to his brother, October 12, 1723, Sebastien Rasles gives a vivid account of Abenaki warfare as waged against the English.]

The manner in which these tribes make war renders a handful of their warriors more formidable than a body of 2 or 3,000 European soldiers would be. As soon as they have entered the enemy's country, they divide into separate companies—one of thirty warriors, another of forty, and so on. They say to some: "To you is given this hamlet to eat" (that is their expression), to others: "To you is given this village," etc. Afterward the signal is given to strike all together, and at the same time in the different places. Our two hundred and fifty warriors spread themselves over more than twenty leagues of country, where there were villages, hamlets, and houses; and, on the appointed day they made simultaneous attacks, very early in the morning. In one single day they ruined all the English; they killed more than two hundred, and took a hundred and fifty prisoners, while on their side only a few warriors were wounded, and these but slightly. They returned from this expedition to the village, each of them having two canoes laden with booty that he had taken.

During the whole time while the war continued, they carried desolation into all the country that belonged to the English; they ravaged their villages, their forts, and their farms; they took away great numbers of cattle, and seized more than six hundred prisoners.

(Thwaites, ed., *Jesuit Relations*, 67:203–5.)

12. THE FRENCH WATCH FROM THE WINGS, 1724

[Anglo-French conflict usually involved Indian allies as willing—or not so willing—participants. However, from 1723 to 1727, a time of formal peace between France and England, Abenaki resentment of English encroachment and breaches of treaties flared into a war, or wars, that they fought without French support. In Maine, the conflict was known as Dummer's War or Lovewell's War; in Vermont, Chief Grey Lock dictated the character of the conflict. The French

watched nervously from the wings as their allies took on the English unaided, and they feared the consequences of their own inaction. As Father Jean-Baptiste Loyard, missionary to the Maliseets on the Saint John River, predicted in his "Memoir on the Present Condition of the Abenaquis," the Abenakis of Maine grew tired of war, made the best terms they could, and some quit their country. But Grey Lock and the Vermont Abenakis remained defiant and undefeated, and the war petered out without them ever attending a peace conference.[14]]

Should the Court not think proper to assist the Indians publicly in this war, which is waged by the English against them, it seems at least expedient that it complain loudly of the contraventions by the English of the Treaty of Utrecht, adopt measures to put an end to them, and have it settled at the Congress at Cambray, that the English shall not be permitted to molest the Abenaquis by encroaching on their territory and establishing themselves, contrary to the law of nations, in a country of which the said Indians have been from all time in possession.

Otherwise, it will follow that the Abenaquis, tired of the war, will abandon their country, or what is more probable, will, without quitting it, make the best terms they can with the English, who, by means of much larger presents than we can possibly make these Indians, will soon succeed in gaining them over, especially by giving them to understand, as they will not fail to do, that France has cared nothing for them except when she had need of them, whilst now, when it is her interest not to embroil herself with England, she refuses to take any part in their quarrel with the English. This reasoning is within the comprehension of the Indians, and the proof of it would be too plain not to convince them. If, on the contrary, the Court succeed in replacing matters on their ancient footing, and in putting a stop to the usurpations of the English, the Abenaquis, on hearing the fact, will attach themselves more and more to France, without thinking of quitting their country, and we, thereby, shall have completely provided for the security of Canada on the land side.

(O'Callaghan, ed., *Documents Relating to the Colonial History of New York*, 8:940.)

13. PASSPORT FOR AN INDIAN HOSTAGE, 1724

[Even at its height, dawnland warfare did not preclude the possibility of honorable and considerate dealings between Indians and Europeans. In February 1724, Lieutenant Governor Dummer made arrangements for the safe passage of an Abenaki hostage named Saccamakten or Sackamaten to return home on parole, furnishing him with the following passport.]

Whereas Saccamakten (one of the Indian hostages) has obtained my leave to visit the Indian settlemts and see his family and friends in thos parts upon his parol to return back in the space of forty days; These are to require all officers civil and military and to desire persons within this Government and all his Majesties good subjects to suffer the said Saccamaksen to pass forward to Penobscot or other Indian settlemts without lett or molestation and to return back to the English fort at St. Georges River provided he pass and repass peaceably without offering any injury to his Majesties subjects.

(*Collections of the Maine Historical Society*, 2d ser., 10 [1907]: 180–81.)

[Saccamakten fulfilled his commitment to return and, "by his Honesty & Faithfulness," helped secure similar paroles for other Indians.[15]]

14. INDIAN "PIRATES," 1725

[Dawnland fighting took place primarily in the forests, but coastal Indians in captured vessels carried the war to the English on the sea. In July 1724, volunteers from Piscataqua went out after "indian pirets" who had captured a schooner from Marblehead and made the coast unsafe for English fishermen.[16]

The next year, the English again took measures to counter the sea-borne Indian threat.]

It being highly probable that the Indians of Penobscot will speedily be out in the vessels they took last summer from the English and will infest the eastern coast to the great disturbance and loss of those concerned in the fishery.

(William Blake Trask, ed., *Letters of Colonel Thomas Westbrook and Others Relative to Indian Affairs in Maine, 1722–1726* [Boston: George E. Littlefield, 1901], 112; and Mass. Archives, 52:188–90.)

15. LOVEWELL'S FIGHT, 1725

[In the spring of 1725, Captain John Lovewell scored a Pyrrhic victory over the Pigwackets in a battle that became celebrated in history, legend, and verse. Samuel Penhallow's account conveys the desperate nature of the struggle, fought between men who in some cases recognized each other, and the English determination to claim it as a victory. The Indian body count was probably exaggerated, but many Pigwackets retreated to Canada in the wake of the battle.]

Captain *Lovewell* being still animated with an uncommon zeal of doing what service he could, made another attempt on *Pigwackett* with forty four men; who in his going built a small fort near *Ossipy,* to have recourse unto in case of danger, as also for the relief of any that might be sick or wounded. And having one of his men at this time sick, he left the *doctor* with eight men more to guard him. With the rest of his company he preceeded in quest of the enemy, who on *May* the 8th about 10 in the morning, forty miles from said fort, near *Saco* Pond, he saw an *Indian* on a point of land. Upon which they immediately put off their blankets and snapsacks, and made towards him, concluding that the enemy were ahead and not in the rear. Yet they were not without some apprehensions of their being discovered two days before, and that the appearing of one *Indian* in so bold a manner, was on purpose to ensnare them. Wherefore the Captain calling his men together, proposed whether it was best to engage them or not; who boldly replyed, *That as they came out on purpose to meet the enemy, they would rather trust Providence with their lives and die for their country, than return without seeing them.* Upon this they proceeded and mortally wounded the *Indian,* who notwithstanding returned the fire, and wounded Captain *Lovewell* in the belly; upon which Mr. *Wyman* fired and killed him. But their dismantling themselves at this juncture proved an unhappy snare; for the enemy taking their baggage, knew their strength by the number of their packs, where they lay in ambush till they returned, and made the first shot; which our men answered with much bravery, and advancing within twice the length of their guns, slew nine. The encounter was smart and desperate, and the victory seemed to be in our favour, till Captain *Lovewell* with several more were slain and wounded, to the number of *twelve.* Upon which our men were forced to retreat unto a pond, between which and the enemy was a ridge of ground that proved a barrier unto us. The engagement continued ten hours, but although the shouts of the enemy were at first loud and terrible, yet after some time they became sensibly low and weak, and their appearance to lessen. Now whether it was through want of ammunition, or on the account of those that were slain and wounded, that the enemy retreated, certain it is they first drew off and left the ground. And although many of our men were much enfeebled by reason of their wounds, yet none of the enemy pursued them in their return. Their number was uncertain, but by the advice which we afterwards received, they were *seventy* in the whole, whereof *forty* were said to be killed upon the spot, *eighteen* more died of their wounds, and that twelve only returned. An unhappy instance at this time fell out respecting one of our men, who when the fight began was so dreadfully terrified, that he ran away unto the fort, telling those who were there,

that Captain *Lovewell* was killed with most of his men; which put
them into so great a consternation, that they all drew off, leaving
a bag of bread and pork behind, in case any of their company
might return and be in distress.

(Penhallow, *History of the Indian Wars of New England*, 112–14.)

16. PENOBSCOT FOREIGN POLICY, 1728

*[The Abenakis were not a united nation pursuing a single policy, and war
with the English aggravated divisions within tribes.[17] In the wars of the 1720s,
Grey Lock's Missisquoi warriors acted independently of the Abenakis in Maine
and Canada, and, as this extract from a French despatch shows, the Penobscots
also looked to their own interests in formulating policy. Recognizing that their
proximity to the English would expose them to the greatest destruction, the Penobscots played a major role in inducing other tribes to make peace at the Treaty
of Falmouth in July 1727, even ignoring the advice of their priest to do so.]*

An effort was made to encourage those of Panaouamské to
prosecute the war, or at least not to prevent those of St. Francis
and Beccancourt continuing it. But, notwithstanding all the rep-
resentations respecting their common interests, they answered
that they understood better than any one the importance it was
to themselves not to continue the war against the English, and
even to entertain the proposals for peace that had been offered
them, and to arrest the hatchet of their brethren domiciliated
in Canada, the rebound of which would inevitably fall on them,
and that they were resolved, no matter how much they were
forbidden, to visit their brethren of St. Francis and Beccancourt,
in order to represent the danger to which they were exposing
them by continuing the war. They were told, in answer, that the
step they were about to take, was at entire variance with the
interests of the whole nation; that nevertheless there was no wish
to embarrass them. They did proceed thither in fact, and made

the villages of St. Francis and of Beccancourt so sensible of their reasons, that they continued the war only in spite of themselves; and hastened to stop some parties that were already in the field.

As Father Aubery, missionary of St. Francis, heard nothing but peace spoken of, and saw that these Indians thought of nothing but of going to ratify the treaty concluded by those of Panaouamské, and no longer asked for a fort, the project of erecting it disappeared.

80 domiciliated Indians, belonging to St. Francis, Beccancourt and Narantsouak, joined those of Panaouamské and St. John, and all spent the summer in concluding a peace, the conditions of which have been transmitted in writing by Father Lauverjeat to Mr. de Beauharnais.

The missionaries continued to labor diligently to manage the Abenaquis, who serve, even after the recently concluded peace, in which they have renounced neither their religion, their territory nor their union with the French, as a barrier against the encroachments of the English, on the Acadia frontier, where they are partly located and have some French missionaries.

(O'Callaghan, ed., *Documents Relating to the Colonial History of New York*, 8:990–91.)

17. MUSTER ROLLS FROM FORT DUMMER, 1724–1742

[Built in the early 1720s as a defense against Grey Lock's raids, Fort Dummer near present-day Brattleboro, Vermont, was garrisoned by English and Indian soldiers, as these extracts from the fort's muster rolls attest. The Indian recruits came from Schaghticoke (Scaticook, Seaticook) on the Hudson, from the Catholic Mohawk village at Caughnawaga, and from various Hudson River tribes. Their presence gave the garrison a multi-ethnic character typical of Indian-European interactions in the dawnland.[18]]

Name	Rank	Residence	Expedition	Dates of service	Company
Mascamah, Joseph (Indian)	Lt.	Seaticook		5/21/36–5/20/37	Capt. Kellogg
Mascamah, Joseph	Lt.	Seaticook	Ft. Dummer	5/21/39–5/20/40	Capt. Kellogg
Mascamah, Josiah	Lt.		Ft. Dummer	11/21/40–3/4/42	Capt. Willard
Massequun, Joseph (Indian)	Capt.	Seaticook		5/21/37–5/20/37	Capt. Kellogg
Massequun, Joseph	Capt.	Seaticook	Ft. Dummer	5/21/39–5/20/40	Capt. Kellogg
Massequun, Josiah	Capt.		Ft. Dummer	5/21–11/20/40	Capt. Willard
Massequun, Josiah	Capt.		Ft. Dummer	11/21/40–3/42	Capt. Willard
Massequun, Josiah	Capt.			3/5–5/20/42	Capt. Willard
Massequun, Josiah	Capt.		Ft. Dummer	5/21–11/20/42	Capt. Willard
Nahuamuck, William	Pvt.			7/15–10/28	Capt. Canada
Nannatoohan, Joseph (Indian)	Capt.	Seaticook		5/21/36–5/20/37	Capt. Kellogg
Nannatoohan, Joseph	Capt.	Seaticook	Ft. Dummer	5/21/39–5/20/40	Capt. Kellogg
Nannatoohan, Josiah	Capt.		Ft. Dummer	5/21–11/20/40	Capt. Willard
Nannatoohan, Josiah	Capt.		Ft. Dummer	11/21/40–3/4/42	Capt. Willard
Nanatoohan, Josiah	Capt.			3/5–5/20/42	Capt. Willard
Nannatoohan, Josiah	Capt.		Ft. Dummer	5/21–11/20/42	Capt. Willard
Onlessogo, Joseph (Indian)	Col.	Canghawange		5/21/36–5/20/37	Capt. Kellogg
Onlossogo, Joseph (Indian)	Col.	Canghawange		5/21/39–5/20/40	Capt. Kellogg
Thyhansilhan, Joseph (Indian)	Lt. Col.	Canawange	Ft. Dummer	5/21/39–5/20/40	Capt. Kellogg

Name	Rank	Residence	Expedition	Dates of service	Company
Thyhausilhan, Josiah	Lt. Col.		Ft. Dummer	5/21–11/20/40	Capt. Willard
Thyhausilhan, Josiah	Lt. Col.		Ft. Dummer	11/21/40–3/4/42	Capt. Willard
Thyhausilhan, Josiah	Lt. Col.			3/5–5/20/42	Capt. Willard
Thyhausilhan, Josiah	Lt. Col.		Ft. Dummer	5/21–11/20/42	Capt. Willard
Tihansilhau, Joseph	Lt. Col.	Caughawange		5/21/36–5/20/37	Capt. Kellogg
Wattunkameag (Indian)	Pvt.	Hudson's River		4/21–5/31/24	Capt. Timothy Dwight
Waunnoowoozeet (Indian)	Pvt.	Hudson's River		4/21–5/31/24	Capt. Timothy Dwight

(Myron O. Stachiw, ed., *Massachusetts Officers and Soldiers, 1723–1743: Dummer's War to the War of Jenkins' Ear* [The New England Historic Genealogical Society, 1979], 164, 177, 185, 248, 260.)

18. MISSISQUOI IN KING GEORGE'S WAR, 1744

[The Abenaki village at Missisquoi on the north end of Lake Champlain was a center of Abenaki independence and resistance to the English. Grey Lock established his headquarters near there in the 1720s, and in subsequent conflicts, the village served as a forward base for French and Abenaki forays against the English frontier. Missisquoi dispatched war parties against the New England frontier throughout King George's War, but the village itself emerged unscathed from the conflict. The following document shows how the French relied on Missisquoi and hoped that it would function as a bastion of the Catholic religion and a defense for French colonies, attracting Indian recruits and converts from other areas.]

The village of Missisquoi has grown quite considerably since last year. There are actually a number of families there, composed of about 60 warriors, all young men. Monsieur de Beauharnois sent an officer there last summer to sing the war song and to present them with the war belt and hatchet, which they have accepted with great displays of enthusiasm and attachment for the French. They sang the war song for several days without stop. Up to the present, this mission has incurred no more extra expense than the construction of a house, room by room, and the purchase of some furniture and implements of little value for the use of the missionary, a total cost of perhaps 1500#. The missionary earnestly requests that he be able to build a chapel in the same style. It will be necessary to supply the place continually and to add the ornaments. We hope that once this mission is on its feet, some of the Mahicans from the Hudson Valley region will come and settle there.

(National Archives of Canada, MG1 C11A, vol. 81:31–32; editor's translation.)

19. FORMER PLAYMATES FIGHT AT GORHAM, C. 1745

[Northern New England town histories frequently contain brief information on the original inhabitants the first settlers encountered. Such information, often gathered from local memory, adds small pieces to a picture of interaction that stretched across a two hundred-mile frontier. In settlements like Gorham, Maine, settlers and Indians lived alongside one another, tolerated each other's presence and differences, and even played and grew up together. Such peaceful exchanges came to an end when King George's War broke out and the Indians withdrew to join the French.]

Often when war-parties were discovered about Gorhamtown, Indians were seen and recognized as those, who, in time of peace, had made the town their residence. The young men of the settlement more than once met those with whom they had been playmates. In a skirmish, which the inhabitants had with a war-party, one of the young Phinneys recognized a young Indian of his own age, who grew up in town, and with whom he had had many a happy time at play, and in sliding down hill in the winter on birch bark. But the meeting was not for play, but for life or death. A few taunting words passed between them; they both fired at the same moment; the Indian missed, but Phinney brought his game, dead, to the ground.

(Hugh D. McLellan, *The History of Gorham, Maine* [1903; facs. reprint, Somersworth, N.H.: The New England History Press, 1981], 36.)

20. ABENAKI DEFIANCE, 1747

[In King George's War (1744–1748), Abenaki warriors turned back the tide of English settlement in the Connecticut Valley; by the war's end, they had virtually cleared Vermont of its invaders. English militia and garrisons were no match for Abenaki war parties operating in familiar territory, and the Abenakis knew it. In the spring of 1747, an Abenaki war party that had taken Fort Number Two at Westmoreland on the Connecticut River dictated a defiant message to the General Assembly.]

Gentlemen: Whereas there have been very grievous complaints in the province of ——— with respect to ye support and maintenance of your frontiers in a time of war, we your allies while the peace lasted and so long as we received presents from you; but now as we allways are in a time of war subjects to the King of France, have undertaken to free you from such an extraordinary charge by killing and taking captive the people and driving them off and firing their fortification. And so successful have we been in this affair that we have broke up almost all the new settlements in your western frontiers: so yt you need not be one half of charge you were in past in maintaining a war in these parts. For now there are but little else besides the old towns, and if they will not fortifie and defend themselves, we think they ought to be left to our mercy. And for this good service that we have done the province, we humbly ask a suitable reward; but if your honours prefer we will wait till a peace is concluded and then receive it in presents. But in the mean time if some small matter of encouragement be given us we will go on to bring your frontiers to a narrower compass still and make your charges still smaller. But if your honours approve of this our design we humbly request of you to give us information whither it be more acceptable to you that we man your deserted garrisons our selves and eat up the provisions which your poor distrest neighbours leave in ym when they flee in their hurry and confusion or whether we burn up the forts with the provisions; for we assure you we find much more in them than we want for our own support whilst carrying on this business.

Gentlemen, however some may look upon us now yet we can assure you we are your very humble obsequious servants.

Old Town   Pene wanse

Chee Hoose   Prish Fore English

In the name and behalf of others.

(Indian Petition to the Assembly—Number 2 on Connecticut River April 1, 1747, Newberry Library, Chicago, Ayer Mss 423.)

21. INDIAN WARNINGS, 1754

[Regular interaction between Indians and Europeans opened channels of communication between individuals that transcended ethnic loyalties. Also, some Indians adhered to treaty commitments that specified that they warn the English of impending attacks. Captain Samuel Goodwin, writing from Frankfort on the Kennebec River in May 1754, attested to the debt settlers owed to local Indians as war clouds gathered.]

The stragling Indians that have been into Richmond Fort last week have informed the German settlers at Frank Fort that the Canada Indians would certainly fall on English in two Sabbath days more, and that all the old people were to be killed and the young carried to Cannada, and told them to take care of themselves, and they are now all in garrison, and what to do they know not, but intreat your Excellency's favor and protection.

I am further informed by John Howard at Richmond Fort that the Indians that were last in, told him, that the Arresigunticook Indians were gone to fall on the English at Saco River, or thereabouts.

(*Collections of the Maine Historical Society*, 2d ser., 24 [1916]: 10.)

22. KILBURN'S DEFENSE, 1755

[Indians who frequented English settlements in peacetime proved dangerous foes when war broke out, and they earned the settlers' hatred as spies and traitors. An Indian named Philip was trading with Phineas Stevens at Fort Number Four on the eve of the Seven Years' War,[19] and he was probably the same individual who featured in the Indian attack on John Kilburn and his neighbors at the mouth of the Cold River near Walpole, New Hampshire, in 1755.]

In the spring of 1755, an Indian by the name of Philip, who had just learned English enough to be understood, visited Kilburn's log house, under the pretence of being on a hunting excursion and in want of provisions. He was treated with kindness, and furnished liberally with flints, meal, and various other articles which he asked for. Soon after his departure it was ascertained that the same Indian had visited all the settlements on the Connecticut River, with the same plausible story. The conclusion was with Kilburn and his fellow-settlers that Philip was a scout employed by the enemy.

. . . .

Not long after these Indians came out on the eminence east of Kilburn's house. Here the "Old Devil" Philip, as he was now generally called—being the same wily savage who had visited Kilburn's house the season previous—came forward, securing himself behind a large tree, and called out loudly to those in the house to surrender. "Old John, young John," he cried, "I know you; come out here; we give good quarter."

[Kilburn scornfully rejected the offer of quarter and in the fighting that followed "brought down an Indian, who, from his extraordinary size, and other circumstances, appeared to be Philip."]

(Francis Chase, ed., *Gathered Sketches from the Early History of New Hampshire and Vermont* [Claremont, N.H.: Tracy, Kenney & Co., 1856], 65–68.)

23. BOUNTY ON PENOBSCOT SCALPS, 1755

[Despite twentieth-century assertions that Europeans were to blame for introducing scalping into North America, recent scholarship has demonstrated that the practice and rituals of scalping were intertwined in Indian cultures before Europeans arrived. Europeans had their own repertoire of barbarous practices, but colonial governments institutionalized scalping by paying scalp bounties as a mercenary incentive to their citizens and their Indian allies. Scalping became commonplace in backwoods warfare, and frontiersmen expected—and were expected—to lift trophies from Indian enemies: Captain John Lovewell not only paraded scalps through the streets of Boston, he also wore a wig made of Indian scalps.[20] Frontier warfare engendered its own form of brutality among Indians and Europeans alike, as this proclamation, issued during the Seven Years' War, illustrates.]

By His Honour
SPENCER PHIPS, Esq;
Lieutenant-Governour and Commander in Chief, in and over His Majesty's Province of the Massachusetts-Bay in New-England.
A PROCLAMATION

Whereas the Tribe of *Penobscot* Indians have repeatedly in a perfidious manner acted contrary to their solemn submission unto His Majesty long since made and frequently renewed;
I have therefore, at the desire of the House of Representatives, with the advice of his Majesty's Council, thought fit to issue this Proclamation, and to declare the *Penobscot* Tribe of Indians to

be Enemies, Rebels and Traitors to His Majesty King George the Second. And I do hereby require His Majesty's subjects of this Province to embrace all opportunities of pursuing, captivating, killing and destroying all and every of the aforesaid Indians.

And whereas the General Court of this Province have voted that a Bounty of Incouragement be granted and allowed to be paid out of the Publick Treasury, to the marching forces that shall have been employed for the defence of the *Eastern* and *Western* Frontiers, from the *first* to the *twenty-fifth* of this instant November;

I have thought fit to publish the same; and I do hereby promise, that there shall be paid out of the Province-Treasury to all and any of the said forces, over and above their bounty upon inlistment, their wages and subsistence, the premiums or bounty following, *vis.*

For every male *Penobscot* Indian above the age of twelve years, that shall be taken within the time aforesaid and brought to *Boston, fifty pounds.*

For every scalp of a male *Penobscot* Indian above the age aforesaid, brought in as evidence of their being killed as aforesaid, *forty pounds.*

For every female *Penobscot* Indian taken and brought in as aforesaid, and for every male Indian prisoner under the age of twelve years, taken and brought in as aforesaid, *twenty-five pounds.*

For every scalp of such female Indian or male Indian under the age of twelve Years, that shall be killed and brought in as evidence of their being killed as aforesaid, *twenty pounds.*

Given at the Council-Chamber in *Boston,* this third day of *November* 1755, and in the twenty-ninth year of the Reign of our Sovereign Lord GEORGE the Second, by the Grace of GOD of

Great Britain, France and Ireland, KING, Defender of the
Faith, &c.

By His Honour's Command,
J. Willard, Sec.

S. Phips.

GOD Save the KING

(Printed by John Draper, Printer to His Honour the Lieutenant-Governor and Council,
Boston, 1755.[21])

24. VERSE ON A POWDER HORN, 1757

*[The sentiments of common soldiers often go unrecorded in historical nar-
ratives of conflict. The following verse, etched on a powder horn by Jonathan
Hobart at Fort Number Four on the Connecticut River, conveys some of the
private fears of soldiers stationed on the dawnland frontier.]*

I now at Number Four Remain
Tho Tis Again my will
I hope I shall no enemy meet
But what I wound or kill

(From the collection of William M. Guthman.)

25. FRANCE'S ABENAKI ALLIES, 1758

*[The final round of the Anglo-French contest for continental hegemony cost
the Abenakis heavily. Robert Rogers' Rangers burned St. Francis in 1759, and
Lake Champlain Abenakis experienced fighting on their doorsteps for the first
time. During the war, Abenaki war parties performed their usual services for
the French, but the limited authority of Abenaki chiefs, compounded by problems
with interpreters, continued to cause the French headaches. The following extracts from the journal of a French officer illustrate both aspects of the Abenaki
alliance.]*

March 24 [1758]: A party of seven Abnakis from Misiskoui have penetrated, always hunting through the woods, to within twenty leagues of Boston. They have looted and burned a country house, killed three men, and brought back the wife and children. One Abnaki was slightly wounded.

July 13 [1758]: Thefts and robberies by the Abnakis especially. Of all the Indian tribes, the Abnaki is that in which the young men have the least submission to the old men and the chiefs, either in peace or in war.

Council held with the chiefs to take them to task for these disorders. Great difficulty, almost impossibility of stopping them. The interpreters are often the cause. Great defect in the makeup of this country that it is not officers, that is to say, men who have the sentiments of such as well as the name, who serve as interpreters. It was [not] thus formerly. Now this function, which gives the greatest control over the Indians, is given up to vile souls, mercenaries, cruel men, who are occupied only in retaining their control over the Indians, from which they draw a great profit in countenancing all their vices and even in furnishing the means of satisfying them.

(Hamilton, ed., *Adventure in the Wilderness: The American Journals of Louis Antoine de Bougainville 1756–1760*, 199, 242–43.)

26. PENOBSCOT PEACE INITIATIVES, 1760

[Of all the Abenaki tribes, the Penobscots displayed the most friendship toward the English and were the most reluctant to be drawn into war. At the beginning of the Seven Years' War, some even warned the English about impending attacks by the Kennebec and St. Francis Indians.[22] The Penobscots were also among the first to seek peace, but, as Governor Thomas Pownall's message to the Massachusetts Council and House of Representatives in March 1760 reflects, the English remained suspicious of Indian professions of peace and friendship.]

I have received an account from Brigadier Pribble that the Penobscot Indians have again desired peace, and that they have given him all the assurance that could be expected from Indians, and that they are in good earnest, and do now intend to bring in their families. I still remain of opinion that unless these Indians do, as a previous measure, fix their residence somewhere near the frontier, and become domiciliate with us, as most of the Indian tribes have long been with the French in Canada, so as to be responsible in their tribe for the faithful execution of their treaties, there can be no treaty nor peace held with them. Nor can I answer it to our eastern settlers to put their lives and safety in a situation that must be subject to the faith of Indians— While I think our frontiers are much safer under those precautions which we have taken in a state of war. But if the Indians will do this, which I have required, I am ready to make peace with them, and have ordered Brigadier Pribble to send to me here such a deputation of their people as they shall appoint to ratifye and confirm the same.

(*Collections of the Maine Historical Society,* 2d ser., 13 [1909]: 207–8.)

27. ABENAKIS IN THE AMERICAN REVOLUTION, 1777–1778

[The French defeat in 1760 left the Abenakis without allies as English settlers flooded into the dawnland after the war. Some Abenakis withdrew to Canada; others stayed and tried to make the best of things. When the American Revolution broke out, the northern frontier once again stood exposed to enemy attack—this time from the British and their Indian allies. The outbreak of the Revolution presented the Indian peoples of eastern North America with difficult choices. British and American agents competed for their support or their neutrality, and, while most tribes hoped to remain neutral, the pressures to become involved usually rendered that impossible. Eventually, British economic advantages and promises of continued protection, coupled with American encroachments and

ill-timed atrocities, pushed most Indians to side with the Crown. As the following three documents reveal, the situation in the dawnland was rather different and complex, and most Abenakis remained neutral or sided with the Americans during the war.]

[Competition for Indian allegiance and the radical new situation created by the Revolution produced confusion and distress in Indian communities and generated a flurry of movement between Indian villages. In May 1775, the Committee of Brownfield sent the following report by Henry Young Brown to the Massachusetts Congress.]

There are five or six families of *Indians* hunting at *Androscoggin*, about twenty-five miles north of my house. Several of the women and youngsters were at my house last week; one of them expressed much concern about the times; said their men could not hunt, eat, nor sleep; keep calling together every night; courting, courting, every night, all night. O, strange *Englishmen* kill one another. I think the world is coming to an end. Mrs. *Brown* asked which side they would fight. Answered, why should we fight for t'other country, for we never see t'other country; our hunting is in this country. One of them said her brother was a colonel; she wished she could see him; she would tell him not to fight for t'other country, but to fight for this country. One of the party is gone to *Canada*. They wanted powder but got none. Some of them were painted; and as it was the first time they came in paint, it surprised some of our women. I thought it best you should know of their concern and uneasiness, and that one was gone to *Canada*.

(Peter Force, comp., *American Archives*, 9 vols. [Washington, 1837–1873] 4th ser. 2:621.)

[Despite the vigilance of British troops occupying St. Francis and the threats of Governor Guy Carleton to burn their village if they displayed Patriot sympathies, many St. Francis Abenakis left their village and moved back to the

upper Connecticut rather than fight for the British. In accordance with General Philip Schuyler's orders, Colonel Timothy Bedel took every measure to attract and secure the allegiance of these Abenakis. Despite suffering hardships in their new location, the Abenakis afforded protection to the settlements and furnished a company of rangers for service in the Patriot cause. Less than twenty years after Rogers' Rangers torched their village, St. Francis Abenakis and New Hampshire Rangers were serving together to protect the Connecticut Valley.]

Copy of a Letter to Colonel Bedel, Dated Albany, September 11, 1777

Sir: You having informed us that forty five families of the St. Francois Indians are removed from thence and are now near the Lake Memphremagog, and inclined to settle on some part of Connecticut River above Cahoos. As it is of importance to secure as many of the Indians to the interest of the American cause as possible, especially such as reside in Canada, you will therefore please to take measures to remove the above mentioned Indians to some part of Connecticut River, as near the inhabitants as possible. And to induce them more readily to come, you will afford them some assistance in provisions and ammunition for which purpose I furnish you with eight hundred dollars.

(Vermont State Archives, Stevens Papers 3:667.)

[The Penobscots, Passamaquoddies, and other tribes of Maine and Nova Scotia displayed similar Patriot sentiments. Colonel John Allan served as American agent to the eastern tribes, and at the Treaty of Watertown in July 1776, the Micmac and St. Johns Indians agreed to assist the United States. Although like most Indians they had little understanding of the causes of the Revolution, were reluctant to get involved, and at first offered only half-hearted support, some eventually took a more positive stand in favor of the American cause—as their letter to the British commander on St. John's River makes clear. In 1779, Passamaquoddy and Penobscot warriors served with distinction in the expedition

against Penobscot. However, British goods and power won over some of the Indians, split the tribes, and curtailed the subsequent activities of Patriot factions.]

To the British commanding officer at the mouth of the River St. John's.
[11 and 18 August 1778]

The chiefs, sachems, and young men belonging to the River St. John's have duly considered the nature of this great war between Old England and America. They are unanimous that America is right and Old England wrong.

The river, on which you are with your soldiers, belongs from the most ancient times to our ancestors, consequently is ours now, and which we are bound to keep for our posterity.

You know we are Americans; that is our native country. You know the King of England with his evil counsellors has been trying to take away the lands and liberties of our country, but God the King of Heaven, our King, fights for us and says America shall be free. It is so now in spite of all Old England his comrades can do.

The great men of Old England in this country told us that the Americans would not let us enjoy our religion. This is false not true, for America allows everybody to pray to God as they please. You know Old England never would allow that but says you must all pray like the King and the great men at his court. We believe America now is right. We find all is true that they told us, for our old father the King of France takes their part. He is their friend, he has taken the sword and will defend them. Americans is our friends, our brothers and country-men; what they do we do, what they say we say, for we are all one and the same family.

Now as the King of England has no business nor ever had

any on this river, we desire you to go away with your men in peace and to take all those men that has been fighting and talking against America. If you don't go directly, you must take [care] of yourself, your men, and all your subjects on this river, for if all or any of you are killed it is not our faults, for we give you warning time enough to escape. Adieu for ever.

(K. G. Davies, ed., *Documents of the American Revolution 1770–1783, [Colonial Office Series]*, 21 vols. [Shannon: Irish University Press, 1972–1981], 15:185.)

Chapter Five

Commerce and
Coexistence

From first encounters, Indians and Europeans engaged in an exchange of furs and manufactured goods that was initially of mutual benefit but which proved ultimately devastating for the Indian participants. Inset on "A map of the inhabited part of Canada from the French surveys; with the Frontiers of New York and New England . . ." by Claude Joseph Sauthier; *National Archives of Canada, C-7300.*

[Francis Jennings' book The Invasion of America: Indians, Colonial-ism, and the Cant of Conquest, *published in 1975, helped change the way many Americans think about Indian history and the history of their own country. The very title challenged readers to rethink many old assumptions, and Jennings painted a damning portrait of the Puritan English as aggressive, violent, and deceitful invaders of Indian New England. Yet even Jennings was careful to point out that the conquest of America was "a mingling of conflict and coop-eration," in which Indians gradually became dependent on Europeans.[1] For almost two hundred years, Europeans and Indians in northern New England fought, captured, and killed one another; yet, despite underlying tensions and mutual mistrust, peaceful exchanges and coexistence were common between In-dians and Europeans. The relationship was one of cautious and often grudging symbiosis rather than open-armed trust and mutual respect, but, from the very first encounters, Indians and Europeans exchanged information and borrowed from the other's knowledge and skills.*

In the course of trading, each obtained from the other things they prized in exchange for things they valued lightly, and each valued the transaction, al-though not necessarily for the same reasons. European sailors, explorers, and merchants sought out Indian hunters and customers to obtain a cargo of pelts that could be converted into financial profit in the markets of Europe; Indians sought out Europeans as their source of supply for metal goods, woolen clothes, firearms, and alcohol, and to exchange gifts as a way of opening and main-taining good relations.

At early fishing stations on the dawnland's coast, Europeans and Indians shared fishing techniques and skills. Although commercial dry cod fishing uti-lized traditional European techniques, the local subsistence fishery developed an amalgamation of Indian and European strategies for procuring and processing the region's marine resources.[2] As fishing gave way to fur trading, commerce meant power for Indians and Europeans alike. European traders established political connections, a network of tribal allegiances and, in the case of the French at least, valuable kinship ties in Indian societies. Indians recognized that trade with gun-peddling Europeans was the key to survival in a changing world, which was why Bashaba welcomed Samuel de Champlain and assured the French that "no greater good could come to them than to have our friendship."³

Abenaki-European exchanges in the fur trade became a vital component of the barter economies of dawnland communities. French, English, and Indian economic systems overlapped. Individuals moved back and forth from one sphere to another, and Indian trappers lived and traded on the edges of European settlements just as European traders ran their businesses close to Indian villages. Successful commerce required cooperation and a degree of understanding and accommodation by all participants. According to Peter Thomas, trade functioned as a "bridging mechanism" between cultures. "Persistent Indian-English exchanges meant that repeated accommodations had to be made in both cultural systems if open ruptures between the two societies were to be avoided."⁴

European fishermen traded with eastern Abenakis on the coast of Maine early in the sixteenth century, and European trade goods filtered into the area via Indian middlemen from the north.⁵ French traders established extensive connections in Indian country, and Abenaki traders carried their furs to Montreal, Chambly, and Quebec. As early as 1609, Henry Hudson met Indians on the Maine coast who spoke words of French and traded beaver skins to the French for red gowns, knives, copper kettles, and beads. French traders operated out of a post on the Penobscot River after 1635.⁶ The English had trading posts on the Piscataqua and Kennebec rivers and at Casco Bay and Pemaquid by the early seventeenth century. Pynchon's trading post at Agawam (Springfield, Massachusetts) opened trade with the upriver tribes of the Connecticut Valley in the 1630s, and Richard Waldron built a trucking house at Pennacook on the Merrimack in 1668. Fort Dummer, erected near Brattleboro, Vermont, as a military post in 1724, conducted a flourishing trade with Abenakis and other tribes from the north. Following King Williams' War, Massachusetts set up a system of truckhouses in Maine. Posts at St. Georges near Penobscot Bay, at Richmond on the Kennebec, and on the Saco River offered quality goods under government regulation in an effort to attract Abenaki customers away from French and private English traders.⁷

Trading for mutual advantage did not mean that differences disappeared. As Neal Salisbury describes it, trade was "an uneasy interface between the interband exchange networks of the natives and the profit economies and state policies of the English."[8] As such, trade was a learning experience for Indians and Europeans alike. Early explorers and traders often gave offense and missed commercial opportunities by refusing objects that Indians offered as gifts. They gradually learned the importance of gift-giving and mastered the rudimentary protocols of trade. "What the English learned slowly and imperfectly," observe David and Alison Quinn, "was that market forces were not the primary impulses in exchanges of goods and that ceremonial exchanges must precede value for value bargaining."[9] As Europeans learned patience and contacts extended, Indians adjusted their own expectations and seem to have picked up the tricks of the trade more quickly than Europeans grasped native concepts of reciprocal exchange. As early as May 1642, Thomas Gorges, deputy-governor of Maine, complained to his cousin, ". . . the trade of beaver utterly lost, the Indians understanding the valew [sic] of things as well as the Inglish."[10]

In some areas, commerce between Indians and Europeans was such a normal activity that war came as an irritating interruption. For the Indians whose source of supplies dried up in time of war, restoration of trade could prove an important incentive to making peace. An Abenaki who left his traps at Fort Number Four when King George's War broke out stopped by to collect them once peace was restored, and Connecticut Valley Abenakis were trading at Fort Number Four right up to the eve of the Seven Years' War.[11] Increasingly dependent on European goods, Abenaki traders and hunters frequented European communities and became tied to European colonial economies. The economic connection made for lively dawnland societies such as those described by Susanna Johnson and Robert Rogers on the New Hampshire frontier.

The fur trade may have promoted maize horticulture among eastern Abenakis by providing them with a safeguard against crop failures in their unpredictable northern climate.[12] But it also upset traditional harmonies, introduced lethal new diseases, triggered an arms race, and promoted dependency on European market economies. Nevertheless, while the European population remained slight and where Indians and Europeans had to coexist, economic arrangements involved cooperation and interdependency between the inhabitants of the dawnland.

The fur trade was not the only area in which cooperation rather than conflict characterized interaction. Indians and settlers frequently lived in and utilized neighboring territories and had little choice but to cooperate, even though they remained cautious of the other's presence. Colonists generally preferred to obtain Indian land by some kind of purchase: Allowing Indians to run up debts in trade was a surer way of acquiring Indian lands than fighting for them. Yet not all colonial land transactions were real estate frauds in which gullible Indians lost their hunting grounds to greedy Europeans. English laws defended the interests of English colonists, but English justice could be blind, and English courts did not always operate to the disadvantage of the Indians over whom they claimed jurisdiction. Indians and Europeans frequently shared vested interests in maintaining peaceful relations, and there were individuals on both sides who did their best to prevent conflict.]

1. TRADERS' ABUSES, 1624

[Competition between European nations and individuals for Indian trade frequently led to abuse and mistreatment of Indian customers, as the following account by Christopher Levett demonstrates. Rather than take their complaints in person to the king of England, as these Abenakis threatened, Indians learned to play off rival traders, to hold their own in hard bargaining, and to exploit their own economic position to advantage. If abuses continued, they might resort to more extreme measures: In 1631, Kennebec Abenakis killed an English trader who had been cheating them.[13]]

On a certain day there came two savages to his place, who were under the command of Somerset or Conway. I know not whether, at which time they were both with me at my house, but the other two who went to him, knew not so much. But afterwards they understanding of it, came presently over, but left their coats and beaver skins behind them, whereat Somerset and Conway were exceeding angry; and were ready to beat the poor fellows, but I would not suffer them so to do. They presently went over the harbor themselves in their canoe to fetch their goods, but this man would let them have none, but wished them to truck with him. They told him they would not, but would carry them to Captain Levett. He said Levett was no captain, but a jacknape, a poor fellow, etc. They told him again that he was a rogue, with some other speeches, whereupon he and his company fell upon them and beat them both, in so much that they came to me in a great rage against him, and said they would be revenged on his fishermen at sea, and much ado I had to dissuade one of them from going into England to tell king James of it, as he said. . . .

(Christopher Levett, "A Voyage into New England, begun in 1623, and ended in 1624" [London, 1628], *Collections of the Massachusetts Historical Society*, 3d ser., 8 [1843]: 173.)

2. COMPENSATION FOR DAMAGE TO INDIAN CORN, 1641

[From early encounters, encroachments on Indian land were a source of competition and contention, and Indian and European neighbors frequently found themselves in dispute. English colonists certainly coveted and acquired Indian lands, and competition for the best lands inevitably produced friction.[14] But, as the following order of the court at Exeter, New Hampshire, indicates, Indians and Englishmen planted crops alongside each other, and there was some recourse for Indians, even as they found themselves subject to alien laws.]

It is ordered that Goodman ——, shall allow the Indians one bushell of corn for their labor per ——, which was spent by them in re-planting of that corne of theirs which was spoiled by his corne, and he is to make up their losse at harvest, according as that corne may be judged worse than their corne which was nowe hurt.

(Bouton, ed., *New Hampshire Provincial Papers*, 1 [1867], 143.)

[Infringements sometimes generated more drastic responses. In 1688, Saco Abenakis killed some settlers' cows after their complaints about the cattle trampling their corn went unheeded. The English retaliated by seizing Abenaki hostages, and relations deteriorated in King Williams' War. Abenaki killings of English livestock in later years sometimes were a product of hunger rather than hostility.[15]]

3. INDIAN DEED TO JOHN PARKER, 1659

[Colonial records are littered with deeds whereby Indians transferred land to enterprising individuals. Like treaties, these deeds often held a different meaning for Indians and Europeans. As this early deed indicates, Indians often specifically reserved to themselves the right to continue hunting and gathering, fishing and planting, on the lands in question. In some instances such arrangements functioned for a time before disintegrating under the pressure of settlement. More often they revealed differing attitudes toward the land and different concepts of ownership. Initially at least, Indians believed they were selling only the right to use the land, and they sometimes sold the same tract several times over. As William Cronon observes, Indians "thought they were selling one thing and the English thought they were buying another." Such misunderstanding and overlapping titles gave rise to later contentions in which the English sometimes disputed ownership among themselves almost as vehemently as they had with the Indians.[16]]

This instrument witnesseth this 14th June 1659 that I Nanuddemaure, proprietor of these lands hereafter mentioned have let, set and sold all my right, title of the said land and appurtenances of marsh and upland meadow unto John Parker now dwelling upon the said land unto him, his heirs, executors, administrators for ever, for one beaver skin received and the yearly rent of one bushell of corn and a quart of liquor to be paid unto the said Nanudemaure his heirs for ever at or before the twenty fifth day of December being Christmas Day at the dwelling house of the said Parker, reserving out of the aforesaid land liberty unto me my heirs to fish, fowl and hunt, also to set ottertraps without molestation. The aforesaid land being bounded as followeth: beginning at the first high head upon the south-west side of Sagadehock River and so running up the said river unto Winegance Creek being by estimation six miles or thereabouts, and all the tract of land southwestward unto the eastern part of

Casco Bay. To confirm the truth hereof I have hereunto set my
hand the day and year abovewritten.

The mark X of   The mark X of
Nanuddemaure   Robinhood Sagamore.
Witnesses
    Henry Jocelyn
    Richard R. F. Foxwell
    Roger Spencer
Robinhood acknowledged this before me in May 1666

                    Henry Jocelyn, Justice of the Peace

(*Collections of the Maine Historical Society,* 2d ser., 24 [1916]: 227–28.)

4. THE EVIL EFFECTS OF TRADE, 1668

*[In 1668, Captain Richard Waldron established a trading post at Penna-
cook, New Hampshire, which was probably the first European house built there,
since a settlement was not made until 1726. In June of that year, Thomas
Dickinson was murdered by an Indian. The affair caused considerable excitement at the time, and evidence was gathered to ascertain the truth about what
had happened. The following testimony reveals both the disastrous effects of
unrestrained trade on Indian communities and the willingness of Indian leaders
to maintain good relations with their new neighbors by meting out punishments
for such injuries.]*

Tohanto, Sagurmoy, Weecanumpee, Sagurmoy, Pacohauntee,
Quampecun, Pehaugun, Nascum, and Monamusque, antient Indians,[17] being examined how and why the Englishman was
killed, say that one Thomas Payne, and the Englishman that is
slayne, sent several Indians to theyre masters Captain Walderne's, and Mr. Peter Coffin's, to Pascataque, who told those
Indians that they should bring from them, gunns, powder, shott
and cloath. But insteade thereof Captain Walderne and the

sayde Peter Coffin retourned those Indians back to Pennycooke loaded only with cotton cloath and three rundlettes of liquors, with which liquors the said examinants say, that there were at least one hundred of Indians drunk for one night, one day, and one half together; in which time of their being soe drunk, the said examinants farther say that all Indians were come from the sayd trucking house, only one which remayned there drunk, who killed the sayd Englishman, the other Englishman being at ye said tyme at ye sayd fort.

. . . And said examinants also farther say, that they telling him the sayd murtherer, that they must kill him for it, to which the murtherer answered he was willing to dye for it, and that he was much sorry for the death of the said Englishman, or with words to the same effect. After which murther was committed and done, (which was about eight weeks since, as the examinants say,) that they with other Indians belonging to the sayd fort, sate in counsel what to doe with the said murtherer; who after some debate thereof passed sentence that the said murtherer should be shott to death, which sentence was accordingly performed the then next ensuing day about noone; who, they the said examinants father say, dyed undauntedly, still saying yt he was much sorry for ye said Englishman's death.

(Bouton, ed., *New Hampshire Provincial Papers*, 3 [1870], 214–16; also, Mass. Archives, 30:154–61.)

5. FLUCTUATIONS IN THE FUR TRADE, 1685

[This brief comment by the Baron de Lahontan shows both the reach and the instability of French trade with dawnland Indians in the seventeenth century. Sokokis, Mahicans, and Pennacooks from the southern edges of the dawnland traveled long distances to trade at Chambly, but the attraction of English trade and the threat of Mohwak ambush were major considerations for the Abenakis and sources of constant concern for the French.]

... In former times this place had a great trade in beaver-skins, which is now decayed: for the Soccokis, the Mahingans, and the Openangos, used formerly to resort thither in shoals, to exchange their furs for other goods; but at present they are retired to the English colonies, to avoid the pursuit of the Iroquese.

(Reuben G. Thwaites, ed., *New Voyages to North-America by the Baron de Lahontan*, 2 vols. [Chicago: A. C. McClurg, 1905], 1:90.)

6. THE ANGLO-ABENAKI FUR TRADE, 1693

[Colonel Ledger's memorial on trade with the Indians in New England, dated February 1692/93, includes information on the nature of the trade, insight into the Indian dependence it promoted, and comment on its value to both parties: as a source of supply to the Indians and a source of leverage to the English.]

The peltry of yt countrey is generally and more espetialy in ye eastern parts taken by ye Indian natives, and from them purchased by ye English with severall commodities, viz blanketing and linnen for cloathing, corne, kettles, iron, steel, liquors, powder, lead, shot and gunns etc at very great rates, which turns to ye great advantage of ye concerned but is of fatall consequence to ye publick by supplying their enemys with ye necessaryes of their own destruction, as may appear by ye vast depredations made on many but most immediately those parts where it hath been so done. In ye year 1688 when ye Indians first broke with ye English ye Government then took such care that no person upon what pretence soever should trade or be concerned with either French or Indian by which means ye Indians were so distressed for want of fire-arms powder and lead that they scarcely did subsist and ye cheifs of them came to make supplication for a peace in ye moneth of April 1689. . . .

(*Collections of the Maine Historical Society*, 2d ser., 10 [1907]: 1.)

7. SOCIAL REPERCUSSIONS OF CONTACT
AND COMMERCE

[It is well known that commerce with Europeans wrought change and up-heaval among American Indians. Alcohol produced demoralization and social chaos, diseases caused demographic disaster, firearms and metal weapons inten-sified intertribal warfare, and manufactured goods eroded native technology. As the following comment by Nicholas Perrot suggests, interaction with Europeans also produced changes in traditional Indian values and behavior. Things once freely given now assumed a market value in the eyes of Indians who had grown accustomed to trading with profit-minded Europeans.]

This sort of reception is ordinary among the savages; in point of hospitality, it is only the Abenakis, and those who live with the French people, who have become somewhat less liberal, on account of the advice that our people have given them by placing before them the obligations resting on them to preserve what they have. At the present time, it is evident that these savages are fully as selfish and avaricious as formerly they were hospit-able. Although they are no less haughty than they were before, they have fallen very low in sordidness, even so far as to beg; and notwithstanding all that, the most singular thing is, that they not only consider themselves so necessary to those who aid them to live, but regard those very persons as their inferiors and in-capable of excelling them. Those of the savages who have not been too much humored [by the French] are attached to the ancient custom of their ancestors, and among themselves are very compassionate. If anyone of them is in want, they at once unite their efforts to assist him.

(Nicholas Perrot, "Memoir on the Manners, Customs, and Religion of the Savages of North America," in Emma Helen Blair, ed., *The Indian Tribes of the Upper Mississippi Valley and Region of the Great Lakes*, 2 vols. [Cleveland: The Arthur H. Clark Co., 1911], 1:134–35.)

8. WANALANCET AND JONATHAN TYNG, 1685–1697

[Recurrent dealings built up individual relationships over the years. In some cases, these relationships were clearly exploitative, but others produced a degree of mutual respect. The following extracts hint at the mixture of self-interest and respect that developed in the relationship between Jonathan Tyng of Dunstable and the Pennacook chief, Wanalancet.]

Deed of Sale from the Indians to Jonathan Tyng, 10 October, 1685

By this deed Wanalansit (the only surviving son of Passorono-way who was the great and chief sachem upon Merrimack River to whom the rest of the Indians paid tribute), in consideration of 70 shillings, together with sevll other Charges expended on and gifts and kindnesses shown him by Jonathan Tyng of Dunstable on Merrimack River in the Massachusetts Colony, absolutely conveyed to the said Tyng, his heirs and assigns for ever "One tract of land situate lying and being *on the said Merrimack River* and to lye full 6 English miles on each side of said river, the said river lying in the center of it, to begin at a place commonly called by the Indians *Pennicook* and commonly known by the English by that name, to begin on *said* river 3 miles up *the river beyond that place in Pennicook* where the old Indian ffort now standeth, and so to ascend *up said river untill you come to the Great Pond,* which pond is full of small islands, which pond is the utmost northward to which Major Simon Willard Esqr went with his company when sent by the General Court up said river on discovery."

HABEND the said tract of land with all the islands in said river with all the rivulets on each side said river from 6 miles wide on each side said river from end to end, to said Tyng, his heirs and assigns for ever with covenants of a good title, of warranty, and of quiet enjoyment. Which deed was 27 October 1685 duly acknowledged, and recorded 10 November 1686.

(Albert Stillman Batchellor, ed., *New Hampshire Provincial Papers*, 19 [1891], 356–57.)

[Wanalancet retired to St. Francis or some other northern location shortly after the sale, but in the spring of 1692, "ye old sachem Wonnalansett" returned to Dunstable under a flag of truce and told Tyng he wished to live in peace with the English. Tyng informed the Massachusetts authorities, who had the Pennacook detained in prison in Cambridge and then sent to Boston for questioning. Then, according to a petition submitted by Jonathan Tyng in May 1697, the sagamore requested that he be removed to Tyng's house. The governor approved the request.]

and ordered me to supply him with necessary provisions and promised it should be payd out of ye publick. Your petitioner also paid his expences coming to Boston and his returne, kept him with food and good part of his cloathing for almost four years, who then dyed, I was also at some small charge to bury him, he having shewed him self friendly to ye English in ye former war and now, authority would not suffer him now in his old age to be ill treated.

(Petition of Jonathan Tyng, May 27, 1697, Mass. Archives, 30:426.)

[Tyng got his reward: In June 1699, he was granted the management of the trade with the Pennacooks.[18]]

9. THE MAGNET OF TRADE, 1700

[The English recognized that they could not compete with the spiritual influence exerted by French Jesuits among the Abenakis, but they hoped the price and quality of English trade goods would wean the Indians away from their French priests, as this letter from William Stoughton in December 1700 suggests.]

This Government have lately erected a trading house with a fortification, and settled a garrison at Casco Bay for accommodating of trade with the Indians and by kind usage and treatment of them therein hope to oblige them and to divert their conversation and commerce with the French and have likewise made provision for trade with them at Saco Fort and other places, and by meanes of their drawing thither to gain the advantage for instructing them in the true Christian Religion. To which end two English ministers are sent to reside in the eastern parts, one at the fort at Saco, and the other at Casco Fort.

(*Collections of the Maine Historical Society,* 2d ser., 10 [1907]: 85.)

10. INDIAN MURDER, ENGLISH JUSTICE, 1726

[During Dummer's War, a number of Indian volunteers served in English militia companies. Most were Mahicans and Mohegans, but some Abenakis also served. In August 1725, an Indian volunteer named Joseph Quasson murdered a fellow Indian volunteer, John Peter, at Cape Porpoise. English colonial authorities assumed that their jurisdiction extended over Indians and demanded it in one conference after another. Jurisdictional treatment of Indians varied somewhat, depending upon the colony imposing its justice, the tribe involved, and the time and circumstances; but individual Indians living in white communities "were placed under the ordinary courts just like the colonists." Quasson was tried and convicted before the Superior Court. Englishmen who murdered Indians sometimes met with similar conviction and punishment at the hands of English juries, but this was not always the case.[19]]

The jurors for our Sovereign Lord the King upon their oath present Joseph Quasson, an Indian, of Yarmouth in the County of Barnstable for that the said Joseph Quasson at Cape Porpus, or Arendel in the County of York, and while he was in the public service of the province as a soldier about the twentyeth day of August last, not having the fear of God before his eyes, but being moved and instigated by the Devil, and of his malice forethought, with force and arms an assault did make on the body of one John Peter, an Indian of Yarmouth in the County of Barnstable in the peace of God and the King then and there being, viz as a soldier in the public pay and service of the province and with a gun value forty shillings that was charged with powder and ball, which he the said Joseph Quasson held in his hands, and levelled at, and shot the said John Peter in at the groin, on the upper part of his thigh, wounding the said John Peter mortally; so that he the said John Peter for a few days viz three or four languished, and then dyed, of the wound given him as aforesaid by the bullet shot at him by the said Joseph Quasson. And so the juriors aforesaid upon their oaths to say that the said Joseph Quasson did then [and] there wilfully and feloniously kill and murther the said John Peter against the peace of our Sovereign Lord the King and the law. Upon this indictment the said Joseph Quasson being arraigned, pleaded not guilty, and for tryal put himself upon God and his countrey. A jury being sworn to try the issue; after a full hearing of the evidences in behalf of his Majesty, and the prisoners defence, went out to consider the case, and returned their verdict therein upon oath by Daniel Simpson their Foreman, that is to say, that the said Joseph Quasson is guilty. It's therefore considered and ordered by the Court, that the said Joseph Quasson shall suffer the pains of death.

(*Province and Court Records of Maine*, 6 vols. [Portland: Maine Historical Society, 1928–1975], 6:234.)

[Quasson was hanged by Sheriff Jeremiah Moulton on the seashore about a mile from the York gaol where he had been imprisoned. Some three thousand people are reported to have turned out to witness the execution. Moulton submitted a bill of five pounds, two shillings, for carrying out the execution; the county treasury paid him in full for his part in seeing English justice done in a case involving two Indian English soldiers.[20]]

11. RESTORING PEACEFUL RELATIONS, 1727

[In time of war, many Abenakis took refuge in Canada and the northernmost reaches of their territory. But the exodus was often only temporary, and bands returned home once peace was restored. As this letter from Lieutenant Governor Dummer to Colonel Wheelwright in May 1727 shows, the English were not averse to having the Indians return to the neighborhood of their settlements and even took measures to ensure they were able to resume their war-torn lives in peace.]

I have received from the Eastern Indians very full testimonies of their peaceable temper and intentions and as a mark of their entire confidence in our friendship, many of them (who have been driven by the late war into the Government of Canada) are now returning back with their families to their old habitations near our borders, and they have desired I would take the proper methods for their safety in their hunting near us; more particularly at Connecticut and Kennebeck River.

These are therefore to desire and direct you to take effectual care that the inhabitants of the frontier towns in your country be notified hereof, and that they give no molestation to the said Indians in their hunting and fishing, but treat them with kindness and friendship, and that they avoid all occasions of quarrelling with them, which is absolutely necessary in order to preserve the peace. You must more especially restrain the people on Kennebunk River from any resentment of the injury done to our people there, for I have taken proper measures for satisfaction.

(*Collections of the Maine Historical Society,* 2d ser., 10 [1907]: 397.)

12. FLUCTUATING PRICES, 1727

[Indians quickly learned the market value of the pelts they traded and became suspicious at any drop in the prices European traders offered for their furs. This

letter from Lieutenant Governor Dummer to Captains Heath and Smith, May 27, 1727, shows the English, anxious to retain their Abenaki customers, taking pains to explain that fluctuating prices stemmed from market forces, not the dishonesty of English traders.]

Sir

I received your letter by Captain Saunders, and observe what you mention of the uneasiness of ye Indians upon the fall of the price of the bever. To satisfy them in this matter, you must shew them by your invoice that our goods are likewise fallen especially rum (which is much lower in proportion than bever). That it was agreed at ye treaty that they should have the utmost for their furrs that they would fetch in the market at Boston. That we then told them that the prices of goods were not fixed but would frequently change according to the circumstances of trade. And when they come to Boston they will have liberty to try the merchants and shop keepers here [and] they will find that we have allowed them the full price of every thing we have bought and sold our goods to them at very easy and moderate rates. And they will certainly find that no other people will give them so much for their furrs nor sell goods so cheap to them as we do.

(*Collections of the Maine Historical Society*, 2d ser., 10 [1907]: 398–99.)

13. GOODS FOR THE ABENAKIS: REGISTER OF THE KING'S STOREHOUSE AT QUEBEC, 1729

[Europeans regularly supplied their Indian allies with goods and provisions. The following extract from the registers of the French storehouses in Quebec provides examples of the things the French gave visiting Abenakis.]

June 12
Delivered to an Abenaki Indian for eight days' rations
Sixteen pounds of bread

four pounds of bacon
four pounds of powder
eight pounds of lead
> June 25
> Delivered to five Indians from Norridgewock for four days' rations

fourteen pounds of bread
ten pounds of bacon
two and one half pounds of powder
five pounds of lead
one pound of tobacco
> July 4
> Delivered to ten Abenaki Indians from the mission of R. P. Rasle for four days' rations

eighty pounds of bread
twenty pounds of bacon
two pounds of tobacco

(Chicago Historical Society; editor's translation)

14. DISBURSEMENTS FOR ENTERTAINING INDIANS, 1730

[Frontier outposts served as more than just garrisoned defenses and trade centers. As the following account shows, they also functioned as a rendezvous and catered to visiting Indians in a variety of ways.]

Memorandum. Sundry disbursements for entertaining the Indians at Richmond Fort on divers occasions from December 22nd unto May 31, 1730 (being 18 months) conformable to a resolve of the Honorable Court in that respect.—

Decbr 23 1728—To the old blind squa of Abomazeen who lay about ye fort healpless being that ye Governour shoud marcy on her for Christs sake

15—10

Feb.1, 1729. To sundry sachems who came to ye fort upon hearing that Governour Burnett had sent them a letter   1–10–0

" 22. To the said sachems who came to wright an answer to ye
Governours letter aforesaid   18–9

March 19. To Toxus and his captains upon their coming to
inform me that they were designed for Boston to pay their
complements to the Governour   1–6–2

July 11. To the said Toxus and companions in provisions and
drink while the country sloop lay wind bound at Arrowsick
viz three dayes   2–9–3

" 13 To the widow of Soccarexes (some time an hostage at Castle
William and who led the English army through ye woods to
Penobscot) viz. to ye said squa a blanket at 20 shillings and
to her child in provisions at sundry times 10 shillings, 4
pence   1–10–4

" To the sachem Nemmaggeen and ye other Indians of St Francois who came to express their friendship and send their complements to ye Governor   –15–9

August 30. To Wyworney and Sosep whome I had sent to
receive a message from the Governour who came and received ye same and 5 Days afterwards returned with an
answer   –17–11

Oct. 3d. To Toxus and 30 more Neridgawalk men who came to
be informed wheither Goverer Burnet was dead (as they had
heard) and to know who succeeded him in the Government   1–7–6

Jany 30, 1730. To Toxus, Jumawit, Sabadis, Wyworney and sundry other chief Indians representing ye Neridgewalk, Saco,
Amoscogin and Shepscut Indians to inquire what they were
to expect from Colonel Dunbars precedings at Pemaquid and
wheither his Honour ye Lieut. Governour was concerned in
yt matter   1–5–8

Brought over   12–17–2

March 10th To the Indians who came to receive his Honour the Lieut. Governour answer to ye aforesaid message   14–1

    To John Hegon who lay by the fort healpless by reason of his arme being broken in two places   17–8

20 To 4 captains who came to informe me of the death of Toxus their sachem   3–9

″ At their barying ye said Toxus 31 shillings, 7 pence 1–15–4

30 To three messengers from Penobscot to acquaint that Wesnunganit the sachem of ye tribe was dead   4–6

Apr. 30. To an Indian at sundry times during ye 18 months aforesaid who secretly informs me of the counsels and determination of the French and Indians from time to time 4–3–5

June 30, 1730———   Total———   £20–12–2

(Collections of the Maine Historical Society, 2d ser., 23 [1916]: 233–35.)

15. ABUSES IN TRADE, 1736

[The fur trade was carried on in circumstances that were open to abuse by unscrupulous merchants, and unfair practices were a common cause of Indian complaint and official response. The following extract from a conference held in Boston with visiting Indians suggests the variety of ways in which traders could shortchange their customers.]

Another grievance is that the truckmaster tells us our beaver is not of full price notwithstanding it is taken in cold weather (out of ice and snow) and will allow us but the price of fall beaver, when other traders allow us full price with the spring beaver and this is the price allowed by all traders everywhere else, and we are allowed no more than fall beaver price, till late in the winter, or early in the spring by the truckmaster.

(*Collections of the Maine Historical Society,* 2d ser., 23 [1916]: 236.)

16. REMEDYING ABUSES IN TRADE, 1727, 1738

[Truckmasters operated under government regulation²¹ and could be held accountable for their dishonest dealings, as the two extracts below attest. Abenakis visiting Boston in the winter of 1727 brought evidence before the Council that their trader had been cheating them in the prices he paid for their beaver pelts. As the action taken in that case and the following letter from Secretary Josiah Willard to John Noyes in 1738 demonstrate, the English authorities recognized that a fair trade was essential to retaining Indian custom and allegiance.]

As to your complaint respecting the trade of, have fully examined into the matter, and find that the truck master for St. Georges has very much mistaken his orders. I nor the General Court do approve of his conduct. I have chosen and appointed a new truck master in his room and ordered restitution to be made for the damage the Indians have sustained by his mistakes to the value of £77.

And if hereafter there should be any mistakes (as I hope there will be none) I desire you will alwaies inform me of such mistakes, and I shall very readily rectify them as I have done now.

("Conference with the Indians, Jan 3 1727," *Collections of the Maine Historical Society,* 2d ser. 23 [1916]: 229.)

Sir

I am directed by the Governor and Council to acquaint you that the Indians of the Penobscot Tribe now in town have made divers complaints against you as to your conduct as truck master, particularly that you made them pay for bread, tobacco and other things that were wet and damnified by the sinking of the boat the same price as if the things were good and merchantible, and that when some of their people bring small quantities of feathers and small pieces of fur, you throw their things away and refuse to trade with them and bid them to trade with the French, and in general that you treat them with great roughness and ill temper.

To these complaints the Board expect youre answer, and that in the mean time you do every thing consistent with the other parts of your duty to make the Indians easy and well satisfied in their trade with you.

("Letter to John Noyes, 1738," *Collections of the Maine Historical Society*, 2d ser., 11 [1908]: 185.)

17. ENGLISH TRADE COUNTERS FRENCH CATHOLICISM, 1742

[Recognizing that Jesuit influence gave the French a tremendous advantage among the tribes, the English placed increasing importance on trade as a means of competing for Abenaki allegiance. Massachusetts Governor Shirley describes the competition in this letter to the Duke of Newcastle, August 30, 1742.]

Since I had the honour of writing my last to your Grace, I have visited the eastern parts of this province at the distance of about sixty leagues by sea with the several forts there, and have had an interview and treaty with the Penobscott and other Indian tribes bordering on those settlements. These tribes by means of some intermarriages of the French among 'em and French missionaries being constantly resident with 'em at their headquarters in the woods, who thereby gain an influence over 'em from their childhood, are always so far in the French interest as to take their part in time of war, and sometimes by their instigation enter into war with the English in a time of peace between the two Crowns, upon which occasions they have ever broke up our frontier eastern settlements and destroyed many families, and kept the province in a continual alarm. And as the only hold which this Government has had upon 'em, has been to supply 'em with a trade upon cheaper terms than the French can, it has ever been its policy to maintain truck or trading houses in their neighbourhood in order to keep 'em dependent upon us for their cloathing, corn, rum and other provisions and necessaries. These circumstances have made it thought advisable upon the accession of a new Governour that a good understanding and friendship should be renewed and cultivated with 'em by his having an interview and conference with 'em, and hearing and redressing their complaints, which I thought the more necessary at this crisis, when an expectation of a French war had in great measure prepared 'em for a rupture with us. . . .

(*Collections of the Maine Historical Society*, 2d ser., 11 [1908]: 251.)

18. CHARLESTOWN, NEW HAMPSHIRE, IN 1744

[Where European population was sparse, colonists and Indians often lived side-by-side without hostility and cooperated in economic endeavors. Looking back fifty years to her first visit at age fourteen to Charlestown on the Connecticut River, Mrs. Susanna Johnson (later Hastings) recalled her initial impressions of an isolated frontier community where Indians lived in frighteningly close proximity.]

When I approached the town of Charlestown, the first object that met my eyes was a party of Indians holding a war dance: a cask of rum, which the inhabitants had suffered them to partake of, had raised their spirits to all the horrid yells and feats of distortion which characterize the nation. I was chilled at the sight and passed tremblingly by. At this time Charlestown contained nine or ten families, who lived in huts not far distant from each other. The Indians were numerous, and associated in a friendly manner with the whites. It was the most northerly settlement on Connecticut River, and the adjacent country was terribly wild. A saw mill was erected, and the first boards were sawed while I was there. The inhabitants commemorated the event with a dance, which took place on the new boards. In those days there was such a mixture on the frontiers of savages and settlers, without established laws to govern them, that the state of society cannot easily be described. . . .

("Captivity of Mrs. Johnson," in *Indian Narratives* [Claremont, N.H.: Tracy & Bros., 1854], 131.)

[Gorham, Maine, was in a similar situation at about the same time. Prior to 1745, the neighboring Ossipees, Pigwackets, and Androscoggins were "much more numerous" than the settlers, and Gorhamtown was "thought to be far into the wilderness." The Indians, however, "were not troublesome, otherwise than by continual begging and stealing from the settlers," and the latter realized that "their situation made it for their interest to keep on good terms with their neighbors when the sacrifice was not too much." Relations remained generally harmonious until King George's War, and the English and Indian children "were always at play together."[22]

19. JUSTICE FOR A PENOBSCOT, 1750

[In the vicious frontier warfare that frequently erupted between Indians and Europeans, Indians all too often fell victim to European vengeance and violence irrespective of their actual involvement in the conflict. However, as the following order of the New Hampshire Superior Court demonstrates, English justice could retain a measure of impartiality, even in time of war.]

An Indian man of Penobscot (as he saith) by ye name of Nambrous being committed to his Majesties goal in Portsmouth by warrant from Samuel Hart Esq. Justice of the Peace for said province for attempting to kill Moses Wright of Dover by stabbing him with a knife in the arm and body—no evidence appearing against him, the said Indian—to convict him, it is considered by the court that the said Indian be acquitted and discharged. And inasmuch as the Indian nations are making warr upon his Majesties subjects in New England, therefore ordered that his Excellency the Governour be informed of this courts order to discharge the said Indian and that this court can hold him no longer, to the intent that his Excellency may take order as he shall think fit concerning him.

This order passed September 26, 1750.

Which [order] being read at the Board and in as much as the tribe to which the said Indian belongs having committed hostilities against his Majestys subjects of the neighboring Governments, the Council advised his Excelency to give the sheriff orders to detain the said Indian and his squaw that is now with him til further order of the Governour and Council.

(Bouton, ed., *New Hampshire Provincial Papers*, 6 [1872], 9.)

20. INDIANS REQUEST REGULATION OF RUM, 1751

[Alcohol was a crucial component of trade with Indians and a cause of disturbance in Indian communities. Colonial authorities denounced its effects and tried to restrict its use in trade, albeit with little effect. Indians too complained about the use of alcohol in trade and asked that measures be taken to limit its use, as this extract of a letter dated September 12, 1751, from the Penobscot sachem, Squadook, to the governor of Massachusetts, indicates.]

Brother once more, we dont like a great deale of rum. It hinders our praiers. We buy to much of it it hurts our souls. It is not you but we that doe it. One kegg and one bottle is enough for one man, the women must have none. This we ask of you the Governour and Council. The women buy and sell to the men and are debauched thereby. I believe you will think I speak well, rum is the cause of quarrels amongst us. I expect your answer to this.

(*Collections of the Maine Historical Society*, 2d ser., 23 [1916]: 427.)

21. REGULATING ENGLISH HUNTERS, 1764

[After seven years and more of fighting in North America, Britain was anxious to regulate the situation on the frontiers of her colonies. Since encroachment on Indian lands was clearly the greatest cause of unrest, British policy found expression in the Royal Proclamation of 1763, restricting settlement beyond the Appalachians, and in repeated instructions to royal governors to restrain their people from trespassing on Indian lands, making illegal purchases, and abusing

the Indians in trade. Regulating the frontier was a difficult task, for European hunters and settlers beyond the reach of British laws had few qualms about trespassing on Indian lands, which they felt had been opened to them by the defeat of the French and their Indian allies. By 1764, the Penobscots were complaining that white hunters were depleting their beaver population. Nevertheless, as the following exchange of letters and Governor Bernard's explanation to the Massachusetts House of Representatives show, measures were taken to protect Indian rights, trespassers were not always blind to reason, and some men in authority had a vision of how relations could be improved. Unfortunately, attempts to stop overhunting failed, the Indians were left with little choice but to join in the slaughter before the beaver disappeared, and the Penobscot fur trade was virtually dead by 1820.[23]]

To the English Hunters on Quontabagook Pond, Fort Pownall, March 24 1764

Gentlemen

The Indians complain heavily of the injury you do them, in hunting upon a stream which they had taken up. There is a law against English hunting at all, but it is hardly yet in force; still I cant but hope that you are so friendly to the Commonwealth that you won't give the Indians any just cause of complaint. The little advantage you may make will be a poor compensation to you if by this means you should be the authors of disturbing the peace and quiet of your country. Therefore I earnestly intreat you to quit the streeam you are upon, and which it plainly appears the Indians have the best right to, but if you will not and any mischief ensues, I cannot see how you can acquit yourselves. If you are apprehended after the Act takes place, you are liable to a fine and forfeit your fur, and I shall certainly use my endeavours to have the Act duly executed.

I am yours etc

Their answer received upon a piece of birch bark marked with a Pin—Captain Goldthwait

Sir

This comes to let you know that I have seen the Indians you sent your letter with, and they have given it to us, and we have not set any traps where they have any, and we would be very glad, you would tell the Indians that we would hunt upon the pond, that we were upon it first, and there were no signs of any Indians upon it when we came here. If there were any traps upon it we would not have sat any here, and as we were here first we think it is our right to hunt here, but if they are not satisfied we will go home.

So I remain your humble servant,
Hans Robinson

Fort Pownall, March 28, 1764

Gentlemen,

I received your note by Arexes, and am sorry to tell you, that there is an absolute occasion for you to leave the pond, which you are upon, and which the Indians say and demonstrate they have the best right to. I wish you could accomodate yourselves otherwise for the little time which you have a right to hunt, but if you are determined to continue where you are I fear what will be the consequence. It is as much as I can do now to pacify the Indians, and I hope you'll consider what injury may be done the province by your not complying with my request, I am Gentlemen

Your very good Friend etc
Thomas Goldthwait

Governor Francis Bernard to the Council and House of Representatives, June 5, 1764

It seems to me that all the uneasiness of the Indians arises from two things, the settling of the English and their hunting; which indeed are but one cause, as they fear the one only because it is productive of the other. And indeed they have great reason to be alarmed at the extension of English hunting; their very existence depends upon its not being permitted. And it is with great justice they complain how hard it is that the English who have many ways of living will interfere with the Indians in the only business by which they subsist. For this purpose at last session an Act was passed to prevent English hunting: but it was enacted only for one year and the activity of it was postponed to such a distant day, that the very mischiefs it was intended to prevent had like to have been produced by that defect only. This spring before the Act took place, a quarrell happened between some English and Indian hunters at a pond near Fort Pownall. Happily Captain Goldthwait got timely notice of it. The Act had not gained its activity, and therefore he could use no other authority than persuasion, which luckily had the effect. If blood had been drawn in this quarrel, it would probably have turned the scale in favour of an Indian insurrection: so nicely are the politicks of those people at this time ballanced.

It is therefore high time that these matters were finally adjusted, and I make no doubt but that the jealousy of the Indians may be removed by very easy and plain means. If they were to be called together and had liberty to unbosom their minds; if they were patiently heard and their grievances readily addressed; if they were assured that English hunting would be effectually prevented; if they were told that the settlements in those parts, being chiefly intended for fishery and not for husbandry, were not likely in ages to come to extend up into the country so as to incommode them; if they were treated in such a manner as would show that we do not neglect or despise them; and if at the same time they were given to understand that we should insist upon our right to settle the country in such parts as were convenient for us; I make no doubt that a firm and lasting accommodation with the Indians might be established and that country be intirely freed from the apprehension of danger from Indian irruptions. . . .

(*Collections of the Maine Historical Society*, 2d ser., 13 [1909]: 337–38, 340, 344.)

22. ROBERTSON'S LEASE, 1765

[The fur trade was not the only economic sphere where Indians and Europeans worked out mutually satisfactory arrangements. The following document details a lease of lands by Missisquoi Abenakis to a trader from St. Johns. The arrangements evidently held, since Robertson operated a sawmill and trading house at the falls of the Missisquoi River for several years.]

Know all men by these presents, that we, Daniel Poorneuf, Francois Abernard, Francois Joseph, Jean Baptiste, Jeanoses, Charlotte, widow of the late chief of the Abenackque nation at Missisque, Mariane Poorneuf, Theresa, daughter of Joseph Michel, Magdalene Abernard, and Joseph Abomsawin, for themselves, heirs, assigns, etc., do sell, let, and concede unto Mr. James Robertson, merchant of St. Jean, his heirs, etc., for the space of ninety one years from the 28th day of May, 1765, a certain tract of land lying and being situated as follows, viz: being in the bay of Missisque on a certain point of land, which runs out into the said bay and the river of Missisque, running from the mouth up said river near east, one league and a half, and in depth north and south running from each side of the river sixty arpents, bounded on the bank of the aforesaid bay and etc., and at the end of the said league and a half to lands belonging to Indians joining to a tree marked on the south side of the river, said land belonging to old Abernard; and on the north side of said river to lands belonging to old Whitehead; retaining and reserving to the proprietors hereafter mentioned, to wit; on the north side of said river five farms belonging to Pierre Peckenowax, Francois Nichowizet, Annus Jean, Baptiste Momtock, Joseph Comprent, and on the south side of said river seven farms belonging to Towgisheat, Cecile, Annome Quisse, Jemonganz, Willsomquax, Jean Baptiste the Whitehead, and old Etienne, for them and their heirs, said farms contain two arpents in front nearly, and sixty in depth.

Now the condition of this lease is, that if the aforesaid James Robertson, himself, his heirs, and assigns or administrators, do pay and accomplish unto the aforesaid Daniel Poorneuf et als, their heirs, etc., a yearly rent of fourteen Spanish dollars, two bushels of Indian corn, and one gallon of rum, and to plow as much land for each of the above persons as shall be sufficient for them to plant their Indian corn every year, not exceeding more than will serve to plant one quarter of a bushel for each family, to them and their heirs and assigns; for which and every said article well and truly accomplished the said James Robertson is to have and to hold for the aforesaid space of time, for himself, his heirs, etc., the aforesaid tract of land as mentioned aforesaid, to build thereon and establish the same for his use, and to concede to inhabitants, make plantations, cut timber of what sort or kind he shall think proper for his use or the use of his heirs, etc., and for the performance of all and every article of the said convenant and agreement either of the said parties bindeth himself unto the other firmly by these presents.

(Original, National Archives of Canada, RG 68, reel 3945, liber A, folio 179; true copy, University of Vermont, Wilbur Collection, Stevens Family Papers, folder #9.)

23. THE AUTOBIOGRAPHY OF A CRIMINAL,
1772–1775

[Henry Tufts spent three years, from the spring of 1772 to the spring of 1775, among the Abenakis of western Maine. Tufts was, at various times in his life, a thief, a counterfeiter, an army deserter, a farm worker, a fortune teller, a bigamist, a doctor, and an itinerant preacher. He was often in jail and on one occasion was sentenced to hang, but his sentence was commuted to life imprisonment. Tufts escaped to lead a new life as a reformed character, passing the rest of his days in Lemington, Maine. He visited the Abenakis in the hope of finding a cure for a dangerous knife wound in his thigh, sustained in an accident. After he recovered his health, he stayed with the Abenakis and studied their medical practices. He learned their language and lived with an Abenaki woman, Polly Susap, the niece of chief Tomhegan. His autobiography provides information about Abenaki life in the little-known area between Lake Memphremagog and Lake Umbagog at a time when most Abenakis were assumed to have migrated to Canada. There have been some doubts about the authenticity of Tufts' narrative, and Tufts himself was certainly a slippery character, but ethnologist Gordon Day is convinced that Tufts saw what and whom he described. The Abenaki chief Swanson is probably Swashan or Swassin, who served with Washington and on the upper Connecticut Valley in the Revolution and was one of the signatories of Philip's land grant in 1798. Tomhegan was the Abenaki chief who led the raid on Bethel in August 1781. Molly Ockett became well known to settlers in the region for her skills as a physician, and the stories and reminiscences that grew up made her almost a legend in the area after her death in 1816. Tufts' rare narrative, first published in 1807, was reprinted in 1930 as The Autobiography of a Criminal.[24] *He traveled to Pigwacket (Fryeburg, Maine), then journeyed thirty more miles before locating the Abenakis' wigwams at what he called Sudbury, Canada, but which in fact became Bethel, Maine.]*

On my approach, their chief, whose name was Swanson, gave me a very cordial reception, and presently ordered his domestics to prepare dinner. Meanwhile we commenced a prolix confabulation, in the course of which I acquainted him with my circumstances, and the design I had formed of residing in Canada for a season. He seemed pleased with my intentions, and gave me free toleration to reside in his tribe during pleasure. To these instances of benignity, he superadded another, which was to enjoin Molly Occut, at that time the great Indian doctress, to superintend the recovery of my health. At my departure he gave me a general invitation to visit his house whenever I saw fit, or might stand in need of his assistance, and this I assured him I should never fail to do.

Those formalities over, I felt myself at liberty to shape my conduct, as inclination or convenience might dictate. Recovery of health was my first and earliest concern, so I made direct application to the lady for such medicines as might be suitable to my complaints. She was alert in her devoirs, and supplied me for present consumption, with a large variety of roots, herbs, barks and other materials. I did not much like even the looks of them; for to have contemplated an encounter with the formidable forrage might have staggered the resolution, doubtless, of a much greater hero than myself. However I took the budget with particular directions for the use of each ingredient.

My kind doctress visited me daily, bringing me new medicinal supplies, but my palate was far from being gratified with some of her doses, in fact they but ill accorded with the gust of an Englishman. Nevertheless, having much faith in the skill of my physician, I continued to swallow with becoming submission, every potion she prescribed.

Her means had a timely and beneficial effect, since from the use of them, I gathered strength so rapidly, that in two months, I could visit about with comfort.

Returning health inspired my breast with new-born hope, and was a source of lasting consolation. And now curiosity prompting me to visit the Indian settlements in this department, in order to become more intimately acquainted with their customs and modes of life, I followed the daily practice of traveling from place to place, until I had visited the whole encampment, and from the best conjectures I could frame on the subject, found there might be about three hundred inhabitants in this quarter. The entire tribe, of which these people made a part, was in number about seven hundred of both sexes, and extended their settlements, in a scattering, desultory manner, from Lake Memphremagog to Lake Umbagog, covering an extent of some eighty miles. Finding traveling to agree with my feelings I continued the salutory exercise, every day, for several months, until my health was restored in as full and perfect a manner, as I had possessed that blessing at any former period. This happy restoration to pristine ability I attributed principally to the good offices of my doctress, who during my convalescence, was indefatigible in her care and attention. Her character was, indeed, that of a kind and charitable woman. . . .

. . . .

Since beginning to amend in health under the auspices of madam Molly, I had formed a design of studying the Indian practice of physic, though my intention had hitherto remained a profound secret. Indeed I had paid strict attention to everything of a medical nature, which had fallen within the sphere of my notice. Frequently was I inquisitive with Molly Occut, old Plilips, Sabattus and other professed doctors to learn the names and virtues of their medicines. In general they were explicit in communication, still I thought them in possession of secrets they cared not to reveal.

(*A Narrative of the Life, Adventures and Sufferings of Henry Tufts, Now residing at Lemington, in the District of Maine, In substance as compiled from his own mouth* [Dover, N.H.: Samuel Bragg, Jun. 1807], 69–71, 73.)

[Despite being well aware of the evil effects of alcohol among Indians, Tufts resorted to trading his furs to the English for rum, which he dispensed to his

Abenaki hosts as a means of winning their trust and learning their medicinal secrets. After his return to the settlements, he later utilized the knowledge and skills he acquired to work as a doctor.]

24. A FRONTIER RENDEZVOUS, 1776

[When the American Revolution first broke out, settlers and Indians in the upper Connecticut Valley took alarm and sought refuge in safer locations. Colonists retreated to hastily erected blockhouses. Once the initial excitement died down, however, people returned home and resumed their everyday life. Jonathan Elkins' family returned to Peacham, Vermont, where his father ran a trading store. The Elkins' home served as a frontier outpost, but it also functioned as a meeting place for Indians, soldiers, and traders. Among the visitors was the Abenaki chief, Joseph Louis Gill, discussed in chapter 6.]

. . . my Farthers house was the out post during the war. the Indins made it thair home, all our scouts stopped thair. In fact it was a place of randevews, for scouts, Indins and desarters.

The friendship showed to the Indins brought numbers of thair cheafs in, to larn if it was true what they had heard of our kindness. Gill the cheff of the St Frances tribe came to our house and stayed nearly a week, we treted him with all the hospatality posable. He could speak but few words of English. I understood many words of the Indin dialect, and between us we could make each other under stand, so that he appeared to be quite happy. The cheaffs from the Cagnawagah tribe came here also, and every friendship was showed that was possable for us to do. And in the course of the war I became so much acquanted with them, that I knew thair language so well, they would apply to me for my assistance to settle difficultys between each other, in which I was verry sucsesful; and by my under standing so much of their language when strangers of them met thay would converse about the war, and in some instances, have been able to convince them of errors they had imbibed so that thair friendship appeared to be secuard, and I believe was the case.

("Reminiscences of Jonathan Elkins," manuscript in the Vermont Historical Society, reprinted in *Collections of the Vermont Historical Society* 3 [1943]: 268.)

25. PERSISTENT ABENAKIS, 1800

[Abenaki patterns of migration and dispersal encouraged many Europeans to think they had died out or gone to Canada by the end of the eighteenth century. But many Abenakis remained in and around the areas of their original habitation, where they came into occasional contact with newly arrived settlers and left their names in local town histories as the "last" of their tribe.]

Several families moved into Troy and Potton [Vermont] in 1799, and in the winter of 1800, a small party of Indians, of whom the chief man was Captain Susap, joined the colonists, built their camps on the river, and wintered near them. These Indians were represented as being in a necessitous and almost starving condition, which probably arose from the moose and deer (which formerly abounded here) being destroyed by the settlers. Their principal employment was making baskets, birch-bark cups and pails, and other Indian trinkets. They left in the spring and never returned. They appeared to have been the most numerous party, and resided the longest time of any Indians who have ever visited the valley since the commencement of the settlement.

(Abby M. Hemenway, *The Vermont Historical Gazeteer*, 5 vols. [Claremont, N.H.: Claremont Manufacturing Co., 1877] 3:315.)

[Captain John Susap had served with the Americans during the Revolution. Molly Ockett was also one of the band.]

Chapter 6

Captives and
Culture Crossings

Jean Vincent D'Abbadie, Baron de Saint Castin (1652–1707), the French nobleman who spent thirty years of his life among the Indians of Penobscot Bay. *Collections of the Maine Historical Society.*

During the course of some two hundred years of dawnland encounters, many individuals found themselves living in other cultures or on the edges of their own. Captives abducted in Indian raids, priests ministering in Indian villages, traders doing business in Indian country, and Indians praying in French missions or studying in English schools—all crossed cultural boundaries to some degree. Some chose an alternative culture freely; some adjusted to it only after time and coercion; and others returned to their parent culture with changed outlooks, new skills, and valuable contacts that enabled them to play crucial intermediary roles on dawnland frontiers.[1]

Capture by Indians was commonly regarded as a fate worse than death, and the narratives recounted by some of the survivors frequently portrayed dawnland Indians as bloodthirsty savages who preyed on defenseless women and children. New England captivity narratives usually present a story of bondage and redemption, in which the captive endures countless sufferings in Indian hands before returning home by escape or ransom.

Closer examination of Indian captivities reveals a more complex phenomenon. Captive-taking was a long-established practice in Indian warfare and fulfilled important cultural functions, since captives were often adopted to take the place of deceased relatives. Escalating warfare in the northern woodlands— and the French practice of purchasing captives to bolster their colony or to exchange them for French prisoners—increased the level of captive-taking. Over sixteen hundred people were carried off from New England between 1677 and 1760. Scores disappeared without a trace, many into Indian villages, while others took up life in New France.[2]

Many captives suffered appalling conditions and mistreatment, but Indians with adoption in mind often showed their prisoners kindness and consideration once they were out of danger from pursuit. Adoption into Indian society initiated a new life for captives, and some succumbed to it completely. Many captive children grew up thinking of themselves as Indians. Others adjusted to the new life while memories of home and hopes of returning faded. Gradually, home became the Indian community where they had spent most of their lives and to which they had become bound by marriage and children.

French Canada offered a common alternative to Indian captivity or English redemption. The French regularly bought prisoners from their Indian allies, and the Abenakis regularly carried New England captives to new homes in New France. The majority of English captives who did not return home spent their lives with the French.[3]

English colonial authorities feared the lure of Indian life and the effects of living in Indian country. Indian ways offered the newcomers an education in New England living, but Massachusetts Bay and Connecticut each took measures to prevent their people from running off to live in Indian country. Long before Hector St. Jean De Crèvecour feared the effects that an education in Indian country might have on his children, Hannah Swarton regretted that she had moved to the frontier settlement of Casco Bay, "thereby Exposing our Children to be bred Ignorantly like Indians." Englishmen who "went Indian" earned the wrath of the authorities, and "renegades" could expect cruel treatment at the hands of vengeful former neighbors.[4] Men like Thomas Morton and Edward Ashley aroused concern and contempt; men like Sebastien Rasles or the Baron de Saint Castin who lived among the Indians were automatically assumed to be foreign agents working to evil purpose. Settlers who adjusted to life in Indian country earned the disdain of coastal elites and foreign visitors: As late as 1794, after traveling through the Maine backcountry, the French statesman Charles-Maurice de Talleyrand wrote that the inhabitants "still resemble too much the natives of the country whom they have replaced."[5]

Nevertheless, Europeans regularly crossed cultural boundaries. In De Crèvecoeur's words, Indian society exerted an "imperceptible charm." On dawnland frontiers, Abenakis, French, and English interacted and intermingled. European men cohabited with Indian women; French traders lived like Indians in Indian country; English captives spent years in Indian villages and entered French-Canadian society via Indian captors; Indian neophytes resided in French mission villages under Jesuit tutelage; a handful of Indians even spent time in English schools and society; and a number of remarkable individuals crossed cultures and operated in and between Indian and European society. Dawnland frontiers were never clearly drawn ethnic boundaries; they were porous cultural borderlands that produced their own crop of bicultural individuals.]

1. EDWARD ASHLEY, 1629

[Englishmen who took up residence with Indians deeply troubled William Bradford and the authorities of Plymouth Colony. English communal endeavors repudiated such individual activities; English ethnocentrism balked at such choices. When Thomas Morton settled at Ma-re-Mount, he alarmed the English not only by selling guns and rum to the Massachusett Indians but also by mingling freely with the Indian women and, in Governor Bradford's eyes, promoting anarchy and atheism. Morton was arrested and deported by the Plymouth authorities. Like Morton, Edward Ashley aroused Bradford's ire on commercial and moral grounds. In 1629, Ashley and his partner Isaac Allerton began to monopolize the Indian trade of the Penobscot River. This was bad enough, but Bradford had additional cause for concern.]

. . . for though he had wite and abilitie enough to manage the business, yet some of them knew him to be a very profane yonge man; and he had for some time lived amonge the Indeans as a savage, and wente naked amongst them, and used their manners (in which time he got their language), so they feared he might still rune into evill courses (though he promised better), and God would not prosper his ways.

(William T. Davis, ed., *Bradford's History of Plymouth Plantation, 1606–1646* [New York: Charles Scribner's Sons, 1908], 256.)

[Eventually, Plymouth had Ashley arrested for selling guns to the Indians, but in 1635 the French captured the post at Penobscot and established their own trading settlement of Pentagoet.[7]]

2. "A DESCRIPTION OF AN INDIAN SQUA," 1672

[European men cohabited with Indian women for reasons of love, lust, loneliness, and political and commercial expediency. French and Indians intermarried regularly; between English and Indians such arrangements were less common and therefore attracted comment and demanded explanation. Henry Tufts explained his inducement in marrying an Abenaki woman as "to remedy

the want of a female companion, while in these rude regions," and reflected upon "the nature of man to need such helps and conveniences, as smooth the asperities and soften the rugged condition of life." Sexual intercourse, he said, was "not the smallest of these advantages" and Polly Susap "supplied to me the place of a wife, though without the fashionable appelation." Although the English worried over marriage or other long-term sexual arrangements, more casual sexual encounters raised less of a specter. English commentators often displayed a fascination with Indian women as "dark beauties," and John Josselyn found a poem that aptly expressed his views on what James Axtell calls "intercultural dalliance."8]

> Whether White or Black be best
> Call your senses to the quest;
> And your touch shall quickly tell
> The Black in softness doth excel,
> And in smoothness; but the ear,
> What, can that a colour hear?
> No, but 'tis your Black ones wit
> That doth catch, and captive it.
> And if slut and fair be one,
> Sweet and fair, there can be none;
> Nor can ought so please the tast
> As what's brown and lovely drest:
> And who'll say, that that is best
> To please ones sense, displease the rest?
> Maugre then all that can be sed
> In flattery of White and Red:
> Those flatterers themselves must say
> That darkness was before the day:
> And such perfection here appears
> It neither wind nor sun-shine fears.

(John Josselyn, *New England's Rarities Discovered* [Boston: William Veazie, 1865 original edn. 1672, 158].)

3. INDIAN CAPTIVITIES: THE PURITAN VIEW

[To the Puritans, conflict with Indians constituted a Holy War waged in the wilderness against the forces of Satan. Indian raids were a form of divine punishment visited upon erring communities, and Indian captivities tested the moral fiber of individuals. Laced with Biblical quotations and scriptural allusions, Puritan captivity accounts often took the form of a sermon in which the greater the trials confronting the individual, the greater the ultimate triumph over the forces of evil.[9] Consequently, descriptions of the sufferings inflicted on captives by Indians are legion in the records. Cotton Mather typifies the themes of many diatribes.]

. . . Truly the dark places of New-England where the Indians had their unapproachable *kennels* were habitations of cruelty; and no words can sufficiently describe the cruelty undergone by our captives in those habitations. The cold, and heat, and hunger, and weariness, and mockings, and scourgings, and insolencies endured by the captives would enough deserve the name of *cruelty;* but there was this also added unto the rest, that they must ever now and then have their friends made a sacraface of devils before their eyes but be afraid of dropping a tear from those eyes lest it should upon that provocation be next their own turn to be so barbarously sacrificed.

(Cotton Mather, *Magnalia Christi Americana*, 2 vols. [Hartford: Silas Andrus and Son, 1853], 2:597–98.)

4. THE CAPTIVITY OF MARY ROWLANDSON

[Mary Rowlandson was one of twenty-four people taken prisoner when Indian raiders sacked Lancaster, Massachusetts, in 1676. The account that she produced of her experiences while in Indian hands became one of the most famous captivity narratives, containing as it did the classic elements of Indian "savagery," Christian bondage, and ultimate redemption. Mary described her Indian

attackers as "hell hounds" who fell on the Christian inhabitants of Lancaster like wolves tearing at sheep. During the course of her captivity, Mary found herself in the camp of Metacom or King Philip near South Vernon on the banks of the Connecticut River in Vermont, where the Indians were regrouping to renew the offensive against the English. Mary's encounter with these Indians hardly justified her portrayal of her captors as merciless heathens. The Indians tried to comfort her, and Metacom even invited her to his lodge. The Indians' consideration—and the chief's respectful offer of tobacco—made little impression on this strong-willed Puritan woman, but she nonetheless found a useful niche in the temporary Indian community.]

. . . We travelled on till night; and in the morning, we must go over the river to Philip's crew. When I was in the cannoo, I could not but be amazed at the numerous crew of pagans that were on the bank on the other side. When I came ashore, they gathered all about me, I sitting alone in the midst. I observed they asked one another questions, and laughed, and rejoyced over their gains and victories. Then my heart began to fail and I fell a weeping which was the first time to my remembrance, that I wept before them. Although I had met with so much affliction, and my heart was many times ready to break, yet could I not shed one tear in their sight; but rather had been all this while in a maze, and like one astonished. But now I may say as Psalm 137.1: By the Rivers of Babylon, there we sat down: yea, we wept when we remembered Zion. There one of them asked me, why I wept. I could hardly tell what to say, yet I answered, they would kill me. No, said he, none will hurt you. Then came one of them and gave me two spoon-fuls of meal to comfort me, and another gave me half a pint of pease; which was more worth than many bushels at another time. Then I went to see King Philip, he bade me come in and sit down, and asked me whether I woold smoke it (a usual complement nowadayes amongst saints and sinners) but this no way suited me. For though I had formerly used tobacco, yet I had left it ever since I was first taken.

It seems to be a bait, the Devil layes to make men loose their precious time. I remember with shame, how formerly, when I had taken two or three pipes, I was presently ready for another, such a bewitching thing it is; but I thank God, he has now given me power over it. Surely there many who may be better imployed than to ly sucking a stinking tobacco-pipe.

Now the Indians gather their forces to go against North-Hampton:[10] over-night one went about yelling and hooting to give notice of the design. Whereupon they fell to boyling of ground-nuts, and parching of corn (as many as had it) for their provision; and in the morning away they went. During my abode in this place, Philip spake to me to make a shirt for his boy, which I did, for which he gave me a shilling. I offered the mony to my master, but he bade me keep it; and with it I bought a piece of horse flesh. Afterwards he asked me to make a cap for his boy, for which he invited me to dinner. I went, and he gave me a pancake, about as big as two fingers; it was made of parched wheat, beaten, and fryed in bears grease, but I thought I never tasted pleasanter meat in my life. There was a squaw who spake to me to make a shirt for her *Sannup*, for which she gave me a piece of bear. Another asked me to knit a pair of stockins, for which she gave me a quart of pease.

(Lincoln, ed., *Narratives of the Indian Wars 1675–1699*, 134–35.)

5. THE ORDEAL OF JOHN GYLES, 1689–1697

[John Gyles was captured at about ten years of age when the French and Indians struck Pemaquid in August 1689. He spent six years among the Indians and almost three more among the French, enduring one of the longest captivities on record that ended in redemption. On his return home, Gyles served the Massachusetts government as an interpreter and negotiator in dealing with the Indians and was granted a commission as an officer on the Maine frontier. The Indians came to respect him as a trustworthy interpreter and valuable inter-

mediary: One Indian speaker declared, "We look upon Capt. Gyles as a Captain of the Tribes in our Parts." Gyles died in 1754 or early 1755.[11]

Instances of Abenakis torturing captives are rare, but Gyles' captors were probably Maliseets. Gyles' brother died at Indian hands, and Gyles himself suffered severe beatings at the hands of visiting or refugee Indians (possibly Micmacs) seeking revenge for some of their people who had been killed by English fishermen. The following extracts from his memoirs reveal that attachments between captors and captives could emerge in the midst of brutality and violence.]

. . . Not one of the Indians showed the least compassion, but I saw the tears run down plentifully on the cheeks of a Frenchman that sat behind, which did not alleviate the tortures that poor James and I were force to endure for the most part of this tedious day; for they were continued till the evening and were the most severe that ever I met with in the whole six years that I was captive with the Indians.

After they had thus inhumanely abused us, two Indians took us up and threw us out of the wigwam, and we crawled away on our hands and feet and were scarce able to walk for several days. Sometime after they again concluded on a merry dance, when I was at some distance from the wigwam dressing leather, and an Indian was so kind as to tell me that they had got James Alexander and were in search for me. My Indian master and his squaw bid me run for my life into a swamp and hide, and not to discover myself unless they both came to me; for then I might be assured the dance was over. I was now master of their language, and a word or a wink was enough to excite me to take care of one. I rant to the swamp and hid in the thickest place that I could find. I heard hallooing and whooping all around me; sometimes they passed very near me, and I could hear some threaten and others flatter me, but I was not disposed to dance. If they had come upon me, I had resolved to show them a pair of heels, and they must have had good luck to have caught me.

I heard no more of them till about evening (for I think I slept) when they came again, calling, "Chon! Chon!" but John would not trust them. After they were gone, my master and his squaw came where they told me to hide but could not find me; and, when I heard them say, with some concern, they believed that the other Indians had frightened me into the woods, and that I was lost, I came out, and they seemed well pleased. They told me James had had a bad day of it; that as soon as he was released he ran away into the woods, and they believed he was gone to the Mohawks. James soon returned and gave me a melancholy account of his sufferings. . . .

[Gyles was subsequently handed over to the French and returned to New England.]

Then I threw away my greasy blanket and Indian flap and looked as smart as ———. And I never more saw the old friar, the Indian village, or my Indian master, till about fourteen years after when I saw my Indian master at Port Royal, whither I had been sent by the government with a flag of truce for the exchange of prisoners; and again, about twenty-four years since, he came to St. John's, to Fort George, to see me, where I made him very welcome.

("Memoirs of Odd Adventures, Strange Deliverances, etc., in the Captivity of John Gyles, Esq., Commander of the Garrison on St. George River, in the District of Maine. Written by Himself. Originally published at Boston, 1736," in Samuel G. Drake, ed., *Indian Captivities or Life in the Wigwam* [Auburn: Derby and Miller, 1852], 85, 101.)

6. THE BARON DE SAINT CASTIN (1652–1707)

[Not all individuals who crossed cultural boundaries did so under coercion. The dawnland produced many individuals and several significant figures who moved willingly into Indian country and made their lives in Indian communities. The son of a well-established noble family from the district of Bearn in

the lower Pyrenees, Jean Vincent D'Abbadie, Baron de Saint Castin, arrived in Quebec in 1665 as a young ensign in the famous Carignan-Salières Regiment, and probably served in the Marquis de Tracy's campaign against the Iroquois the following year. In 1670, he went to Penobscot Bay with Hector de Grand-fontain, the new governor of Acadia, was given responsibility for repairing the fort at Pentagouet, and assumed command of its small garrison. He soon estab-lished ties with the local Indians and even stayed with them during the famine of 1672. When Jacques de Chambly took over as governor of Acadia, he kept Castin in place as liaison officer with the Abenakis. In 1674, Dutch privateers allied to Boston overran Pentagouet and tortured Castin. He escaped with In-dian help and reported to Governor Frontenac in Quebec, who recognized his talents and importance and sent him back to Pentagouet charged with securing Abenaki allegiance to the French Crown.

When his brother died in 1674, Jean Vincent became third Baron de Saint Castin at age twenty-two, but instead of returning to France to claim his in-heritance, he returned to Penobscot. He married a daughter of the chief, Ma-dockawando, named Marie Mathilde Pidianske or Pidiwamiska. He remained a vital agent for the French but increasingly became an Abenaki in his sentiments and loyalties and acted independently, even trading with merchants from Boston. His presence and influence among the Abenakis made him the "best hated Frenchman of his time," and the English burned his trading post at Pentagouet in 1687 and on one occasion tried to have him assassinated. His activities during King William's War—leading Abenaki raids on the Maine frontier—earned the conflict the name of "Castin's War," but when peace was restored he resumed trading with Boston.

Finally, in 1701, he returned to France to sort out his affairs. He became bogged down in legal chicanery and died in 1707 without ever seeing the dawnland again.[12] A contemporary traveler, the Baron de Lahontan, left an account of this fascinating individual and Captain John Alden indicated that he played an intermediary role between French and English as well as between Indian and European.]

. . . The Baron of Saint *Casteins*, a gentleman of *Oleron* in *Bearn,* having lived among the *Abenakis* after the savage way, for above twenty years, is so much respected by the savages, that they look upon him as their tutelar God. He was formerly an officer of the *Carignan* Regiment in *Canada;* and upon the breaking of that regiment, threw himself among the savages, whose language he had learned. He married among them after their fashion, and prefered the forrests of *Acadia* to the *Pyrenean* Mountains, that encompass the place of his nativity. For the first years of his abode with the savages, he behaved himself so, as to draw an inexpressible esteem from them. They made him their Great Chief or leader, who is in a manner the soveraign of the nation; and by degrees he has worked himself into such a fortune, which any man but he would have made such use of, as to draw out of that country above two or three hundred thousand crowns, which he has now in his pocket in good dry gold. But all the use he makes of it, is to buy up goods for presents to his fellow-savages, who upon their return from hunting, present him with beaver-skins to a treble value. The governours general of *Canada* keep in with him, and the governours of *New-England* are afraid of him. He has several daughters, who are, all of them, married very handsomly to *Frenchmen,* and had good dowries. He has never changed his wife; by which means he meant to give the savages to understand, that God does not love inconstant folks. 'Tis said, that he indeavoured to convert these poor people, but his indeavours proved successless; so that 'tis in vain for the Jesuits to preach up the Truths of Christianity to them; though after all, these good Fathers are not discouraged, nay, they think that the administring of baptism to a dying child, is worth ten times the pains and uneasiness of living among that people.[13]

(Thwaites, ed., *New Voyages to North-America by the Baron de Lahontan,* 1:327–29.)

[Shortly after he returned from a trip to the Penobscot River in June 1700, Captain John Alden reported to the Earl of Bellomont the gist of a conversation he had with Castin, with whom he had traded for several years.]

Monsieur de St. Castin told him he hoped he should shortly come under the King of England's government, for that he had much rather be a subject of England than a slave to France; he likewise said that the true boundary between England and France to the eastward was the River of Ste Croix and said the English would do well to insist on it vigorously, otherwise the French court would try to cozen them out of it. Captain Alden desired him the said Castin to write by him to the Governour of New England what he had then related about the boundary but he said he could not venture to do such a thing least his letter should be carried to Quebec. He, vizt. St. Castin told Captain Alden that the Jesuits has taken indefatigable pains to stir up the Indians everywhere to make war upon the English and said they were very wicked in so doing. I desired Captain Alden to put what he told me in writing by way of memorial, and set his name to it but he desired to be excused, saying that St. Castin was his friend and correspondent, and he, viz. Alden, could not do anything that would expose Monsieur de St. Castin. This I immediately writ down after Captain Alden had left me.

Monsieur de St. Castin is said to be a gentleman of good family who leaving France on some disgust in his youth, came and settled on Penobscot River, married the chief sagamore's daughter, speaks the Indian tongue, lives after the Indian manner, and is become chief or sagamore of the Penobscot Indians consisting in about 130 families, being grown rich by trade. 'Tis said the French governours of Canada and St. Johns have sent several times to him to go to them, but he would not go near them. He professes great kindness to the English and speaks English. He gave advice to some of the late gouvernours here, of the designes of the French against this countrey, and the return he had was the sending a frigat and some souldiers, who ravaged his country and burnt the wigwams or homes of him and his Indians, which faithless action he complains of to this day.

(*Collections of the Maine Historical Society*, 2d ser., 10 [1907]: 57–59.)

7. INDIANS DECLINE AN ENGLISH EDUCATION FOR THEIR CHILDREN, 1701

[*Relatively few Indians adjusted to life in European society, and it was a source of discomfort to English authorities that more colonists preferred Indian society than vice versa. The English devoted considerable effort toward educating Indian children, hoping thereby to begin transforming Indian society and culture—an act they deemed essential to "civilizing" the natives.[14] But Indians regularly resisted European attempts to take away their young people for education, often with good reason, as shown by this extract from a meeting between commissioners from Massachusetts Bay and Abenaki delegates at Casco Bay in June 1701.*]

That to the intent of perfecting our future and mutual friendship and acquaintance we have thought good to offer and invite your sending of some of your children to live amongst us whom we shall take care of both for their maintenance and education and to return them at such times as you shall desire, and that if you are any ways inclineable to have your young men see England and King William, we shall send them whereby you may be better informed of the circumstances of our nation.

[*The Indians requested time to consider this proposition and the council adjourned until the next day, when the Indians gave their answer.*]

We conclude not to send any of our children to England, because Moxus his son when he was sent to France, he died there. And we conclude not to send any of our children to Boston because we formerly had two of our children at Boston, called John and Robin, which we believe have by this time learned to read and write English enough, and they never yet have returned amongst us. . . .

[The commissioners replied:] Those two children were taken in war, and disposed of by those to whom they did belong, and we hear that one of them is dead and the other is now in London where he is well provided for, and we believe he hath lost his language and that he will not incline to return, but if he be willing, we shall use our endeavours to procure him.

[Indians:] You ought to force him to come home for we have a great mind to see him. We forced some of our captives to return home.

(*Collections of the Maine Historical Society*, 2d ser., 10 [1907]: 92–93.)

8. JOHN WILLIAMS' CHILDREN, 1704

[In February 1704, after an arduous trek from Canada, Hertel de Rouville and a war party of 200 French and 142 Indians fell on Deerfield, Massachusetts, and left the town a smoking ruin. They killed 47 inhabitants and carried off 109 captives in a desperate flight up the frozen Connecticut River. The town minister, the Reverend John Williams, spent two and a half years in captivity and, when he returned, produced a graphic account of the captives' experiences. Published in Boston in 1707 under the title, The Redeemed Captive Returning to Zion, *Williams' narrative sold one thousand copies in the first week and became a classic example of captivity literature. Williams' wife was among those who fell under the Indians' tomahawks on the flight upriver, but his children received kind treatment, as this extract from his narrative describes.]*

My youngest daughter, aged seven years, was carried all the journey and looked after with a great deal of tenderness. My youngest son, aged four years, was wonderfully preserved from death; for, though they that carried him or drew him on sleighs were tired with their journeys, yet their savage cruel tempers were so overruled by God that they did not kill him, but in their pity he was spared and others would take care of him; so that four times on the journey he was spared and others would take care of him, till at last he arrived at Montreal where a French gentlewoman, pitying the child, redeemed it out of the hands of the heathen. My son Samuel and my eldest daughter were pitied so as to be drawn on sleighs when unable to travel. And though they suffered very much through scarcity of food and tedious journeys, they were carried through to Montreal. And my son Stephen, about eleven years of age, [was] wonderfully preserved from death in the famine whereof three English persons died and after eight months brought into Chamble.

(John Williams, *The Redeemed Captive* [Springfield, Mass.: H. R. Huntting Co., 1908], 29–30.)

[Almost more alarming for Williams than Indian tomahawks was the threat of English Puritans falling into Jesuit hands. The Reverend's worst fears were realized in the person of his daughter, Eunice. Though his other children returned home, Eunice remained with the Indians, married a Caughnawaga, and embraced Catholicism. She lived with the Indians for more than eighty years. Other women and girl captives found safety, solace, and society in the convent schools and Catholic religion of New France. At least seventy-eight women and girls from New England remained with the French and Indians. Many married Frenchmen, some stayed with the Indians, and others took vows in convents. Captured at Wells, Maine, in 1703, Esther Wheelwright spent several years with the Abenakis before being handed over to the French and becoming a nun. Eventually, she became mother superior of the Ursuline convent in Quebec. But captives who established new family ties and loyalties did not necessarily abandon old ones: Mary Storer, captured in the same raid as Esther Wheelwright, married Jean St. Germaine and lived in Montreal, but she kept up correspondence with her New England relatives and returned to visit Rhode Island.[15]]

9. ANOTHER SIDE TO THE DEERFIELD RAID, 1704

[The attack on Deerfield became infamous in the annals of the northern frontier as a dramatic example of French perfidy and Indian savagery. However,

as the following statement reveals, the Deerfield raiders had more than just murder and mayhem on their minds.]

Some of our captives then in Canada, knowing the enterprize that was on foot, sent several letters unto their friends, which the enemy did carefully put into a bag, and hung it upon the limb of a tree in the high-way; which letters were afterwards found, and gave satisfaction of those that were then alive among them.

(Penhallow, *History of the Indian Wars of New England,* 13.)

10. COMPANIONS IN CAPTIVITY, 1708

[English men and women who were hauled off into captivity by the French or Indians were not entering closed societies. They were likely to encounter fellow New Englanders in various stages of acculturation—some of them on their second "go around"—in Indian villages and French communities. Joseph Bartlett, a soldier at Haverill, was captured during a raid in August 1708 and taken via Lakes Winnepausaukee and Champlain to an Indian village near Montreal.]

One of them then took me by the hand, and, after a lengthy speech, gave me to an old squaw, who took me into another wigwam. Here, after a little crying and whimpering, she made me put off my Indian stockings and my blanket, and gave me others; and she warmed some water, and washed the red paint and grease from my face and hands. There was another family lived in the same wigwam. An English woman, who belonged to one of the French nuns, came in, and told me I need not fear for I was given to this squaw in lieu of one of her sons, whom the English had slain; and that I was to be master of the wigwam; but she being a papist, I placed little reliance on her assertions. The old squaw was very kind to me. I staid here about two weeks; and then went to another fort about eighteen miles distant. . . .

After I had been a short time at the other fort, there was brought in by the Indians an Englishman named Martin Kelcock[16] who lived in the same wigwam with me. I found him of great benefit to me, as he understood and could well explain their language. He had been taken by them some years previous, but escaped, and was afterwards re-taken. We lived together till February; but we endured much from the severity of the weather, being poorly clad, and destitute of proper food. . . .

(*A Narrative of the Captivity of Joseph Bartlett among the French and Indians. Written by Himself* [published for the Purchaser, 1807], 7–8; copy in the New Hampshire Historical Society.)

11. "GOD'S MERCY SURMOUNTING MAN'S CRUELTY," 1724

[Captives frequently fell prey to petty and vicious treatment. Quaker Elizabeth Hanson was captured when a French and Indian war party raided Dover, New Hampshire, in the summer of 1724. She suffered dread and misery at the hands of an Indian master who vented frustration at his own misfortunes by threatening captives. But as Elizabeth Hanson's aptly titled account demonstrates, not all Indians participated in such persecution, and sometimes common experience and gender forged bonds stronger than those of race or birth.[17]

Then the Indian, my master, left me; but his wife's mother came and sat down by me, and told me I must sleep there that night. She then going from me a little time, came back with a small skin to cover my feet withal, informing me that my master intended now to kill us, and I, being desirous to know the reason, expostulated, that in his absence I had been diligent to do as I was ordered by him. Thus, as well as I could, I made her sensible how unreasonable he was. Now, though she could not understand me nor I her, but by signs, we reasoned as well as we could.

She therefore makes signs that I must die, advising me by pointing up with her fingers, in her way, to pray to God, endeavoring
by her signs and tears to instruct me in that which was most
needful, viz. to prepare for death which now threatened me.
The poor old squaw was so very kind and tender, that she would
not leave me all that night, but laid herself down at my feet,
designing what she could to assuage her son-in-law's wrath, who
had conceived evil against me, chief, as I understood, because
the want of victuals urged him to it. My rest was little this night,
my poor babe sleeping sweetly by me.

. . . .

Some few weeks after this, my master made another remove,
having as before made several; but this was the longest ever he
made, it being two days' journey, and mostly upon ice. The first
day's journey the ice was bare, but the next day, some snow
falling, made it very troublesome, tedious, and difficult traveling; and I took much damage in often falling; having the care
of my babe, that added not a little to my uneasiness. And the
last night when we came to encamp, it being in the night, I was
ordered to fetch water; but having sat awhile on the cold ground,
I could neither go nor stand, but [was] crawling on my hands
and knees. A young Indian squaw who came to see our people,
being of another family, in compassion took the kettle, and
knowing where to go, which I did not, fetched the water for me.
This I took as a great kindness and favor, that her heart was
inclined to do me this service.

("Elizabeth Hanson's Captivity," in Drake, ed. *Indian Captivities,* 119–20, 123.)

12. ONE WHO CAME BACK AND ONE WHO DIDN'T,
1725

*[Elizabeth Hanson was redeemed after just over a year in captivity but was
obliged to leave one of her daughters among the Indians. Although her father*

literally died trying to recover her, Sarah Hanson remained with the Indians, married a captain in the French-Canadian militia, and spent the rest of her life in Canada.]

I having been about five months amongst the Indians, in about one month after I got amongst the French, my dear husband, to my unspeakable comfort and joy, came to me, who was now himself concerned to redeem his children, two of our daughters being still captives, and only myself and two little ones redeemed; and, through great difficulty and trouble, he recovered the younger daughter. But the eldest we could by no means obtain from their hands, for the squaw, to whom she was given, has a son which she intended my daughter should in time be prevailed with to marry. The Indians are very civil towards their captive women, not offering any incivility by any indecent carriage (unless they be much overgone in liquor,) which is commendable in them so far.

However, the affections they had for my daughter made them refuse all offers and terms of ransom; so that, after my poor husband had waited, and made what attempts and endeavors he could to obtain his child, and all to no purpose, we were forced to make homeward, leaving our daughter, to our great grief, behind us, amongst the Indians, and set forward over the lake, with three of our children, and the servant maid, in company with sundry others, and, by the kindness of Providence, we got well home on the first day of the seventh month 1725.

("Elizabeth Hanson's Captivity," in Drake, ed., *Indian Captivities*, 124–25.)

13. THE CAPTIVITY OF ISABELLA MCCOY, 1747

[Despite the cruelties attributed to Indian raiders by contemporary chroniclers and later writers, warriors rarely if ever raped or behaved indecently toward their female captives. Indians embarking on the warpath frequently practiced sexual abstinence to keep their war medicine pure, and, as James Axtell points

out, no warrior would risk infringing incest taboos by forcing himself on someone who might subsequently be adopted into his family. Moreover, contrary to European assumptions of male dominance and female subservience in Indian society, gender relations in northeastern band societies were typically egalitarian.[18] Testimony to Indians' respectful treatment of women captives is common in literature. Isabella McCoy, captured by Plausawa, Sabatis, and Christi in New Hampshire in 1747, modified her preconcieved opinions of the Abenakis, even though the Indians torched her home.]

They now commenced their long and tedious journey to Canada, in which the poor captive might well expect that great and complicated sufferings would be her lot. She did indeed find the journey fatiguing, and her fare scanty and precarious. But in her treatment from the Indians she experienced a very agreeable disappointment. The kindness she received from them was far greater than she had expected from those who were so often distinguished for their cruelties. The apples they had gathered they saved for her, giving her one every day. In this way they lasted her as far on the way as Lake Champlain. They gave her the last as they were crossing that lake in their canoes. This circumstance gave to the tree on which the apples grew the name of "Isabel's tree," her name being Isabella. In many ways did they appear desirous of mitigating the distresses of their prisoner while on their tedious journey. When night came on, and they halted to repose themselves in the dark wilderness, Plausawa, the head man, would make a little couch in the leaves, a little way from theirs, cover her up with his own blanket, and there she was suffered to sleep undisturbed till morning. When they came to a river which must be forded, one of them would carry her over on his back. Nothing like insult or indecency did they ever offer her during the whole time she was with them. They carried her to Canada, and sold her as a servant to a French family, whence, at the close of that war, she returned home. But so comfortable was her condition there, and her husband being a man of rather a rough and violent temper, she declared she never should have thought of attempting the journey home, were it not for the sake of her children.

(Chase, ed., *Gathered Sketches*, 48–50.)

[Plausawa and Sabatis were killed in New Hampshire in 1753. Their murders fueled the escalating tensions between Abenakis and English that erupted into war in 1754.[19]]

14. CASTIN THE YOUNGER, 1751

[The Baron de St. Castin left several children, two of whom, Bernard-Anselm and Joseph, inherited their father's influence and continued his role among the Abenakis. In 1721, Joseph d'Abbadie described himself as "Abenaquis by my mother. All my life has passed among the nation that has made me chief and commander over it."[20] This translation of a letter from Joseph to Lieutenant Governor Phips in January 1751 shows the younger Castin attempting to operate as an independent intermediary between Indians and Europeans in ways his father would have approved.]

I do myself the honour to write to you to assure you that I could not hinder the Indians of the St Francois and Becancour who made a descent upon you this fall. I did all I could to hinder them with our Indians of Panavauke. I would have hindered them from doing you mischief. I was not heard, because I had not taken up arms against you in the last war, nor in former wars. I am glad to assure you that I will not take up arms against you, if you have a war with the Indians and French. If you will please to grant me what I ask that you will please to leave me at liberty where I am and likewise to give me a protection signed by all your council that I may be secure. I can assure you I have done all in my power to maintain the peace between us.

I conclude with respect, I am your most humble,

and most obedient servant.

Joseph de badis de St Castin

If I might be so bold I would desire to be trusted by the gentlemen who supply Fort St. George, with a small vessel of 15 or 16 tons and a small cargo this spring to go a trading for beaver and other furs along the eastern coast, otherwise to the River St John. If you will grant me this request, I beg you would send me an answer in French.

(*Collections of the Maine Historical Society*, 2d ser., 12 [1908]: 123–24.)

15. SUSANNA JOHNSON AND THE "WHITE CHIEF" C. 1754

[Susanna Johnson and her family were captured when Abenakis raided Charlestown, New Hampshire, in 1754. In the course of the march into captivity—which she likened to a funeral procession—Mrs. Johnson went into labor. The Abenakis stopped, built her a crude shelter, and, after the baby—Elizabeth Captive Johnson—was born (near Reading, Vermont), allowed the new mother to ride while they walked. On arrival at St. Francis, Mrs. Johnson was adopted into the family of Joseph Louis Gill, "the White Chief of St. Francis Abenakis."

Gill was the son of Yankee parents, both of whom were captured as children by the Abenakis and then adopted, baptized as Catholics, and raised as Indians. They lived with the Abenakis the rest of their lives, married, and had seven children, of whom Joseph Louis was the oldest. Raised as an Abenaki, Joseph fought for the French in 1747 against the Miamis, married an Abenaki woman named Marie Jeanne, who bore him two or three children, and emerged as a prominent leader and cultural broker between the Abenakis and Europeans. He was said to be "definitely blond Yankee-English in appearance."

Gill was about forty at the time of Rogers' raid in 1759. The raid was a personal disaster for him. His wife was taken prisoner and died on the march, as did at least one child. In 1763, Gill married the daughter of a French militia captain, Antonie Gamelin, and together they had six sons and two daughters. Gill inherited land from the Gamelin estate, and by the eve of the Revolution, he was fairly well to do. He sent a son and nephews to Dartmouth College. During the Revolution, he gave the British considerable headaches, as the leader of one of the factions at St. Francis. The redcoats—with good reason—suspected

him of espionage and double dealing, although in October 1780 he took an oath
of allegiance to King George. Gill died in 1798 at about seventy-eight years of
age and was buried in the Abenaki church.[21]

Mrs. Johnson remembered Gill as a bicultural individual, living among the
Abenakis and enjoying a prominent position at St. Francis, yet aware of his
English roots and displaying characteristics that betrayed his Yankee heritage.]

I was taken to the house of my new master, and found myself
allied to the first family. My master, whose name was Gill, was
son-in-law to the grand sachem, was accounted rich, had a store
of goods, and lived in a style far above the majority of his tribe.
He often told me that he had an English heart, but his wife was
true Indian blood. Soon after my arrival at his house the interpreter came to inform me I was adopted into his family. I was
then introduced into the family, and was told to call them brothers and sisters. I made a short reply, expressive of gratitude for
being introduced to a house of high rank, and requested their
patience while I should learn the customs of the nation.

("Captivity of Mrs. Johnson," in *Indian Narratives*, 158–59.)

16. TITUS KING "BECOMES" AN INDIAN, 1755

[Titus King was captured near Rice's Fort, Massachusetts, in June 1755,
but his march into captivity took an unusual turn after his Abenaki captors
stopped at the French fort at Crown Point. The fort was a common port-of-call
for returning war parties who felt they could relax their vigilance on the final
stretch of their homeward journey. As the party continued on its journey, the
Abenakis began to prepare King for his new life and adoption when he reached
St. Francis.]

19th: Got up this morning. The Indians seemd to be a lettel
ashamed that they was so drunk last night; they told me that
rum was no good. Now we set out for St. Johns but the Indians
felt so after there drunkness they could not paddel. They told

me I must paddel with the outher Indian that had not been drunk while they layd down and sleept. Now I was a paddeling myself into captivety. Now I had a night and day to compose my mind and bring it to my circumstancses. Nothing remakbel happed this day nor the next.

Saturday 21st: The Indians told me this day that I must be an Indian. They had always told me before that I should go to Montreal but now they told [me] I must go with them to the Indian town. I told them I chose to leve with the French; they told me Frenchman no good, Enlishman no good, Indian very good. At noon they went out of the canoes and spred a blanket on a lettel nole [and] told me to set down. They took out my sleve buttens, pulled of my shurt, put on a old shurt of theres that stand with Indian sweet, put wonpon in my neck, panted my face. I began to think I was an Indian. . . .

June 26th: The Indians that took me told me that I should be given away to outher Indians as there manner is to adopt the Enlish prisons and so make children of them. All the Indians was called tagether on this ocasion. The govenor made a long speach. The famely that I was adopted into gave my Indian master that took me a sute of cloths, came and took me by the hand [and] lead me away to his house. Now I was in new family and in a nere relation to them; became brother to the old Indian and squaw, being in the place of an Indian that was killd the last war. I being in the same relation as he was to them I became a grandfather; they said there grandfather was come to life again. Now all things seemd to be settld a Indian that could speak good Enlish came in to see me and told that the wigwam I was in was my house and pointd to a nother and said that was mine also; and brought a new Indian dress to put on me so I was now drest compliat in Indian dress adoptd amongust [them]. Lived with and dress and painted looked right like a Indaan; this indeed was hard times fore me. . . .

(*Narrative of Titus King of Northampton, Mass. A Prisoner of the Indians in Canada 1755–1758* [Hartford: Connecticut Historical Society, 1938], 10, 13–14.)

17. WHITE INDIAN CHILDREN

[Children proved most susceptible to assimilation into Indian society. Young captives had few strong attachments to their birthplaces, few memories of their early lives, and succumbed most easily to the lure of Indian life. Just as European missionaries and teachers tried to get hold of Indian youths and reeducate them at an impressionable age, so, as Titus King observed, French priests and Abenaki Indians at St. Francis worked successfully to win over youthful captives.[22]]

Now there was above eight or tin young children in this Indian town, an awfull school this for children when we see how quick they will fall in with the Indians ways; nothing seems to be more takeing in six months time they forsake father and mother, forgit thir own land, refuess to speak their own toungue and seeminly be holley swollowed up with the Indians. Then the French prests take great pains to school the Enlish children in there reglion meeting [e]very morning at nine of clok at the toleing of the bell, where they go with the Indian children and are cateksed according to the Romish prinpsels: and this is a taking to the [   ] like there being one and the s[ame] Divel to tempt. I took all the pains with these children I could to keep there hearts att hum, to rember there cattekime and to remember there God, that now he would be a Father to them tha he would help them hume again if they would pray to him; and as often as I could yousd to teach them their catekism, the Lords Prayer and the like. Sume of the oldest of them would give heed to what I said [and] seemed to be turely affected with there eastate, but almost imposable to keep children here: the French prests and Indians use all their powers to disafect them to the Enlish. . . .

(*Narrative of Titus King*, 17.)

18. A CHILD REDEEMED, A CHILD CAPTURED, 1758–1759

[The captive-taking frontier was a two-way street. While English settlers feared the horrors of Indian captivity, Indians were abducted to Europe, taken as prisoners of war, held hostage, and sometimes sold into slavery. The Abenakis who took captive Mrs. Johnson's family in 1754 suffered similar tragedy five years later when Rogers' Rangers burned their village at St. Francis. As a former captive and resident at St. Francis, Mrs. Johnson recalled the sufferings those events caused on both sides of the frontier. The following extract shows how children like her son Sylvanus became "Indianized" during their captivity with the Abenakis. It also illustrates how the attachments formed with one's adopted family during captivity endured when circumstances were changed and tables were turned. The Indian boy whom Mrs. Johnson called Sabatis was Antoine, the only son of Joseph Louis Gill who survived Rogers' raid.]

In October, 1758, I was informed that my son Sylvanus was of Northampton sick of a scald. I hastened to the place and found him in a deplorable situation. He was brought there by Major Putnam, (afterwards General Putnam) with Mrs. How and her family, who had returned him from captivity. The town of Northampton had taken the charge of him. His situation was miserable: when I found him he had no recollection of me; but after some conversation he had some confused ideas of me, but no remembrance of his father. It was four years since I had seen him; he was then eleven years old. During his absence he had entirely forgotten the English language, spoke a little broken French, but was perfect in Indian. He had been with savages three years, and one year with the French; but his habits were somewhat Indian. He had been with them in their hunting expeditions and suffered numerous hardships; he could brandish a tomahawk or bend the bow; but these habits wore off by degrees. I carried him from that place to Lancaster, where he lived a few years with Colonel Aaron Willard.

I lived in Lancaster till October, 1749, when I returned to Old Charlestown. The sight of my former residence afforded a strange mixture of joy and grief; while the desolations of war, and the loss of a number of dear and valuable friends, combined to give the place an air of melancholy. Soon after my arrival Major Rogers returned from an expedition against the village of St. Francis, which he had destroyed, and killed most of the inhabitants.[23] He brought with him a young Indian prisoner, who stopped at my house: the moment he saw me he cried. "My God! my God! here is my sister!" It was my little brother Sabatis, who formerly used to bring the cows for me when I lived at my Indian masters. He was transported to see me, and declared he was still my brother, and I must be his sister. Poor fellow! The fortune of war had left him without a single relation; but with his country's enemies he could find one who too sensibly felt his miseries. I felt the purest pleasure in ministering to his comfort.

("Captivity of Mrs. Johnson," in *Indian Narratives*, 174–75.)

19. ROBERT ROGERS, 1765

[While Frenchmen like Castin seemed to display a natural affinity for living with Indians, Englishmen are often portrayed as blind to the attractions of Indian life. The French certainly developed a more extensive network of Indian relations and imbibed Indian culture to an extent unmatched by their rivals, but it would be wrong to suggest that the English were unaffected by their encounters with the native inhabitants of the dawnland. Men like John Gyles, Phineas Stevens, and the Kellogg brothers acquired substantial knowledge from their Indian captors, which they put to use as culture brokers in later years. In Abenaki history, perhaps no individual stands out as an enemy as clearly as Robert Rogers: "The White Devil!" who led the raid that burned St. Francis. Yet, as the following extract from his memoirs suggests, Rogers' abilities in dawnland warfare owed much to the Abenaki lore and culture he absorbed in early life.]

It would perhaps gratify the curious to have a particular account of my life, preceding the war; but though I could easily
indulge them herein, without any dishonour to myself, yet I beg
they will be content with my relating only such circumstances
and occurrences as led me to a knowledge of many parts of the
country, and tended in some measure to qualify me for the service I have since been employed in. Such, in particular, was the
situation of the place in which I received my early education, a
frontier town in the province of New Hampshire, where I could
hardly avoid obtaining some knowledge of the manners, customs, and language of the Indians, as many of them resided in
the neighbourhood, and daily conversed and dealt with the English. Between the years 1743 and 1755 my manner of life was
such as led me to a general acquaintance both with the British
and French settlements in North America, and especially with
the uncultivated desart, the mountains, valleys, rivers, lakes, and
several passes that lay between and contiguous to the said settlements. Nor did I content myself with the accounts I received
from Indians, or the information of hunters, but travelled over
large tracts of the country myself, which tended not more to
gratify my curiosity, than to inure me to hardships, and, without
vanity I may say, to qualify me for the very service I have since
been employed in.

(*Journals of Major Robert Rogers* [London, 1765], vi–vii.)

[*Rogers was not the only adversary of the Abenakis to proclaim his close
association with them. Even Ethan Allen, notorious with his brother Ira for
dispossessing Abenakis of lands around Lake Champlain, boasted to the Caughnawagas in 1775, "I always love Indians and have hunted a great deal with
them I know how to shute and ambush just like Indian. . . ."*[24]]

20. ABENAKI STUDENTS AT DARTMOUTH COLLEGE, 1777

[The Reverend Eleazar Wheelock devoted twenty-five years of his life to Indian education. Like other colonial educators, he believed that schooling was the key to "civilizing" Indians. After he moved his Indian school from Lebanon, Connecticut, to Hanover, New Hampshire, in 1769, Wheelock recruited Indian students from St. Francis and elsewhere. Joseph Louis Gill sent his son and several nephews to Darmouth College. Some graduated and returned home as teachers and preachers, but others rebelled against the regimen of school life. Like many other schoolmaster/missionaries, Wheelock was unable to appreciate the tenacity with which his students clung to their traditional cultural values.²⁵ On November 1, 1777, Wheelock wrote Joseph Louis Gill a letter that reveals some fundamental differences in notions of work and education, as well as the reluctance of the students in question to fit into Wheelock's mold.]

Mr. Gill

Sir. These come by your son Anthony who seems to have desire to go home and I think it best for him and for you. Yet he should go. I have faithfully done the best I could for him, and the school masters have taken much pains with him—but he dont love his books, but loves play and idleness much better. I hope you will know better than I do what to do with him and for him. I should be willing to do him and you the kindness to carry him through a course of college learning. But unless he should make better proficiency than he has done he will not get through in ten years in which time I can with the same expence educate ———— who will esteem the privilege which has been offered him to be very great, as it really is. If you have another son which you desire I should make tryal of, and will send him to me, I will make a faithful tryal of his disposition and abilities, and do for him accordingly as shall appear best for him, and you shall be wellcome to my labor and expence for him as you are to what I have done for Anthony. But if you or any of your friends shall have a desire to send your sons here for an education it will be best they should be well instructed in the business of farming before they come, or else be told that they must learn it here, as they will have opportunity to do without any interruption or disadvantage to their studies at all and yet only by improving part of the vacation of the school on the farm with my laborers. This will be safest and best for them for if they should not be able in future life to get their living by the business of a learned profession, and wild game should be all gone from the country, as they likely will be within a few years, your sons will be in a very unhappy state if they should not know how to get their living by farming. So we think and so all wise men here practice with their own sons unless they have a good estate to support them and so I think it would be best to do by yours. Some of your children appear to l[ove] play very much and if I would let them would do nothing else thro a whole vacation of the school for three or four weeks together and think hard if I send them into the field with my laborers to learn every branch of labor, if it be only for a few days. And I hear the sons of yours say they had not come here to work and it is best to let you know fully that yours come here to learn everything that will be every way wisest and best for you. It is but a small part of the time that is propsed for them to work in, nor more than will be best for their health and to fit them for their studies. All the vacations in a year in ———— make but 9 weeks, unless they labor and study so hard that their health requires more.

Benedict did not get the English tongue so easie as some do and is not so forward in reading and writing as I could wish.

Joseph and Montuit have done very well. Joseph entered college last August and bids fair to make a good schollar. Montuit will be fit to enter college as soon as he is old enough. I hope these two will be wise learned and useful men, and do much good in the world if their fathers are wise enough to let them go through their learning and not take them away to spoil them as some as have done. I pray God to grant all prosperity to you and your family.

I am

Your hearty friend and well wisher,

Eleazar Wheelock.

(Letter to Sachim Gill, Nov. 1, 1777, Dartmouth College Ms. 777601.)

21. THE RAID ON ROYALTON, 1780

[Indian raids on frontier settlements were accompanied by violence and confusion. Nevertheless, even in the heat of an attack, all was not mindless brutality. In this famous incident from the British and Indian raid on Royalton, Vermont, in October 1780, Mrs. Hannah Handy (Handee) set about relocating her son, who had become separated from her in the attack.]

Wishing to find the commanding officer, and supposing him to be there, she set out to cross the river, and just as she arrived at the bank, an old Indian stepped ashore. He could not talk English, but requested by signs to know where she was going. She signified that she was going to cross, when he, supposing she intended to deliver herself up to them as a prisoner, kindly offered to carry her and her child across on his back; but she refused to be carried. He then insisted upon carrying her child, to which she consented. The little girl cried, and said, "She didn't *want* to ride the old Indian." She was however persuaded to *ride the old Indian,* and they all set out to ford the river.

Having proceeded about half way across, they came to deeper and swifter water, and the old Indian, patting the mother upon the shoulder, gave her to understand that if she would tarry upon a rock near them, which was not covered with water, till he had carried her child over, he would return and carry her also. She therefore stopped, and sat upon the rock till he had carried her daughter and set it upon the opposite shore; when he returned and took her upon his back, lugged her over, and safely landed her with her child.

(Zadock Steele, *A Narrative of the Captivity and Sufferings of Zadock Steele, Related by Himself* [Springfield, Mass.: The H. R. Huntting Co., 1908], 34–35.)

[Mrs. Handee not only found the commanding officer, Lieutenant Richard Horton, and persuaded him to have her son released, she also succeeded in securing the release of eight other children. She lived her old age in Sharon, Vermont, where she recounted her story to Zadock Steele in 1818.]

22. INDIAN CAPTIVITY CONTRASTED, C. 1780

[The forced march into captivity was a harrowing ordeal, punctuated by acts of violence and instances of cruelty. Yet, as Zadock Steele noted when his captors led him across Vermont from Royalton, what captives saw as hardship was often the norm for Indians, and Indian warriors often looked to the welfare of their prisoners.]

On the morning of the 18th they first ordered me to eat my breakfast, urging me to eat as much as I wanted, while, on account of the loss of their provisions at Randolph, they had scarce half an allowance for themselves. I knew not whether to attribute this conduct to their feelings of charity and generosity, a desire to secure my friendship, or a wish to preserve my life under a prospect of procuring gain, or to some other cause.

Indeed they seemed at all times to be willing to "feed the hungry," not even seeing one of the prisoners leisurely to pick a berry by the way, as they passed along, without offering them food; considering this as a token of our hunger.

Their food, however, was very unsavory, insomuch that nothing but extreme hunger would have induced me to eat of it, though I always had a share of their best.

Habituated to a partial covering themselves and excited by

curiosity, they took from me all my best clothes, and gave me blankets in exchange. They often travelled with the utmost celerity in their power, to try my activity, viewing me with looks of complacency, to find me able to keep pace with them. . . .

[Looking back over his captivity with the Caughnawagas and his subsequent term in a British jail under the watch of Tory guards, Steele found it easier to excuse cultural captors than political jailors.]

Who would not shudder at the idea of being compelled to take up their abode with a herd of tawny savages? Yet, alas! when I contrasted the sufferings I endured, while with the Indians, with those afflictions, that were laid upon me by men, who had been from their youth favored with the advantages of civilization, clothed with authority, and distinguished with a badge of honor; I could truly say, the former chastised me with whips, but the latter with scorpions.

An Indian captivity will hardly admit of a comparison with my wretched condition, while in the hands of the British, and under the domineering power of a company of refugees and tories.

(Steele, *A Narrative of the Captivity and Sufferings of Zadock Steele*, 62–63, 162–63.)

23. CONTINUITY AND CHANGE AMONG THE PENOBSCOTS: AN ITALIAN VIEW, 1785

[By the late eighteenth century, Indians and Europeans in northern New England had been interacting and selectively borrowing for some three hundred years. Words, styles of dress, items of technology, beliefs, practices and people passed between cultures with lasting effect. In 1785 Luigi Castiglioni, a Milanese botanist traveling the United States to study New World flora and to see the young Republic for himself, visited the Penobscot village at Old Town, Maine. Although he spent only a few hours at the village and expressed some disdain for the inhabitants, he left a valuable description of Penobscot life. Like most

*casual visitors among eastern Indians around this time, Castiglioni was im-
mediately impressed with the evidence of acculturation he saw, but he also
recorded important elements of continuity in Penobscot society. After centuries
of contact, dawnland Indian life was characterized by a mixture of traditional
ways and European adaptations.]*

Penobscot, or Old Town, as the English call it, on the little
island of the same name, is situated, according to the best maps,
at latitude 45°10′ and 50 miles north of the mouth of the river.
About 20 Indian families live there in their huts, which they call
wigwams, arranged in rows and placed close to each other. These
huts are made of pine trunks fastened at the corners with
strands of bark, and the outside walls, like the roof, are covered
with wide pieces of hemlock bark. Inside there are no partitions,
and their furnishings consist simply of square pieces of the same
bark which serve as seats and some skins or woolen blankets in
which they wrap themselves at night to sleep. Woolen blankets,
as well as guns and other tools now common among the Indians,
are brought to them by European merchants. Before the discovery of America they used—instead of these furnishings—
furs, earthen or terra cotta receptacles, and sharp pieces of flint
that served as arrowheads, knives, and axes. Every Indian is
provided with a gun, a dog, and a canoe—three things that they
consider most necessary, and which therefore they conserve with
the utmost care.

. . . .

[These Indians] descend from the ancient nation of the Abenaki, who once inhabited the regions included under the name
of New England, and they are mixed with the descendants of
the Mohawk who came from Canada and with offspring of
Frenchmen married with Indian women.

Their attire is no longer the ancient one, made of skins, but
European dresses and shirts, and uniforms of French and En-

glish soldiers. A few wear European-style hats, decorated with feathers. Others always go bareheaded, and their long black, glossy hair is cut short over the upper half of the head, while that of the nape comes down to their shoulders. Some paint their faces red and black with various designs, others have the cartilage of their ears cut and hanging down; and others adorn them with silver rings, which sometimes hang even from their nostrils. They also wear, sometimes across their shoulders, sometimes around their necks, canvas bags covered with *wampum* or tiny bugle beads or various colors arranged in patterns. Some have silver bracelets or rings, and others, plaques or medallions of the same metal hanging around their necks. The upper part of their thighs is bare, and they cover their nakedness with a piece of cloth or canvas, ordinarily red in color, which they slip between their thighs and hold up with a band. To this band or belt they attach, by means of a long ribbon, their leggings, that drop from mid-thigh to instep. These are usually scarlet, and sewn from the outside so that they can be easily put on and taken off, with a strip about two or three finger-breadths wide left beyond the seam which they adorn with *wampum* or bugle beads arranged in patterns. Their shoes have neither sole nor heel. They are made of deer or elk skins cured and tanned a hazelnut brown, and very elegantly fashioned. Along the uppers they make an ornamentation with porcupine quills, which they flatten and paint a very pretty red, and on the outside part of the shoe that goes around the instep they put a number of little tassels made of a tin cylinder packed with deer hair colored red, which, as they move, produce a pleasing rustle.

The women also wear European dresses, draped over their shoulders and coming down only to their knees, their legs and feet covered with the same stockings and shoes already described above. They, too, wear earrings, bracelets and similar ornaments, and a few of them have pointed caps decorated with glass beads or *wampum*. When the women are young they have, as I said, pretty, though swarthy, faces, with wide, flat noses; but as they grow old, and perhaps also out of slovenliness, they are utterly disgusting and revolting. Indian women give birth almost without pain. When the children are born, they tie them to a small board with bands, resting their feet on a little piece of wood that joins the board at right angles; and if they are traveling, they carry this behind their shoulders more or less in the same way as the Eskimo do. The occupations of the women consist in raising a little corn, working on the canoes, on stockings, shoes, and other ornaments, and in making birch-bark baskets and pouches, and also dishes and bowls that hold water, which they use on their journeys.

The main occupations of the men are fishing and hunting, which provide them with food, and skins, that they then use to buy what they need from European traders. They have a fixed season for the hunt, during which they leave their villages. When they have to stay in the woods a long time, they build for themselves temporary huts with tree branches to protect themselves against the inclemencies of the season. Their food consists of maize, or corn, and the flesh of beaver, deer, elk, and other animals, or birds, fish, and shellfish. They preserve meat by drying and smoking it. Their ordinary beverages were formerly water and drinks made from the spruce, sugar maple, or birch; but after the introduction of rum and brandy, they preferred to the other healthy beverages these poisons, which wrought there more devastation than war, smallpox, and plague, and continue still to reduce the population and to pervert the excellent qualities of these tribes. The Abenaki are (like the other Indians) sincere and frank in their behavior, and if they never forget an injury, they are incapable of forgetting a favor. The religion of the inhabitants of this village is Catholicism, and a missionary is sent out of Montreal, who lives among them, baptizes the children, performs weddings, and instructs them in religion. A short time ago, however, a number of young Indians, persuaded perhaps by some Presbyterian ministers, changed religion. Hence there arose such dissensions between the two parties that the missionary, fearful every night of being killed, withdrew to an island in Penobscot Bay, where he was followed by some of the older Indians.

(Luigi Castiglioni's *Viaggio: Travels in the United States of North America 1785–1787*. Translated and edited by Antonio Pace. Syracuse: Syracuse University Press, 1983, 37–41. By permission of the publisher.)

[Having noted the inroads of European influences in Indian culture, the itinerant Italian stepped into a Penobscot canoe and resumed his American journey.]

Epilogue

---◆---

The Education of
Henry David Thoreau,
1846–1857

[Two and a half centuries after Champlain and Popham sought out Indian guides for their dawnland expeditions, Henry David Thoreau enlisted the services of Penobscot Indians for his trips through the backwoods of Maine. Like many of his European predecessors, Thoreau entered Indian country with preconceived notions about Indians; like many of his predecessors he found that contact with real Indians challenged some of his assumptions. He admitted "I have much to learn of the Indian."

Thoreau had an enduring interest in Indians. He read widely and he compiled thousands of pages of notebooks about them. But for most of his life he seems to have viewed "the Indian" as a symbol—of nature, freedom, wisdom, a simpler way of life. Like Europeans who imagined "the noble savage," he felt that contact with whites corrupted Indians; yet he feared that holding on to old ways spelled the Indians' doom.

Thoreau's three trips to Maine—in 1846, 1853, and 1857—brought him into extended contact with Indian people, as opposed to the stereotypical Indians of his imagination. His Penobscot guides, Joe Attean in 1853 and Joe Polis in 1857, taught him much about travel and survival in the woods. But they also wore white men's clothes and spoke English. Attean whistled American tunes and worked as a lumberman; Polis, a Protestant, sang Catholic hymns in Penobscot, bought land, hired white laborers to work for him, and subscribed to a newspaper. Thoreau's return trips to Maine and the time he spent with Attean and Polis allowed him a glimpse beneath the surface acculturation that first impressed casual observers. The following extracts illustrate stages in his education about the Indian inhabitants.

In 1846, Thoreau saw Indian Island for the first time. Seeking spiritual rejuvenation in Maine, he was disappointed and depressed by the sight of an Indian taking his pelts to Old Town to trade for alcohol and by the external appearance of the village.]

This picture will do to put before the Indian's history, that is, the history of his extinction. In 1837 there were three hun-

dred and sixty two souls left of this tribe. The island seemed
deserted today, yet I observed some new houses among the
weather-stained ones, as if the tribe had still a design upon life;
but generally they have a very shabby, forlorn, and cheerless
look, being all back side and woodshed, not homesteads, even
Indian homesteads, but instead of home or abroad-steads, for
their life is *domi aut militiæ*, at home or at war, or now rather
venatus, that is, a hunting, and most of the latter. The church is
the only trim-looking building, but that is not Abenaki, that was
Rome's doings. Good Canadian it may be, but it is poor Indian.
These were once a powerful tribe. Politics are all the rage with
them now. I even thought a row of wigwams, with a dance of
powwows, and a prisoner tortured at the stake, would be more
respectable than this.

*[Seven years later, Thoreau was back. This time, instead of cultural decay,
he noted cultural survival. He and Joe Attean spent a night in the hunting
camp of three Abenakis, "two of them apparently mixed Indian and white." The
Indians were drying moose skins and smoking the meat on racks, as they had
done for generations.]*

While lying there listening to the Indians, I amused myself
by trying to guess at their subject by their gestures, or some
proper name introduced. There can be no more startling evidence of their being a distinct and comparatively aboriginal race,
than to hear this unaltered Indian language, which the white
man cannot speak or understand. We may suspect change and
deterioration in almost every other particular but the language
which is wholly unintelligible to us. It took me by surprise,
though I had found so many arrow-heads, and convinced me
that the Indian was not the invention of historians and poets. It
was a purely wild and primitive American sound, as much as
the barking of a *chickaree,* and I could not understand a syllable
of it; but Paugus, had he been there, would have understood it.

These Abenakis gossiped, laughed, and jested in the language in which Eliot's Indian Bible is written, the language which has been spoken in New England who shall say how long? These were the sounds that issued from the wigwams of this country before Columbus was born; they have not yet died away; and, with remarkably few exceptions, the language of their fore-fathers is still copious enough for them. I felt that I stood, or rather lay, as near to the primitive man of America, that night, as any of its dicoverers ever did.

[On his final trip Thoreau consistently referred to his guide as "the Indian." Yet he did not portray Joe Polis as simply a romantic symbol or "the last of his race." Instead, through incident, conversation, and comment, Polis emerged in Thoreau's writing as a complex and interesting individual, one of the most realistic Native American characters in nineteenth-century literature. Ralph Waldo Emerson ranked Joe Polis, along with John Brown and Walt Whitman, as one of the three men most influential in the last years of Thoreau's life. Yet, the writer's parting from his Indian teacher produced no pronouncements on Indian life].

This was the last that I saw of Joe Polis. We took the last train, and reached Bangor that night.

[Like most Europeans before him, Thoreau never quite lost his condescension and his prejudices, but at last, between individuals, there was some understand-ing and quiet respect.¹]

(Henry David Thoreau, *The Maine Woods* [Boston: Ticknor & Fields, 1864], 5, 139–40, 304.)

Notes

Preface (pp. ix–xiii)

1. Things are beginning to change, however, as historians probe the northern frontier; see Gregory H. Nobles, "Breaking into the Backcountry: New Approaches to the Early American Frontier, 1750–1800," *William and Mary Quarterly*, 3d ser., 46 (October 1989): 641–70.

Introduction: Dawnland Frontiers (pp. 1–23)

1. For background on the Abenakis, see William A. Haviland and Marjory W. Power, *The Original Vermonters: Native Inhabitants, Past and Present* (Hanover: University Press of New England, 1981); Dean Snow, "Eastern Abenaki," and Gordon M. Day, "Western Abenaki," in Bruce G. Trigger, ed., *Handbook of North American Indians* (Washington, D.C.: Smithsonian Institution, 1978), vol. 15, *Northeast*, 137–47; 148–59; Kenneth M. Morrison, *The Embattled Northeast: The Elusive Ideal of Alliance in Abenaki-Euramerican Relations* (Berkeley: University of California Press, 1984).

2. For example, Alvin H. Morrison, "Penobscot Country: Disagreement Over Who Lived There in the 17th Century Needs Resolving—If Possible," in William Cowan, ed., *Papers of the Ninth Algonquian Conference* (Ottawa: Carleton University, 1978), 47–54; and Bruce J. Bourque, "Ethnicity on the Maritime Peninsula, 1600–1759," *Ethnohistory* 36 (Summer 1989): 257–84, discusses the population movements that have given rise to disagreement among anthropologists about the identities of Maine's native populations.

3. Lieutenant John Montresor, "Journal of a Scout, 1761," in Kenneth Roberts, comp., *March to Quebec: Journals of the Members of Arnold's Expedition* (1938; reprint, Camden: Down East, 1980), 19.

4. Captain John Smith, "A Description of New England" (London, 1616), in Philip L. Barbour, ed., *The Complete Works of Captain John Smith*, 3 vols. (Chapel Hill: University of North Carolina Press, 1986), 1:329, 339.

5. Christopher Levett, "A Voyage into New England, begun in 1623 and ended in 1624" (London, 1628), in *Collections of the Massachusetts Historical Society*, 3d ser., 8 (1843): 179.

6. Charles E. Clark, *The Eastern Frontier: The Settlement of Northern New England 1610–1763* (New York: Knopf, 1970), chap. 2; D. W. Meinig, *The Shaping of America: A Geographical Perspective on 500 Years of History* (New Haven: Yale University Press, 1986), vol. 1, *Atlantic America, 1492–1800*, 87–90; Faith Harrington, "Sea Tenure in Seventeenth Century New England: Native Americans and Englishmen in the Sphere of Marine Resources, 1600–1630," Ph.D. diss., University of California at Berkeley, 1985.

7. Clark, *Eastern Frontier*, chap. 3 and p. 189; Meinig, *Atlantic America*, 91–92.

On Puritan-Indian relations, see the widely differing interpretations in Alden Vaughan, *New England Frontier: Puritans and Indians 1620–1675,* rev. ed. (New York: W. W. Norton & Co., 1979); and Francis Jennings, *The Invasion of America: Indians, Colonialism, and the Cant of Conquest* (New York: W. W. Norton & Co., 1976); as well as Neal Salisbury, *Manitou and Providence: Indians, Europeans, and the Making of New England, 1500–1643* (New York: Oxford University Press, 1982).

   8. Clark, *Eastern Frontier,* 175, 227, 230; Meinig, *Atlantic America,* 94; Douglas Edward Leach, *The Northern Colonial Frontier 1607–1763* (Albuquerque: University of New Mexico Press, 1974), 131; Jere R. Daniell, *Colonial New Hampshire: A History* (Millwood, N.Y.: KTO Press, 1981), 141; Ralph Stuart Wallace, "The Scotch-Irish of Provincial New Hampshire" (Ph.D. diss., University of New Hampshire, 1984).

   9. Bernard Bailyn, *Voyagers to the West: A Passage in the Peopling of America on the Eve of the Revolution* (New York: Vintage, 1988), 604–37; *Collections of the Vermont Historical Society* 3 (1943): 105–262; Clark, *Eastern Frontier,* 353–54; David C. Smith, "Maine's Changing Landscape to 1820," in Charles E. Clark, James S. Leaman, and Karen Bowden, eds., *Maine in the Early Republic: From Revolution to Statehood* (Hanover: University Press of New England, 1988), chap. 1.

   10. Clark, *Eastern Frontier,* 197ff.

   11. Maps depicting these movements are in Leach, *Northern Colonial Frontier,* 34, 116, 130; and Bailyn, *Voyagers to the West,* 11.

   12. Clark, *Eastern Frontier,* 176; Daniell, *Colonial New Hampshire,* 141, 168; William D. Piersen, *Black Yankees: The Development of an Afro-American Subculture in Eighteenth-Century New England* (Amherst: University of Massachusetts Press, 1988), xi, 15, 19–20.

   13. Alfred Goldsworthy Bailey, *The Conflict of European and Eastern Algonkian Cultures 1540–1700,* 2d ed. (Toronto: University of Toronto Press, 1969), 92; Olive Patricia Dickason, "The French and the Abenaki: A Study in Frontier Politics," *Vermont History* 58 (Spring 1990), 89.

   14. The Indians to whom Smith referred—the "Tarrantines"—were probably Micmacs. Smith, "A Description of New England," 338; compare L. F. S. Upton, *Micmacs and Colonists: Indian-White Relations in the Maritimes, 1713–1867* (Vancouver: University of British Columbia Press, 1979), 26–27; Kenneth Silverman, ed., *Selected Letters of Cotton Mather* (Baton Rouge: Louisiana State University Press, 1971), 144; Cotton Mather, "New Assaults from the Indians," in Alden T. Vaughan and Edward W. Clark, eds., *Puritans among the Indians: Accounts of Captivity and Redemption* (Cambridge: Belknap Press of Harvard University Press, 1981), 137.

   15. Dean R. Snow, *The Archaeology of New England* (New York: Academic Press, 1980), 38.

   16. Reuben Gold Thwaites, ed., *The Jesuit Relations and Allied Documents,* 73 vols. (Cleveland: Burrows Bros, 1896–1901, reprinted), 3:105; Thomas Gorges to Ferdinando Gorges, Jan. 22, 1642, Robert E. Moody, ed., *The Letters of Thomas Gorges, Deputy Governor of the Province of Maine 1640–1643* (Portland: Maine Historical Society, 1978), 110; compare, James Phinney Baxter, ed., *Sir Ferdinando Gorges and His Province of Maine,* 3 vols. (1890 reprint, New York: Burt Franklin, 1967), 2:77. Virginia P. Miller, "Aboriginal Micmac Population: A Review of the Evidence," *Ethnohistory* 23 (Spring 1976): 117–27, discusses the population decline to which Biard refers.

   17. See, for example, Fernand Braudel, *The Structures of Everyday Life: The Limits of the Possible* (New York: Harper & Row, 1985), 70–98; Richard I. Melvoin, *New*

England Outpost: War and Society in Colonial Deerfield (New York: W. W. Norton, 1989), 195; Clark, *Eastern Frontier,* 118, 274–77.

18. William Cronon, *Changes in the Land: Indians, Colonists, and the Ecology of New England* (New York: Hill and Wang, 1983), esp. 14–15, 53; Peter A. Thomas, "Contrastive Subsistence Strategies and Land Use as Factors for Understanding Indian-White Relations in New England," *Ethnohistory* 23 (Winter 1976): 14–15; Smith, "Maine's Changing Landscape to 1820."

19. John Canup, *Out of the Wilderness: The Emergence of an American Identity in Colonial New England* (Middletown, Conn.: Weslyan University Press, 1990), chaps. 3–5; compare, for example, Carl Bridenbaugh, "Right New-England; or, The Adaptable Puritans," *Proceedings of the Massachusetts Historical Society* 88 (1976): 3–18, reprinted in Bridenbaugh, *Early Americans* (New York: Oxford University Press, 1981), 77–91. Bridenbaugh pays less attention to interactions with Indians but discusses the "reciprocal influences operating between man and nature that transformed the Englishmen of 1640 into the Yankees of 1690." He portrays New England Puritans as "amazingly flexible" rather than rigid in their responses to their new world.

20. For example, Alaric Faulkner, "Gentility on the Frontiers of Acadia, 1653–1674: An Archaeological Perspective," paper presented at the Dublin Seminar for New England Folklife, 1989, finds that French entrepreneurs and "would-be aristocrats" in coastal outposts retained fashionable trappings of status even as they struggled with the harsh realities of life on the dawnland frontier.

21. Chester B. Price, "Indian Trails of New Hampshire," *New Hampshire Archaeologist* 8 (1956): 2–13; John Moody, "The Native American Legacy," in Jane C. Beck, ed., *Always in Season: Folk Art and Traditional Culture in Vermont* (Montpelier: Vermont Council on the Arts, 1982), 58.

22. John McPhee, *The Survival of the Bark Canoe* (New York: Farrar, Straus, Giroux, 1975), 55; Nathaniel Bouton, ed., *New Hampshire Provincial Papers,* 7 vols. (Concord, Nashua and Manchester, 1867–1873), 3 (1869): 290.

23. James Axtell, *After Columbus: Essays in the Ethnohistory of Colonial North America* (New York: Oxford University Press, 1988), 179. For additional studies of European reactions to first encounters, see Robert F. Berkhofer, *The White Man's Indian: Images of the American Indian from Columbus to the Present* (New York: Alfred A. Knopf, 1978), part 1; Gary B. Nash, *Red, White, and Black: The Peoples of Early America* (Englewood Cliffs, N.J.: Prentice Hall, 1974), 34–43; Thomas D. Matijasic, "Reflected Values: Sixteenth Century Europeans View the Indians of North America," *American Indian Culture and Research Journal* 11 (1987): 31–50; Alfred A. Cave, "Richard Hakluyt's Savages: The Influence of 16th Century Travel Narratives on English Indian Policy in North America," *International Social Science Review* 60, no. 1 (1985): 3–24. On the French in particular, see Cornelius Jaenen, *Friend and Foe: Aspects of French-Amerindian Culture Contact in the Sixteenth and Seventeenth Centuries* (New York: Columbia University Press, 1976), chap. 1 and Olive Patricia Dickason, *The Myth of the Savage* (Edmonton: University of Alberta Press, 1984). For a discussion of early Indian views of Europeans, see Axtell, *After Columbus,* chap. 8. For Verrazzano's account, see chapter 1 of this book, document 2.

24. Kenneth M. Morrison, "Montagnais Missionization in Early New France: The Syncretic Imperative," *American Indian Culture and Research Journal* 10, no. 3 (1986), 1–23. For discussion of the question, "Were Indian Conversions Bona Fide?" see Axtell, *After Columbus,* chap. 7. James P. Ronda, "'We Are Well as We Are': An

Indian Critique of Seventeenth Century Christian Missions," *William and Mary Quarterly,* 3d ser., 34 (1977): 66–82; and Cornelius J. Jaenen, "Amerindian Views of French Culture in the 17th Century," *Canadian Historical Review* 45 (1974): 261–91, offer additional insights.

25. Jennings, *Invasion of America*; David L. Ghere, "Mistranslation and Misinformation: Diplomacy on the Maine Frontier, 1725–1755," *American Indian Culture and Research Journal* 8 (1984): 3–26.

26. Leach, *Northern Colonial Frontier,* 109–25; Daniell, *Colonial New Hampshire,* 108–14; Daniel S. Smith, "The Demographic History of Colonial New England," *Journal of Economic History* 32 (1979): 179.

27. Fred Anderson, *A People's Army: Massachusetts Soldiers and Society in the Seven Years's War* (New York: W. W. Norton, 1985), 27–28.

28. See chapter 4 of this book, documents 4 and 24.

29. Clark, *Eastern Frontier,* 263; Hugh D. McLellan, *History of Gorham, Maine* (1903; facs. reprint, Somersworth, N.H.: New England History Press, 1980), 36–38; "Captivity of Mrs. Johnson," in *Indian Narratives* (Claremont, N.H.: Tracy & Brothers, 1854), 135; "The Last of the Pennacooks," *Farmer's Monthly Visitor* 13, nos. 9–10 (September–October 1853): 293.

30. Massachusetts Archives, 32:99; "Journal of Phineas Stevens," in Newton D. Mereness, ed., *Travels in the American Colonies* (New York: Macmillan Co., 1916); Bouton, ed., *New Hampshire Provincial Papers,* 6:236; "Account Book of Phineas Stevens, kept at Fort #4, Charlestown, N.H., 1752–1756," University of Vermont, Bailey/Howe Library, Stevens Family Papers, Box 1, folder 8, microfilm copy at the Silsby Library, Charlestown, N.H.

31. Compare, Richard White, *The Roots of Dependency: Subsistence, Environment, and Social Change among the Choctaws, Pawnees and Navajos* (Lincoln: University of Nebraska Press, 1983), 318–19.

32. Peter A. Thomas, "Bridging the Cultural Gap: Indian/White Relations," in John W. Ifkovic and Martin Kaufman, eds., *Early Settlement in the Connecticut Valley* (Historic Deerfield, Inc., and Institute for Massachusetts Studies, Westfield State College, 1984), 5–21. Compare the relative stability in relations between settlers and Indians in the 1640s and 1650s in Neal Salisbury, "Social Relationships on a Moving Frontier: Natives and Settlers in Southern New England 1638–1675," *Man in the Northeast* 33 (1987): 89–99.

33. For example, Harry Andrew Wright, ed., *Indian Deeds of Hampton County* (Springfield, Mass.: 1905), 125–27, 129–33; "Lease of certain lands on the Missisquoi River by Abenakis of Missisquoi to James Robertson," University of Vermont, Bailey/Howe Library, Stevens Family Papers, Box 9, folder 1.

34. Reuben G. Thwaites, ed., *New Voyages to North-America by Baron de Lahontan,* 2 vols. (Chicago: A. C. McClurg and Co., 1905), 1:90; "A Narrative of the Captivity of Mrs. Johnson," in *Indian Narratives,* 131, 140.

35. Melvoin, *New England Outpost: War and Society in Colonial Deerfield,* 153–54.

36. James Axtell, "The White Indians of Colonial America," *William and Mary Quarterly,* 3d ser., 32 (1975): 55–88, reprinted in *The European and the Indian: Essays in the Ethnohistory of Colonial North America* (New York: Oxford University Press, 1981); Alden T. Vaughan and Daniel K. Richter, "Crossing the Cultural Divide: Indians and New Englanders, 1605–1763," *Proceedings of the American Antiquarian Society* 90, part 1 (October 1980): 23–99; Colin G. Calloway, "An Uncertain Destiny:

Indian Captivities on the Upper Connecticut River," *Journal of American Studies* 17 (1983): 189–210.

37. For the western Abenaki phase of the dispersal, see Colin G. Calloway, *The Western Abenakis of Vermont, 1600–1800: War, Migration, and the Survival of an Indian People* (Norman: University of Oklahoma Press, 1990), or his "Green Mountain Diaspora: Indian Population Movements in Vermont, c. 1600–1800," *Vermont History* 54 (1986): 197–228.

Chapter 1: First Encounters (pp. 25–56)

1. Braudel, *The Structures of Everyday Life*, 63. H. P. Biggar, ed., *Works of Samuel de Champlain*, 6 vols. (Toronto: Champlain Society, 1922–36), 1:278, 393; *Dictionary of Canadian Biography* (University of Toronto Press, 1966), 1:506. Vaughan, *New England Frontier*, 22–23, 69–75; Canup, *Out of the Wilderness*, 94–95; Neal Salisbury, "Squanto: Last of the Patuxets," in David G. Sweet and Gary B. Nash, eds., *Struggle and Survival in Colonial America* (Berkeley: University of California Press, 1981), 228–46. I am grateful to Harald Prins for drawing my attention to Messamouet.

2. David B. and Alison M. Quinn, eds., *The English New England Voyages 1602–1608* (London: The Hakluyt Society, 1983), 117.

3. J. B. Harley, "Victims of a Map: New England Cartography and the Native Americans," paper presented at the "Land of Norumbega Conference," Portland, Me., December 1988.

4. J. R. Miller, *Skyscrapers Hide the Heavens: A History of Indian-White Relations in Canada* (Toronto: University of Toronto Press, 1989), 23–24.

5. C. O. Sauer, *Sixteenth Century North America: The Land and the People as Seen by the Europeans* (Berkeley: University of California Press, 1971), 6. James F. Pendergast, "Native Encounters with Europeans in the Sixteenth Century in the Region Now known as Vermont," *Vermont History* 58 (Spring 1990), 113–18, discusses the insubstantial evidence that Cabot landed on the Gulf of Maine or elsewhere on the New England coast.

6. Quinn and Quinn, eds., *The English New England Voyages*, 8–9, 88.

7. Joseph Nicolar, *The Life and Traditions of the Red Man* (Bangor, Me.: C. H. Glass & Co., 1893), 31, 98; compare, William S. Simmons, *Spirit of the New England Tribes: Indian History and Folklore, 1620–1984* (Hanover: University Press of New England, 1986), 67–68, 71–72; Peter Nabokov, ed., *Native American Testimony: An Anthology of Indian and White Relations* (New York: Thomas Y. Crowell, 1978), 1–17; and Christopher L. Miller, *Prophetic Worlds: Indians and Whites on the Columbia Plateau* (New Brunswick, N.J.: Rutgers University Press, 1985).

8. Floating islands or island canoes are familiar motifs in the folklore of Algonquian peoples in northern New England and eastern Canada; Simmons, *Spirit of the New England Tribes*, 65–66; Bruce G. Trigger, *Natives and Newcomers: Canada's "Heroic Age" Reconsidered* (Montreal: McGill-Queens University Press, 1985), 126; Thwaites, ed., *Jesuit Relations*, 5:119–21.

9. Verrazzano had met Narragansett Indians farther south who knew nothing of European trade and had given freely to the Europeans.

10. The term "pulse" referred to seed-bearing plants, such as beans and peas. These Indians may have produced no such crops, but elsewhere in northern New England, Indians were growing beans, squash and corn long before Europeans arrived.

11. ". . . such as showing their buttocks and laughing." Wroth, *Voyages,* 141n.

12. H. P. Biggar, ed., *The Voyages of Jacques Cartier* (Ottawa: Publications of the Public Archives of Canada, 1924), 49–53.

13. Bruce J. Bourque and Ruth Holmes Whitehead, "Tarrantines and the Introduction of European Trade Goods in the Gulf of Maine," *Ethnohistory* 32 (1985): 322–41; "Divers Voyages and Northern Discoveries," in Samuel Purchas, ed., *Hakluytus Posthumus, or Purchas His Pilgrims,* 20 vols. (Glasgow: Maclehose and Sons, 1905–1907), 13:346–47.

14. The "baske" or Biscay Shallope was a style of boat developed by Basque fishermen for whaling and later adopted for a variety of uses.

15. A port in the Bay of Biscay.

16. Dean R. Snow, "The Ethnohistoric Baseline of the Eastern Abenaki," *Ethnohistory* 23 (1976): 293–94, discusses the name Bessabez or Bashaba and the tendency of English writers to confuse it for a title rather than as the name of a single important leader. For further discussion, see Alvin H. Morrison, "Membertou's Raid on the Chouacoet 'Almouchiquois'—The Micmac Sack of Saco in 1607," in William Cowan, ed., *Papers of the Sixth Algonquian Conference* (Ottawa: National Museum of Canada, 1975), 145–58.

17. Micmacs and probably Montagnais.

18. For detailed observations on this encounter, see Quinn and Quinn, eds., *The English New England Voyages,* 267–270nn.

19. Crew member Owen Griffin had previously gone ashore with the Abenakis.

20. For example, *Collection de Manuscrits . . . Rélatifs à la Nouvelle-France,* 4 vols. (Quebec: Imprimérie à Coté et Cie, 1883–1885), 2:116, 3:182–85; Trigger, *Natives and Newcomers,* 130, 133, 173; Axtell, *After Columbus,* 149–52.

21. Davies' journal ends at this point. The remainder of the narrative comes from William Strachey's "Historie of Travaile into Virginia," also reproduced in Burrage, ed., *Early English and French Voyages.*

22. Quinn and Quinn, eds., *The English New England Voyages,* 411 n. 3. James P. Ronda, *Lewis and Clark among the Indians* (Lincoln: University of Nebraska Press, 1984), chap. 2, provides an excellent analysis of the Teton encounter.

23. Thwaites, ed., *The Jesuit Relations and Allied Documents,* 2:45–47, 3:223; Kenneth M. Morrison, *The Embattled Northeast: The Elusive Ideal of Alliance in Abenaki-Euramerican Relations* (Berkeley: University of California Press, 1984), 74.

24. G. M. Wrong, ed., *The Long Journey to the Country of the Hurons* (Toronto: The Champlain Society, 1939), 138.

25. Snow, "The Ethnohistoric Baseline of the Eastern Abenaki," 299–300; Snow, *The Archaeology of New England,* 55–56.

26. Near what is now Fryeburg, Maine.

Chapter 2: Frontiers of Spirit and Soul (pp. 57–89)

1. James Axtell, *The Invasion Within: The Contest of Cultures in Colonial North America* (New York: Oxford University Press, 1985), forms the first volume of a trilogy examining *The Cultural Origins of North America.*

2. Trigger, *Natives and Newcomers,* 201, 293–95; Axtell, *The Invasion Within,* 49–54, 71ff.

3. "Traces of an Indian Legend," *The Catholic World* 22 (1875–1876): 278–81;

National Archives of Canada, Ottawa, MGI C¹¹A, 9:373. Gordon M. Day, *The Mot Loups of Father Mathevet* (Ottawa: National Museum of Man, 1975).

4. Axtell, *The Invasion Within*, 248; Thwaites, ed., *Jesuit Relations*, 28:225, 62:161; Alaric and Gretchen Faulkner, *The French at Pentagoet 1635–1674: An Archaeological Portrait of the Acadian Frontier* (The New Brunswick Museum and the Maine Historic Preservation Commission, 1987), 43.

5. National Archives of Canada, National Map Collection, M3/900/1713; Peter A. Thomas, "In the Maelstrom of Change: Indian Trade and Culture Process in the Middle Connecticut River Valley, 1635–1665" (Ph.D. diss., University of Massachusetts, 1979), 375–77; *Calendar of State Papers, Colonial Series, America and the West Indies* (London: His Majesty's Stationery Office), 1700:401.

6. *Collections of the Maine Historical Society*, 2d ser., 23 (1916): 268.

7. Axtell, *The Invasion Within*, chaps. 5–6; Morrison, *The Embattled Northeast*, chap. 3, quotation at p. 99, Bigot reference at p. 221; Robert Conkling, "Legitimacy and Conversion in Social Change: The Case of French Missionaries and the Northeastern Algonkian," *Ethnohistory* 21 (1974): 1–24; George R. Hammell, "Mythical Realities and European Contact in the Northeast During the Sixteenth and Seventeenth Centuries," *Man in the Northeast* 33 (1987): 63–87. Compare, John Webster Grant, *Moon of Wintertime: Missionaries and the Indians of Canada in Encounter since 1534* (Toronto: University of Toronto Press, 1984); William Blake Trask, ed., *Letters of Colonel Thomas Westbrook and Others Relative to Indian Affairs in Maine, 1722–1726* (Boston: George E. Littlefield, 1901), 2; E. B. O.'Callaghan, ed., *Documents Relating to the Colonial History of the State of New York*, 15 vols. (Albany: Weed, Parsons, & Co., 1855), 9:441.

8. Axtell, *The Invasion Within*, 250–52; *Collections of the Maine Historical Society* 4 (1856): 129, 131; 2d ser., 11 (1908): 13; 23 (1916): 29; Silverman, ed., *Selected Letters of Cotton Mather*, 244.

9. Axtell, *The Invasion Within*, chap. 6; Conkling, "Legitimacy and Conversion."

10. In fact, Abenakis frequently requested that the liquor trade be stopped or at least curtailed.

11. For controversial discussion of the idea that Indian hunters "declared war" on animals, see Calvin Martin, *Keepers of the Game: Indian-Animal Relationships and the Fur Trade* (Berkeley: University of California Press, 1978). Focusing on the neighboring Micmac, as well as the Ojibwa, Martin hypothesizes that Indian overkill in the fur trade era took the form of a "war of retaliation" by natives who blamed the animals for visitations of epidemic disease. Dean Snow considers Martin's explanation oversimplified and inadequate for the eastern Abenakis; see Shepard Krech, III, *Indians, Animals and the Fur Trade: A Critique of Keepers of the Game* (Athens, Ga.: University of Georgia Press, 1981), 59–71.

12. On Eliot's work among the Indians of southern New England, see Axtell, *The Invasion Within*, 218–41; Neal Salisbury, "Red Puritans: The 'Praying Indians' of Massachusetts Bay and John Eliot," *William and Mary Quarterly*, 3d ser., 31 (January 1974): 27–54; and Henry W. Bowden and James P. Ronda, eds., *John Eliot's Indian Dialogues: A Study in Cultural Interaction* (Westport, Conn.: Greenwood Press, 1980). On Wanalancet, see Colin G. Calloway, "Wanalancet and Kancamagus: Indian Strategy and Leadership on the New Hampshire Frontier," *Historical New Hampshire* 43 (Winter 1988): 264–90.

13. James P. Ronda, "The Sillery Experiment: A Jesuit Indian Village in New France, 1637–1663," *American Indian Culture and Research Journal* 3 (1979): 1–8. On

migration to another key mission, see Gordon M. Day, *The Identity of the St. Francis Indians* (Ottawa: National Museum of Man, 1981).

14. Mather himself.

15. *Collections of the Maine Historical Society,* 2d ser., 23 (1916): 29.

16. *Dictionary of Canadian Biography* 2 (1969): 524–44.

17. Quoted in Morrison, *The Embattled Northeast,* 178.

18. J. Pickering, ed., "A Dictionary of the Abnaki Language in North America (1691–1722)," *Memoirs of the American Academy of Arts & Sciences,* new series, 1 (1833): 375–565.

19. For a discussion of this famous attack, see Fannie H. Eckstorm, "The Attack on Norridgewock, 1724," *New England Quarterly* 7 (1934): 541–78; and Kenneth Morrison, "Sebastian Racle and Norridgewock, 1724: The Eckstorm Thesis Reconsidered," *Maine Historical Society Quarterly* 14 (1974): 76–97. On the history of Norridgewock, see Harald E. L. Prins and Bruce J. Bourque, "Norridgewock: Village Translocation on the New England-Acadian Frontier," *Man in the Northeast* 33 (1987): 132–58.

20. O'Callaghan, ed., *Documents Relating to the Colonial History of New York,* 8:937–38.

21. White Head (La Tête Blanche) was the war chief Grey Lock; *Dictionary of Canadian Biography* 3 (1974): 265–67; Colin G. Calloway, "Gray Lock's War," *Vermont History* 55 (1987): 212–27.

22. Jerome Atecuando was a chief at St. Francis and a noted orator of the Abenakis; *Dictionary of Canadian Biography* 3 (1974): 20–21.

23. Colonel Allan to Lovell, July 17, 1779, Solomon Lovell Papers, Massachusetts Historical Society, Boston.

Chapter 3: Dawnland Diplomacy (pp. 91–131)

1. For numerous examples of such proceedings, see *Collections of the Maine Historical Society,* 2d ser., 23 (1916): passim.

2. National Archives of Canada, MG 18, H-27:235, quoted in Cornelius J. Jaenen, "Characteristics of French-Amerindian Contact in New France," in Stanley Palmer and Dennis Reinhartz, eds., *Essays on the History of North American Discovery and Exploration* (College Station: Texas A & M University Press, 1988), 91.

3. For example, *Collections of the Maine Historical Society,* 2d ser., 11 (1908): 461–63.

4. David Ghere, "Mistranslations and Misinformation: Diplomacy on the Maine Indian Frontier, 1725–1755," *American Indian Culture and Research Journal* 8 (1984): 3–26; and his "Abenaki Factionalism, Emigration and Social Continuity: Indian Society in Northern New England, 1725–1760" (Ph.D. diss., University of Maine, 1988).

5. See document 1 of this chapter, and Calloway, "Wanalancet and Kancamagus."

6. Clark, *Eastern Frontier,* 263; Mass. Archives 29:36off.; *Collections of the Maine Historical Society,* 2d ser., 11 (1908): 173; 23 (1916): 257–62.

7. James Axtell, ed., "The Vengeful Women of Marblehead: Robert Roules' Deposition of 1677," *William and Mary Quarterly,* 3d ser., 31 (1974): 650–52.

8. *Collections of the Maine Historical Society,* 1st ser., 4 (1856): 145–67, for the full text of the proceedings at Falmouth.

9. For discussions of Anglo-Abenaki treaties, see Ghere, "Mistranslations and Misinformation" and Morrison, *The Embattled Northeast*, 109–13, 128, and passim.

10. The treaty is in *Collections of the Maine Historical Society*, 3:361; and Bouton, ed., *New Hampshire Provincial Papers*, 3:693. See also James Phinney Baxter, *The Pioneers of New France in New England* (Albany: Joel Munsell's Sons, 1894), 68–84.

11. Henry F. DePuy, *A Bibliography of the English Colonial Treaties with the American Indians* (New York: Lenox Club, 1917), 14.

12. Morrison, *The Embattled Northeast*, 107, 169–71; Jennings, *Invasion of America*; Ghere, "Mistranslations and Misinformation"; James H. Merrell, *The Indians' New World: Catawbas and Their Neighbors from European Contact through the Era of Removal* (Chapel Hill: University of North Carolina Press, 1989), 150.

13. Jennings, *Invasion of America*, 314–16.

14. Calloway, "Wanalancet and Kancamagus," 277–79.

15. Morrison, *The Embattled Northeast*, 128.

16. The word is "also" in the printed text of the treaty, but it is clear from the signatures that it should read "alias."

17. The brothers Father Jacques and Father Vincent Bigot were "toward Amonoscogin" on the Kennebec River; Sebastien Rasles was at Norridgewock.

18. Ghere, "Mistranslations and Misinformation." A full account of the negotiations is in *Collections of the Maine Historical Society* 3 (1853): 377–447.

19. For a similar example, see *Collections of the Maine Historical Society*, 2d ser., 23 (1916): 208–9.

20. The French governor.

21. Stevens probably refers to the treaty at St. George's Fort in 1752.

22. The Mohawks referred to here were the Caughnawagas; the possibility of Ottawa involvement stemmed from their relationship to the Caughnawagas and Abenakis in the emerging confederacy of Canadian nations. The Seven Nations of Canada developed as a loose confederacy of tribes from the mission communities along the St. Lawrence. It included the Hurons of Lorette, the Mohawks of Caughnawaga, the Mohawks of St. Regis, the Abenakis of Saint Francis, and the Mohawks, Algonkins and Nipissings from Oka, the Lake of the Two Mountains village.

23. The Tweetwa or Twightee Indians were the Miamis of Ohio; various tribes were called Flat heads.

24. Paul Brodeur, *Restitution: The Land Claims of the Mashpee, Passamaquoddy and Penobscot Indians of New England* (Boston: Northeastern University Press, 1985).

Chapter 4: War in the Dawnland (pp. 133–175)

1. John K. Mahon, "Anglo-American Methods of Indian Warfare, 1676–1794," *Mississippi Valley Historical Review* 45 (1958–59), 254–75; Peter E. Russell, "Redcoats in the Wilderness: British Officers and Irregular Warfare in Europe and America, 1740 to 1760," *William and Mary Quarterly* 3rd ser. 35 (1978), 629–52; Anderson, *A People's Army*, 48.

2. Calloway, *The Western Abenakis of Vermont*, passim.

3. Ray Gonyea, "The 1609 Champlain Expedition," in *The Original People: Native Americans in the Champlain Valley* (Clinton Country Historical Association, 1988), 26.

4. Bruce G. Trigger, "The Mohawk-Mahican War, 1624–1628: The Establishment of a Pattern," *Canadian Historical Review* 52 (1971): 276–86. George T. Hunt,

The Wars of the Iroquois: A Study in Intertribal Trade Relations (Madison: University of Wisconsin Press, 1940), initiated a long-standing debate over the importance of economic competition in seventeenth-century Iroquois warfare.

5. On continuing Iroquois hostilities with the Pennacooks and other tribes, see Gordon M. Day, "The Ouragie War: A Case History in Iroquois-New England Indian Relations," in Michael K. Foster, Jack Campisi, and Marianne Mithun, eds., *Extending the Rafters: Interdisciplinary Approaches to Iroquois Studies* (Albany: State University of New York Press, 1984), 35–50.

6. Onontio was the name for the French governor at Quebec; Tekwirimaeth was Noel Tekwarimat.

7. The Nouthchihuict near the Manathe River appears to be a Montagnais term for a group near the Hudson. Compare Trigger, ed., *Handbook of North American Indians*, 15:211.

8. Bouton, ed., *New Hampshire Provincial Papers*, 1:500–501. See also, Richard R. Johnson, "The Search for a Usable Indian: An Aspect of the Defense of Colonial New England," *Journal of American History* 64 (1977): 623–51.

9. Mass. Archives, 52:231–32, 242–43; Trask, ed., *Letters of Colonel Thomas Westbrook*, 131, 137.

10. Samuel Penhallow, *History of the Indian Wars of New England* (facs. reprint of 1726 edn. Freeport, N.Y.: Books for Libraries Press, 1971), 23.

11. Penhallow, *History of the Indian Wars of New England*, 60.

12. Probably displaced Mahicans from the Albany area.

13. Abenakis besieging St. George's Fort in 1722 were reported to be "headed by ye fryar," Trask, ed., *Letters of Colonel Thomas Westbrook*, 8.

14. Calloway, "Gray Lock's War."

15. Trask, ed., *Letters of Colonel Thomas Westbrook*, 86–87, 91, 99.

16. Mass. Archives, 52:13–14; Trask, ed., *Letters of Colonel Thomas Westbrook*, 63–64; see also, Mass. Archives, 29:154–57; 52:198–99. Compare, Horace P. Beck, *The American Indian as a Sea Fighter in Colonial Times* (Mystic, Conn.: Marine Historical Association, Inc., 1959), and Olive Patricia Dickason, "La 'guerre navale' contre les Britanniques, 1713–1763," in Charles A. Martijn, ed., *Les Micmacs et la Mer* (Quebec: Recherches amérindiennes au Québec, 1986), 233–48.

17. Ghere, "Abenaki Factionalism, Emigration and Social Continuity: Indian Society in Northern New England, 1725 to 1765."

18. Compare the Indian names listed in Captain Richard Bourne's company in 1725; Mass. Archives, 91:139–41; Trask, ed., *Letters of Colonel Thomas Westbrook*, 173–75.

19. "Account Book of Phineas Stevens," 1752:176–77.

20. James Axtell and William C. Strutevant, "The Unkindest Cut, or Who Invented Scalping?" *William and Mary Quarterly*, 3d ser., 37 (July 1980): 451–72; James Axtell, "Scalping: The Ethnohistory of a Moral Question," in his *The European and the Indian: Essays in the Ethnohistory of Colonial North America* (New York: Oxford University Press, 1981), 207–41.

21. The proclamation is printed in *Collections of the Maine Historical Society*, 2d ser., 24 (1916): 62–64.

22. *Collections of the Maine Historical Society*, 2d ser., 12 (1908): 391.

Chapter 5: Commerce and Coexistence (pp. 177–212)

1. Jennings, *Invasion of America,* 39.

2. Harrington, "Sea Tenure in Seventeenth Century New England," esp. 144–71.

3. See chap. 1 of this book, document 4.

4. Thomas, "Bridging the Cultural Gap," 5–21; see also Salisbury, "Social Relationships on a Moving Frontier," 95.

5. Dean Snow, "Abenaki Fur Trade in the Sixteenth Century," *Western Canadian Journal of Anthropology* 6 (1976): 3–11; Bourque and Whitehead, "Trade Goods and Tarrantines on Gulf of Maine."

6. "Divers Voyages and Northerne Discoveries of . . . Henry Hudson," in Samuel Purchas, ed., *Hakluytus Posthumus or Purchas His Pilgrimes,* 13:346–47; Faulkner and Faulkner, *The French at Pentagoet.*

7. Carl Bridenbaugh, ed., *The Pynchon Papers,* vol. 1: *Letters of John Pynchon, 1654–1700* (Boston: Colonial Society of Massachusetts, 1982); "Pennacook Papers," *Collections of the New Hampshire Historical Society* 3 (1832): 212, 214–61; Mass. Archives, 30:154–61; Mary R. Cabot, ed., *Annals of Brattleboro, 1681–1895,* 2 vols. (Brattleboro; E. L. Hildreth and Co., 1921–1922), 1:12; Clark, *Eastern Frontier,* 262; Ronald O. McFarlane, "The Massachusetts Bay Truck House in Diplomacy with the Indians," *New England Quarterly* 11 (March 1938): 48–65.

8. Salisbury, "Social Relationships on a Moving Frontier," 95.

9. Quinn and Quinn, eds., *The English New England Voyages,* 107.

10. Robert E. Moody, ed., *The Letters of Thomas Gorges* (Portland: Maine Historical Society, 1978), 98.

11. Mass. Archives, 32:99; "Journal of Phineas Stevens," in Mereness, ed., *Travels in the American Colonies,* 315–16; Bouton, ed., *New Hampshire Provincial Papers,* 6:236; "Account Book of Phineas Stevens," 176–77.

12. Snow, *The Archaeology of New England,* 56.

13. Morrison, *The Embattled Northeast,* 76.

14. For example, Peter A. Thomas. "Contrastive Subsistence Strategies and Land Use as Factors for Understanding Indian-White Relations in New England," *Ethnohistory* 23 (Winter 1976): 1–18.

15. Morrison, *The Embattled Northeast,* 113; Ghere, "Abenaki Factionalism, Emigration and Social Continuity," 60–62.

16. Roger B. Ray, "Maine Indians' Concept of Land Tenure," *Maine Historical Society Quarterly* 13 (1973): 28–51; Cronon, *Changes in the Land,* 70; Alan Taylor, "'A Kind of War': The Contest for Land on the Northeastern Frontier, 1750–1820," *William and Mary Quarterly,* 3d ser., 46 (January 1989): 3–26. Emerson W. Baker, "'A Scratch with a Bear's Paw': Anglo-Indian Land Deeds in Early Maine," *Ethnohistory* 36 (Summer 1989): 235–56, argues that Indians had more understanding of the deeds they signed than has often been assumed.

17. The sagamore Tahanto later earned local celebrity as an "earnest opposer of the rum traffic": In 1835, a temperance society was formed in Concord, New Hampshire, with the name Tahantoes. Local tradition accorded Pehaungun the dubious (and no doubt incorrect) distinction of being "the last of the Pennacooks" to die at Concord. Nathaniel Bouton, ed., *The History of Concord . . . with a history of the Ancient Penacooks* (Concord: Benning W. Sanborn, 1856), 34–36, 48.

18. Mass. Archives, 30:444.

19. Yasu Kawashima, "Jurisdiction of the Colonial Courts over the Indians in Massachusetts, 1689–1763," *New England Quarterly* 42 (1969): 532–50; Vaughan, *New England Frontier*, 190, 201; Canup, *Out of the Wilderness*, 186–87. See also, Yasumide Kawashima, *Puritan Justice and the Indian: White Man's Law in Massachusetts, 1630–1763* (Middletown, Conn.: Wesleyan University Press, 1986); and Lyle Koehler, "Red-White Power Relations and Justice in the Courts of Seventeenth Century New England," *American Indian Culture and Research Journal* 3, no. 4 (1979): 1–31. Vaughan, *New England Frontier*, chap. 7, presents a favorable view of Puritan justice in relation to Indians.

20. *Province and Court Records of Maine*, 6 vols. (Portland: Maine Historical Society, 1928–1975), 6:xix–xx.

21. For example, *Collections of the Maine Historical Society*, 2d ser., 23 (1916): 23–26.

22. McLellan, *History of Gorham, Maine*, 35–36.

23. Joseph Chadwick, "An Account of a Journey from Fort Pownal—now Fort Point—up the Penobscot River to Quebec, in 1764," *Bangor Historical Magazine* 4 (1889): 141–48, cited by Dean Snow in Krech, ed., *Indians, Animals and the Fur Trade*, 68–69.

24. Edmund Pearson, ed., *The Autobiography of a Criminal: Henry Tufts* (New York: Duffield and Co., 1930); Gordon M. Day, "Henry Tufts as a Source on the Eighteenth Century Abenakis," *Ethnohistory* 21 (Summer 1974): 189–97. On Molly Ockett, see Catherine S. C. Newell, *Molly Ockett* (Bethel, Me.: Bethel Historical Society, 1981).

Chapter 6: Captives and Culture Crossings (pp. 213–251)

1. For a broader discussion of these questions, see A. Irving Hallowell, "American Indians, White and Black: The Phenomenon of Transculturation," *Current Anthropology* 4 (1963): 519–31; James A. Clifton, "Altered Identities and Cultural Frontiers," in Clifton, ed., *Being and Becoming Indian: Biographical Studies of North American Frontiers* (Chicago: Dorsey Press, 1985); and Axtell, *The Invasion Within*.

2. Vaughan and Richter, "Crossing the Cultural Divide"; Axtell, "The White Indians of Colonial America"; Calloway, "An Uncertain Destiny"; Emma Lewis Coleman, *New England Captives Carried to Canada Between 1677 and 1760 During the French and Indian Wars* (Portland, Me.: The Southworth Press, 1925).

3. Vaughan and Richter, "Crossing the Cultural Divide," 51, 60–62, 84–85.

4. James Axtell, "The Scholastic Philosophy of the Wilderness," in *The European and the Indian*, 131–67; Silverman, ed., *Selected Letters of Cotton Mather*, 398; Nathaniel B. Shurtleff, ed., *Records of the Governor and Company of Massachusetts Bay in New England*, 5 vols. (Boston, 1853–1854), 1:88; J. Hammond Trumbull, ed., *The Public Records of the Colony of Connecticut*, 15 vols. (Hartford, 1850), 1:78, 530; Hector St. John De Crèvecoeur, *Letters from an American Farmer* (London: J. M. Dent, 1962), 215; "A Narrative of Hannah Swarton," quoted in Laurel Thatcher Ulrich, *Good Wives: Image and Reality in the Lives of Women in Northern New England 1650–1750* (New York: Oxford University Press, 1983), 181. Joshua Tefft, a notorious renegade in King Philip's War, was hanged, drawn, and quartered when captured among the Narragansetts; Colin G. Calloway, "Rhode Island Renegade: The Enigma of Joshua Tefft," *Rhode Island History* 43 (November 1984): 136–45. See also, Calloway, "Nei-

ther White Nor Red: White Renegades on the American Indian Frontier," *Western Historical Quarterly* 17 (1986): 43–66.

5. Quoted from forthcoming work by Alan Taylor in Gregory H. Nobles, "Breaking into the Backcountry: New Approaches to the Early American Frontier, 1750–1800," *William and Mary Quarterly*, 3d ser., 46 (October 1989): 644.

6. Crèvecoeur, *Letters from an American Farmer*, 214–16, 221; see also, Leonard W. Labaree, ed., *The Papers of Benjamin Franklin* (New Haven: Yale University Press, 1961), 4:481–83.

7. Neal Salisbury, *Manitou and Providence: Indians, Europeans, and the Making of New England 1500–1643* (New York: Oxford University Press, 1982), 157–63, 281n, discusses Morton and Ashley as does Canup, *Out of the Wilderness*, 101–25; Faulkner and Faulkner, *The French at Pentagoet*.

8. *Narrative of the Life, Adventures, and Sufferings of Henry Tufts*, 77–78. Axtell, *The European and the Indian*, 152–55, discusses the European attraction to Indian women (and the relative lack of Indian interest in European women); Rayna Green examines the persistent white fascination with Indian women in "The Pocahontas Perplex: The Image of Indian Women in American Culture," *Massachusetts Review* 26 (Autumn 1975): 698–714.

9. Vaughan and Clark, eds., *Puritans among the Indians*, 1–10; Richard Slotkin, *Regeneration Through Violence: The Mythology of the American Frontier, 1600–1800* (Middletown: Conn.: Wesleyan University Press, 1974), 94–96; Roy Harvey Pearce, "'The Ruines of Mankind': The Indian and the Puritan Mind," *Journal of the History of Ideas* 13 (1952): 200–217; William S. Simmons, "Cultural Bias in the New England Puritans' Perception of Indians," *William and Mary Quarterly*, 3d ser., 38 (1981): 56–72; David L. Minter, "'By Dens of Lions': Notes on Stylization in Early Puritan Captivity Accounts," *American Literature* 45 (1975): 335–47; Peter N. Carroll, *Puritanism and the Wilderness: The Intellectual Significance of the New England Frontier 1629–1700* (New York: Columbia University Press, 1969), 76–79, 212.

10. The Indians launched an attack on Northampton in March 1676 but were repulsed by the colonists.

11. Vaughan and Clark, eds., *Puritans among the Indians*, 93; *Collections of the Maine Historical Society*, 2d ser., 23 (1916): 228, and passim, for Gyles' services as interpreter.

12. *Dictionary of Canadian Biography* 2 (1969): 4–7; Paul Chasse, "The D'Abbadie De Saint-Castins and the Abenakis of Maine in the Seventeenth Century," in Philip P. Boucher, ed., *Proceedings of the Tenth Meeting of the French Colonial Historical Society, 1984* (Lanham, Md.: University Press of America, 1985), 59–73; *Documentary History of the State of Maine*, 6:424–27; Clarence J. d'Entremont, "The Children of the Baron de Saint-Castin," *French Canadian and Acadian Genealogical Review* 3 (Spring 1971): 9–28; John E. Godfrey, "Jean Vincent, Baron De Saint Castin," and "Castin the Younger," *Collections of the Maine Historical Society*, 1st ser., 8 (1876): 39–92; Herbert Milton Sylvester, *Indian Wars of New England* (3 vols. New York: Arno Press, 1979 reprint of 1910 original), 2:387–89, 428.

13. Lahontan belittles Jesuit efforts and underestimates their success among the Abenakis of Maine.

14. Margaret Connell Szasz, *Indian Education in the American Colonies, 1607–1783* (Albuquerque: University of New Mexico Press, 1988). Bobby Wright, "'For the Children of the Infidels?': American Indian Education in Colonial Colleges," *Amer-*

ican Indian Culture and Research Journal 12, no. 3 (1988): 1–14, examines the pecuniary motives behind English education efforts.

15. On Eunice Williams, see Alexander Medlicott, Jr., "Return to This Land of Light: A Plea to an Unredeemed Captive," *New England Quarterly* 38 (1965): 202–16; on Esther Wheelwright, Ulrich, *Good Wives*, 211. Coleman, *New England Captives Carried to Canada*; also, Barbara Austen, "New England Female Captives in Canada, 1689–1763," paper presented at the Dublin Seminar for New England Folklife, 1989. Mary Storer Papers, Massachusetts Historical Society, Boston.

16. Martin Kellogg was brother of Joseph Kellogg and later became schoolteacher to the Indian students at Stockbridge, Massachusetts.

17. Ulrich, *Good Wives*, 231.

18. Eleanor Burke Leacock, *Myths of Male Dominance: Collected Articles on Women Cross Culturally* (New York: Monthly Press, 1981), 133–82; see also, James Axtell, ed., *The Indian Peoples of Eastern America: A Documentary History of the Sexes* (New York: Oxford University Press, 1981), 103–4, 134–39.

19. Correspondence relating to their murder is in Bouton, ed., *New Hampshire Provincial Papers*, 6 (1872): 262–66.

20. Thwaites, ed., *Jesuit Relations*, 67:111, quoted in Bourque, "Ethnicity on the Maritime Peninsula," 272.

21. John C. Huden, "The White Chief of the St. Francis Abenakis—Some Aspects of Border Warfare, 1690–1790," *Vermont History* 24 (July 1956): 199–210; (October 1956): 337–55; Coleman, *New England Captives Carried to Canada*, 361–65. *Dictionary of Canadian Biography*, 4 (1979), 293–94. Gill's Abenaki name was Magouaouidombaouit. Huden thought this meant "English lover" but Thomas M. Charland translated it as "friend of the Iroquois."

22. Erwin H. Ackernecht, "'White Indians': Psychological and Physiological Peculiarities of White Children Abducted and Reared by North American Indians," *Bulletin of the History of Medicine* 15 (1944): 15–36; J. Norman Heard, *White into Red: A Study of the Assimilation of White Persons Captured by Indians* (Metuchen, N.J.: The Scarecrow Press, 1973), 102–4, 119–37; Axtell, "The White Indians of Colonial America," 81–82; Vaughan and Richter, "Crossing the Cultural Divide," 63–65.

23. In fact, Rogers greatly exaggerated the extent of his victory at St. Francis. See, for example, Gordon M. Day, "Rogers' Raid in Indian Tradition," *Historical New Hampshire* 17 (1962): 3–17.

24. Quoted in Charles A. Jellison, *Ethan Allen, Frontier Rebel* (Taftsville, Vt.: The Countryman Press, 1969), 137. The Caughnawagas and other Indians around Montreal were not fooled by Allen's rhetoric—some of them helped the British capture him when he made his abortive attack on the city shortly afterward.

25. Szasz, *Indian Education in the American Colonies, 1607–1783*, 9–13, 220–21, 260. Missionary Joseph Fish, a contemporary of Wheelock, encountered such resistance among the Narragansetts of Rhode Island that he finally gave up his mission. Writing in the spring of 1772, he complained, "I know not What method to take, nor Argument or Motive to Use, to engage them to Attend the Lecture or regard the School. It Seems as if the Devil holds them fast in Chains." William S. Simmons and Cheryl L. Simmons, eds., *Old Light on Separate Ways: The Narragansett Diary of Joseph Fish, 1765–1776* (Hanover: University Press of New England, 1982), 89. For insights into the experiences of some other Indian students who attended Moor's Charity School and Dartmouth College, see James Dow McCallum, ed., *Letters of Eleazar Wheelock's Indians* (Hanover: Dartmouth College Publications, 1932).

Epilogue (pp. 253–257)

1. Robert F. Sayre, *Thoreau and the American Indians* (Princeton: Princeton University Press, 1979), esp. xiii and chap. 6.

Bibliographical Essay

Manuscript sources for Indian and European encounters in northern New England are scattered through repositories in the United States, Canada, Great Britain, and France. The Massachusetts State Archives in Boston and the National Archives of Canada in Ottawa have particularly important collections. An exhaustive bibliography of published works that have bearing on the subject would be too long and would provide little guidance as to which publications are the most informative. Readers should consult the endnotes for specific references. The following short bibliographical essay identifies selected published works that contain significant amounts of material on Abenakis and Europeans or that have some direct relevance to northern New England.

General

James Phinney Baxter, ed., *Documentary History of the State of Maine*, 24 vols. (Portland: *Collections of the Maine Historical Society*, 2d series, 1869–1916) is probably the most useful single collection of printed primary documents on the history of Indians and Europeans in northern New England. It contains letters, treaty proceedings, and other materials essential to understanding Maine's early history. Nathaniel Bouton, ed., *New Hampshire Provincial Papers*, 7 vols. (Concord, Nashua, and Manchester, 1867–1873) contains a wide range of documents and some useful items on Indian relations, although it is less rich than the Maine collections. Despite its New York focus, Edward O'Callaghan, ed., *Documents Relative to the Colonial History of the State of New York*, 15 vols. (Albany: Weed, Parsons, 1853–1887) also contains some valuable materials for Indian-European encounters in northern New England. The *Collection de Manuscrits contenant Lettres, Mémoires, et Autres Documents Historiques Relatifs à la Nouvelle-France*, 4 vols. (Imprimerie à Côté et Cie, 1883–1885) reproduces some important French documents. James Phinney Baxter, *The Pioneers of New France in New England, with Contemporary Letters and Documents* (Albany: Joel Munsell's Sons, 1894) also reproduces original sources.

Secondary works that concentrate on Indians and Europeans in northern New England are relatively few. Students may need to draw upon broader studies on New England in general, the Northeast, and eastern Canada, where Indian-European interactions followed some similar patterns. Many nineteenth-century histories either ignored Indians completely or portrayed them in distorted and one-dimensional fashion. More sophisticated ethnohistorical studies in the late twentieth century allow for better appreciation of Indian cultures and deeper understanding of the processes of interaction.

James Axtell's works, *The European and the Indian: Essays in the Ethnohistory of Colonial North America* (New York: Oxford University Press, 1981), *The Invasion Within: The Contest of Cultures in Colonial North America* (New York: Oxford University Press, 1985), and *After Columbus: Essays in the Ethnohistory of Colonial North America* (New York: Oxford University Press, 1988), are essential reading for anyone interested in the interaction of Indians and Europeans in northeastern North America. In clear and elegant style, Axtell discusses questions of methodology, moral judgments in history, and the various ways in which Indians and Europeans dealt with, understood, and tried to convert each other.

Other examples of the ethnohistory of colonial New England include Francis Jennings' provocative book, *The Invasion of America: Indians, Colonialism, and the Cant of Conquest* (New York: Norton, 1976); and Neal Salisbury, *Manitou and Providence: Indians, Europeans, and the Making of New England, 1500–1643* (New York: Oxford University Press, 1982). Alden T. Vaughan offers a more favorable view of Puritan relations with the Indians in *New England Frontier: Puritans and Indians 1620–1675*, rev. ed. (New York: Norton, 1979). Although it is now quite old and focuses on Canada, Alfred Goldsworthy Bailey, *The Conflict of European and Eastern Algonkian Cultures 1540–1700*, 2d ed. (Toronto: University of Toronto Press, 1969) is still extremely useful for its insights into culture change. Cornelius Jaenen examines the French arena of contact in *Friend and Foe: Aspects of French-Amerindian Contact in the Sixteenth and Seventeenth Centuries* (Toronto: University of Toronto Press, 1976).

Dean R. Snow gives a valuable overview of *The Archaeology of New*

England (New York: Academic Press, 1980), with considerable material on the Abenakis; and Howard S. Russell looks at *Indian New England Before the Mayflower* (Hanover: University Press of New England, 1980), with particular emphasis on agriculture. William S. Simmons compiles oral traditions from southern New England in *Spirit of the New England Tribes: Indian History and Folklore, 1620–1984* (Hanover: University Press of New England, 1986).

Emerging studies of the northern New England frontier are discussed in Gregory H. Nobles, "Breaking into the Backcountry: New Approaches to the Early American Frontier, 1750–1800," *William and Mary Quarterly*, 3d ser., 46 (October 1989): 641–70. William Cronon's excellent study of *Changes in the Land: Indians, Colonists, and the Ecology of New England* (New York: Hill and Wang, 1983) is applicable to the north in some areas and provides a stimulating framework for understanding the new world in which Indians and Europeans met and lived. Laurel Thatcher Ulrich also broadens the picture of frontier life with *Good Wives: Image and Reality in the Lives of Women in Northern New England 1650–1750* (New York: Oxford University Press, 1983). More general studies of the northern frontier include Charles E. Clark, *The Eastern Frontier: The Settlement of Northern New England 1610–1763* (New York: Knopf, 1970); and Douglas Edward Leach, *The Northern Colonial Frontier 1607–1763* (Albuquerque: University of New Mexico Press, 1974). Jere R. Daniell, *Colonial New Hampshire: A History* (Millwood, N.Y.: KTO Press, 1981) contains a chapter on the Pennacooks of New Hampshire. Richard I. Melvoin, *New England Outpost: War and Society in Colonial Deerfield* (New York: W. W. Norton, 1989) offers a good study of a colonial frontier society, just to the south of the dawnland.

The Abenakis

The standard work on the archaeology and anthropology of the western Abenakis is William A. Haviland and Marjory W. Power, *The Original Vermonters: Native Inhabitants Past and Present* (Hanover: University Press of New England, 1981), which is especially useful for the period prior to 1600. Colin G. Calloway describes western Abenaki experiences in the wake of contact in *The Western Abenakis of Vermont, 1600–1800: War, Migration, and the Survival of an Indian People* (Norman: University of Oklahoma Press, 1990). *Vermont History* 58 (Spring 1990) contains three essays on aspects of European contact with the Vermont

Abenakis and their neighbors. All studies on the western Abenakis are indebted to Gordon M. Day, whose publications include *The Identity of the St. Francis Indians* (Ottawa: National Museum of Man, 1981), and "Western Abenaki" in Bruce G. Trigger, ed., *Handbook of North American Indians* (Washington, D.C.: Smithsonian Institution, 1978) vol. 15, *Northeast*.

The eastern Abenakis of Maine are discussed in Fannie Hardy Eckstorm, "The Indians of Maine," in Louis C. Hatch, ed., *Maine: A History*, 3 vols. (New York: The American Historical Society, 1919), chap. 3; Dean R. Snow, "Eastern Abenaki," in Trigger, ed., *Handbook of North American Indians*; and Snow's "The Ethnohistoric Baseline of the Eastern Abenaki," *Ethnohistory* 23 (Summer 1976): 291–306. Kenneth M. Morrison examines the eastern Abenakis' struggle to survive between New France and New England in *The Embattled Northeast: The Elusive Ideal of Alliance in Abenaki-Euramerican Relations* (Berkeley: University of California Press, 1984). Charles M. Starbird's brief book is informative on *The Indians of the Androscoggin Valley* (Lewiston, Maine: Lewiston Journal Printshop, 1928). Bruce J. Bourque tackles the complex question of "Ethnicity on the Maritime Peninsula, 1600–1759," *Ethnohistory* 36 (Summer 1989): 257–84. Readers of French should also consult André Sévigny, *Les Abénaquis: Habitats et Migrations (17ᵉ et 18ᵉ siècles)* (Montreal: Les Editions Bellarmin, 1976).

For information on Indian cultural survivals in the nineteenth and twentieth centuries, see Frank G. Speck, *Penobscot Man: The Life History of a Forest Tribe in Maine* (Philadelphia: University of Pennsylvania Press, 1940); and Fanny Hardy Eckstorm, *Old John Neptune and other Maine Indian Shamans* (Portland: The Southworth-Anthoensen Press, 1945; Marsh Island Reprint, University of Maine at Orono, 1980). Joseph Nicolar relates myths and legends from the Penobscots in *The Life and Traditions of the Red Man* (Bangor: C. H. Glass and Co., 1893).

Journalist Paul Brodeur pulls together some useful history about the Indians of Maine as background for his book on the legal disputes culminating in the landmark settlement of 1980 in *Restitution: The Land Claims of the Mashpee, Passamaquoddy, and Penobscot Indians of New England* (Boston: Northeastern University Press, 1985).

Eunice Nelson, *The Wabanaki: An Annotated Bibliography* (Cambridge, Mass.: American Friends Service Committee, 1982) provides a guide to the literature on Indians in the dawnland and pays particular attention to those appropriate for use in schools and to the ethnocentrism that renders others unsuitable. Since *The Wabanaki* was published, other more balanced and sympathetic treatments have appeared, giving students and teachers a wider choice of materials. The stories collected and told by Joseph Bruchac, *The Wind Eagle and Other Abenaki Stories* (Greenfield Center, N.Y.: Greenfield Review Press, 1985), and *The Faithful Hunter: Abenaki Stories* (Greenfield Center, N.Y.: Greenfield Review Press, 1988), provide brief and enjoyable introductions to Abenaki lore and culture. *The Wabanakis of Maine and the Maritimes: A Resource Book about Penobscot, Passamaquoddy, Maliseet, Micmac, and Abenaki Indians* (Bath, Maine: American Friends Service Committee, 1989) compiles excellent materials for classroom use for grades 4 through 8; while *Finding One's Way: The Story of an Abenaki Child* (Franklin, Vt.: Northwest Supervisory Union, Title IV Indian Education Program and the Abenaki Self-Help Association, various editions) raises issues of identity vital to present-day Abenakis. Colin G. Calloway, *The Abenaki* (New York: Chelsea House, 1989) is a historical overview suitable for high school students or as a brief introduction for college freshmen.

Chapter 1: First Encounters

H. P. Biggar, ed., *The Works of Samuel de Champlain*, 6 vols. (Toronto: The Champlain Society, 1922–1936) is the most complete edition of the works of the French explorer and provides important material from his encounters with Indian people on the coast of Maine and Lake Champlain as well as in Canada. Convenient collections of the most significant accounts of early English explorers in the region are provided in Henry S. Burrage, ed., *Early English and French Voyages* (New York: Charles Scribner's Sons, 1932); and, with excellent commentary, in David B. and Alison M. Quinn, eds., *The English New England Voyages, 1602–1608* (London: The Hakluyt Society, 1983). Carl Ortwin Sauer provides the background in *Sixteenth Century North America: The Land and the People as Seen by the Europeans* (Berkeley: University of California Press, 1971); Morrison, *The Embattled Northeast*, recounts first contacts in Maine; Salisbury, *Manitou and Providence*, includes information on New England; and Bruce G. Trigger, *Natives and Newcomers: Canada's 'Heroic Age' Reconsidered* (Montreal: McGill-Queens University Press, 1985) analyzes comparable encounters in Canada. Karen Ordahl Kupperman gives a more general consideration of East Coast encounters in *Settling with the Indians: The Meeting of English and Indian Cultures in America, 1580–1640* (London: Dent, 1980).

Chapter 2: Frontiers of Spirit and Soul

Reuben G. Thwaites, ed., *The Jesuit Relations and Allied Documents: Travels and Explorations of the Jesuit Missionaries in New France 1610–1791*, 73 vols. (Cleveland: The Burrows Brothers Co., 1896–1901; reprint, New York: Pageant Book Co., 1959) is the basic source for any study of relations between missionaries and Indians in the Northeast. Axtell, *The Invasion Within*, Morrison, *The Embattled Northeast*, and Trigger, *Natives and Newcomers* all discuss the religious dimensions of contact. Mary Celeste Leger provides a history of the relationship between the Catholic Church and the Abenakis in Maine in *The Catholic Indian Missions in Maine, 1611–1820* (Washington, D.C.: Catholic University of America, Studies in American Church History, 1929), vol. 8.

Chapter 3: Dawnland Diplomacy

Copies of treaties with the Indians of Maine are reproduced in the *Collections of the Maine Historical Society*; for example, Frederic Kidder, "The Abenaki Indians: Their Treaties of 1713 and 1717, and a Vocabulary, with a Historical Introduction," *Collections of the Maine Historical Society*, 1st ser., 6 (1859): 229–63. David L. Ghere subjects some of these treaties to scrutiny in "Mistranslations and Misinformation: Diplomacy on the Maine Indian Frontier, 1725–1755," *American Indian Culture and Research Journal* 8 (1984): 3–26. Also relevant is Roger B. Ray, "Maine Indians' Concept of Land Tenure," *Maine Historical Society Quarterly* 13 (1973): 28–51.

Chapter 4: War in the Dawnland

Useful primary sources for warfare in northern New England include Charles H. Lincoln, ed., *Narratives of the Indian Wars 1675–1699* (New York: Charles Scribners' Sons, 1913); Benjamin Church, *The History of the Eastern Expeditions of 1689, 1690, 1692, 1696 and 1704 against the Indians and the French* (Boston: J. K. Wiggin and Wm. Parsons Lunt, 1867); and Edward Wheelock, ed., *Penhallow's Indian Wars* (1726; facs. reprint, Freeport, N.Y.: Books for Libraries Press, 1971). Samuel Adams Drake provided narratives of conflict in *The Border Wars of New England, Commonly Called King William's War and Queen Anne's War* (New

York: Charles Scribners' Sons, 1897), and *A Particular History of the Five Years French and Indian War in New England and Parts Adjacent* (reprint, Freeport, N.Y.: Books for Libraries Press, 1970). Herbert Milton Sylvester provides a detailed account of the conflicts in *Indian Wars of New England,* 3 vols. (original edn. 1910; reprint, New York: Arno Press, 1979). Historians have written more about Indian-white warfare in northern New England than any other aspect of contact, but much of the writing is outdated and heavily ethnocentric, if not downright racist. Francis Parkman's multi-volume *France and England in North America* (Boston: Little, Brown and Co., 1865–1897, and various editions) contains much detail on Abenakis in its panoramic narrative, but bias and distortion pervades Parkman's works. Many other nineteenth- and early twentieth-century writings were no better. Students should go instead to Morrison, *The Embattled Northeast;* or to Calloway, *The Western Abenakis of Vermont 1600–1800, and "Grey Lock's War," Vermont History* 55 (Fall 1987): 212–27. Although it deals with Massachusetts, Fred Anderson, *A People's Army: Massachusetts Soldiers and Society in the Seven Years' War* (New York: W. W. Norton, 1985) offers good insights into the nature of soldiers and service in the New England colonies.

Chapter 5: Commerce and Coexistence

Dean Snow, "Abenaki Fur Trade in the Sixteenth Century," *Western Canadian Journal of Anthropology* 6 (1976): 3–11; and Bruce J. Bourque and Ruth Holmes Whitehead, "Tarrantines and the Introduction of European Trade Goods in the Gulf of Maine," *Ethnohistory* 32 (1985): 327–41, discuss the early fur trade. Peter A. Thomas provides excellent analysis of the processes of exchange and culture contact in Sokoki country in "Contrastive Subsistence Strategies and Land Use as Factors for Understanding Indian-White Relations in New England," *Ethnohistory* 23 (Winter 1976): 1–18; in his "The Fur Trade, Indian Land, and the Need to Define Adequate 'Environmental' Parameters," *Ethnohistory* 28 (1981): 359–79; and in his "In the Maelstrom of Change: The Indian Trade and Cultural Process in the Middle Connecticut River Valley, 1635–1665" (Ph.D. diss., University of Massachusetts, 1979). Emerson W. Baker, "'A Scratch with a Bear's Paw': Anglo-Indian Land Deeds in Early Maine," *Ethnohistory* 36 (Summer 1989): 235–56 studies seventeenth-century deeds for the light they shed on

Anglo-Indian relations and finds that, rather than being cheated, Indians often engaged in transactions that they understood.

Chapter 6: Captives and Culture Crossings

Captivity narratives went through numerous reprintings and are available in various editions and compilations, such as Samuel G. Drake, ed., *Indian Captivities or Life in the Wigwam* (Auburn: Derby and Miller, 1852). For northern New England, *Indian Narratives* (Claremont, N.H.: Tracy Bros., 1854); and Francis Chase, ed., *Gathered Sketches from the Early History of New Hampshire and Vermont* (Claremont: Tracy, Kenney and Co., 1856; reprint, Heritage Books, 1987) contain interesting accounts. Alden T. Vaughan and Edward W. Clark select some of the most useful captivity narratives and provide an introduction to the genre in *Puritans Among the Indians: Accounts of Captivity and Redemption 1676 to 1724* (Cambridge: Belknap Press of Harvard University Press, 1981). Emma Lewis Coleman amassed information on individual captives in *New England Captives Carried to Canada Between 1677 and 1760 During the French and Indian Wars* (Portland, Me.: The Southworth Press, 1925). James Axtell's essay on "The White Indians of Colonial America," is reprinted in *The European and the Indian*; Alden T. Vaughan and Daniel K. Richter examine numbers in "Crossing the Cultural Divide: Indians and New Englanders, 1605–1763," *Proceedings of the American Antiquarian Society* 90, pt. 1 (1980): 23–99; and Colin G. Calloway looks at "An Uncertain Destiny: Indian Captivities on the Upper Connecticut River," *Journal of American Studies* 17 (August 1983): 189–210. John C. Huden, "The White Chief of the St. Francis Abenakis," *Vermont History* 24 (1956): 199–219, 337–55, gathered the information that was then available on Joseph Louis Gill.

Index

Library of Congress Cataloging-in-Publication Data
Calloway, Colin G. (Colin Gordon), 1953–
    Dawnland encounters : Indians and Europeans in Northern New
England / compiled and edited with an introduction by Colin G.
Calloway.
        p.   cm.
    Includes bibliographical references.
    ISBN 0–87451–526–2 (alk. paper)
    1. Abnaki Indians—History—Colonial period, ca. 1600–1775.
2. Abnaki Indians—Government relations.   3. Frontier and pioneer
life—New England—History.   4. Abnaki Indians—Social life and
customs.   I. Title.
E99.A13C354   1990
974'.004973—dc20   90–38192

LEGEND

PENOBSCOT : TRIBAL NAME

— - — - NATIONAL BOUNDARY (U.S / CANADA)

— - — STATE AND PROVINCIAL BOUNDARIES

• ● PRESENT DAY CITIES

ST. LAWRENCE

QUEBEC
N.B.

MALISEET

MONTAGNAIS / NASKAPI

CANADA
U.S.A.

QUEBEC ●

CHAUDIERE R.

ALGONKIN

AROSAGUNTICOOK
(ST. FRANCIS)

NORRIDGEWOCK

PENOBSCOT

PASSAMAQUODDY

AROOSTOOK R.

ST. CROIX R.

PENOBSCOT R.

MACHIAS R.

MONTREAL ●

RICHELIEU R.

ST. FRANCIS R.

CANADA
U.S.A.

MISSISQUOI

MISSISQUOI R.

LAKE
CHAMPLAIN

A B E N A K I

COWASUCK

CONNECTICUT RIVER

ANDROSCOGGIN R.

PIGWACKET

KENNEBEC R.

WAWENOCK

PORTLAND ●

MOHAWK

SOKOKI

MERRIMACK R.

PENNACOOK

ATLAN

WAPPINGER

MAHICAN

ALBANY ●

NIPMUC

WAMPANOAG

BOSTON ●
PLYMOUTH
CAPE COD

HUDSON RIVER

MOHEGAN /
PEQUOT

NARRAGANSETT

NEW YORK ●